SEARCHING FOR MODERN MEXICO:

DISPATCHES FROM THE FRONT LINES OF THE NEW GLOBAL ECONOMY

NATHANIEL PARISH FLANNERY

Floricanto Press

Floricanto Press
7177 Walnut Canyon Rd.
Moorpark, California 93021
(415) 793-2662
www.FloricantoPress.com
ISBN-13: 978-0-915745-82-1
"Por nuestra cultura hablarán nuestros libros. Our books shall speak for our culture."
Roberto Cabello-Argandoña and Leyla Namazie, Editors

Table of Contents:

"We pursue modernity in her incessant metamorphoses yet we never manage to trap her. She always escapes: each encounter ends in flight."

—Octavio Paz

Preface

Boys on rafts work their way across the river in front of an official border crossing bridge.

I moved to Mexico after graduating from the International Affairs master's program at Columbia University in June 2013. Over the previous four years I traveled to the U.S.'s southern neighbor while I worked to finish my degree. By the time I graduated I had worked for over five years as a Latin America analyst on Wall Street and I did a brief stint at a Latin America-focused think tank in Manhattan. I had always worked at a desk, however, and although I had done some freelance reporting in Mexico, the on-the-ground reality of Mexico's borderland was still new terrain for me. I scheduled a ride-along with a squad of border patrol officers and headed out to Mexico's *frontera*. I watched Border Patrol officer Hugo Rivera, a wide-chested man with short black hair, rest his hand on the barrel of his AR-15 assault rifle. Standing on the damp mud bank of the river, we scrutinized the men on rafts crossing the international boundary and pulling up to the water's edge.

§ § §

The water, burbling with energy from the morning rain, churns cocoa-colored as it passes by the row of sand bags. I watch Rivera grip his gun in front of his body and stare out at a dozen barefoot young men with skinny arms, long jean shorts, and faded, baggy t-shirts who strain to balance on the wooden slats that are mounted on the top of their gargantuan inner tube rafts.[1] The boys heave their long wooden poles into the mud of the riverbed on the downstream side of their boats, struggling against the current, and slowly push their passengers towards the northern side of the border. The young men pass right next to the chain-link fence that girds the cement bridge between the custom agents at the official border crossing. For locals, inner tubes are an easier and less complicated mode of transport for quick trips south of the border.

The sky is slightly overcast, but the gray outlines of the mountain peaks on the other side of the border poke through the haze in the distance. Rivera has grown accustomed to summer's suffocating heat, but today the air is cool and muggy. The seconds pass slowly as the rafts approach. He analyzes the details of his surroundings in a tense, awkward silence as the men on rafts pull up on the shoreline. "This is an informal crossing," Rivera explains, gazing out at the rafts without expression or judgment. "This is where the migrants cross. Hondurans, Guatemalans, Nicaraguans, El Salvadorians [pass through here]," he adds.[2]

Tasked with fighting drug trafficking and trying to arrest criminals who might rob or kidnap migrants, Rivera has built a career patrolling the border.

Rivera, however, is nowhere near the U.S. He patrols Mexico's southern border at the Suchiate River that abuts Guatemala, 2,432 miles south from the tall metal fence that separates the dusty, arid border crossing between San Diego and Tijuana. He and his men defend the new front line for drug trafficking and people smuggling in the Americas. Here there are no walls or elaborate electronic surveillance equipment. Rivera and his officers patrol in trucks exploring terrain that few people from the U.S. have visited or understand.

Southern Mexico couldn't be more different from the dry, sparsely populated areas that straddle the U.S.'s southern border. Dense, leafy trees and thick tangles of bushes jut up from both sides of the river. The landscape is dominated by one color: green.

The official border crossing here is a small scratch of modernity barely visible in the rugged, verdant landscape. The rafts drift in and out; small, silent, and impossible to monitor or track. Out on the water, a teenage boy balances with a bicycle on top of an inner tube boat. A southbound raft hauls several yellow and white cardboard cases of Victoria beer, one of the brands that has helped turn Mexico into the world's most successful beer exporter. But such signs of economic progress are hard to find in Chiapas, a place that is perhaps most known around the world for being the home of the masked Zapatista rebels who rose up against Mexico's government in 1994. Today the state is one of the least industrialized and most insular areas of Mexico. It is a place riven by political rivalries, corruption, and feuds between local union groups. To get to work on the border, Rivera sometimes has to pass through barricades set up by militant teachers' unions. He's battled cartel gunmen, but seems more intimidated by the teachers. The unions have the power to bring the state to a standstill and can even detain Rivera and his officers at a roadblock. If the protests turn violent Rivera knows he faces a grave risk. He carries a gun, but in Chiapas real power is held by wealthy landowners, political chieftains, and union leaders.

Border Patrol officers from Chiapas's state police stand guard by the edge of the Suchiate River look south towards Guatemala.

Many studies of Mexico start by zooming in on the U.S.-Mexico border and analyzing the complex cultural, business, and political ties that link the two countries. Movies produced in L.A. often do the same, setting up scenes in dusty desert border towns, but never venturing into the complex and fascinating Mexican states that sit far from the *frontera* with the U.S. At a time when Mexico is often at the center of public discourse in the U.S., however, it's important to find a new point of entry to re-introduce Mexico.

§ § §

As I finish the final edits on this manuscript, I've now lived in Mexico City for over five years. A few years ago I worked as a freelance journalist writing articles about Mexico's culture, politics, economy, and security problems for magazines and news outlets such as *The Atlantic, Foreign Affairs, The Guardian, InSight Crime,* and *Outside*. Now I work doing political risk analysis and advising foreign investors on risks and opportunities in Mexico and Latin America. I have written analytical reports for the Americas Society, IHS Global Insight, Albright Stonebridge, The Economist Intelligence Unit, the Open Society Foundation, The Ford Foundation, and other prestigious consultancies and organizations. I've spoken with investment bankers, lawyers, economists, and other affluent urban professionals and entrepreneurs and also visited many of the most remote parts of the country. While working on this book I rode along with State and Federal Police patrols and tagged along with squads of cartel-fighting vigilantes. Over the last twelve years I've pored over books about Mexico's economic history and anthropological studies of the country's remote, indigenous communities and analyzed data on crime, income levels, and demographic trends. Over time I've come to understand Mexico as a country defined by its disparities.

The state of Chiapas is one of the most inscrutable places in Mexico. It's a rugged region with an economy that remains mostly pre-industrial and almost neo-colonial. More than any other state in Mexico, Chiapas has struggled to adjust to the new reality of 21st century globalization. Chiapas represents many of the paradoxes of Modern Mexico. It is a patchwork of tiny agrarian hamlets that is knit together by community ties and government social programs. Within Chiapas there's a clear sense that the state needs more attention from the government.

Elite landowners built many of Mexico's most brutal colonial plantations and post-colonial haciendas in Chiapas. The state is still home to entrenched poverty and deep-seated inequality, two intransigent characteristics that have not been erased in the two and a half decades since Mexico joined the North American Free Trade Agreement (NAFTA) with the U.S. and Canada in 1994. Nearly eight out of ten of the state's residents work in odd jobs, off the books in the "informal" economy.[3] Chiapas also has the highest poverty rate in Mexico.[4] Eight of every ten residents in Chiapas live in families that have an income of less than two thousand dollars per year.[5]

Most of the state's problems derive from the fact that more than twenty years after Mexico signed up to NAFTA and embraced global trade, communities in many parts of Chiapas remain largely isolated from the outside world. There is no state in Mexico that better represents the country's struggle to transform into a modern industrial economy.

Chiapas, however, is in no way representative of

the more positive trends taking place in other parts of the country. Mexico is home to thirty-two states and nearly two thousand five hundred towns. Each section of the country has a unique cuisine, culture, and economic reality. Overall, however, Mexico is best characterized as a country with fifteen billionaires and more than fifty-three million people who live below the official poverty line.[6] When you travel from the posh, modern business districts of cities such as Tijuana and Guadalajara into the remote regions of Oaxaca and Chiapas, it becomes clear that Modern Mexico is a brutally unequal country.

Mexico built up a strong middle class in the post-WWII boom, a golden age of economic growth that was fueled by protectionism and state-led industrialization, an experiment that ultimately proved unsustainable. After a series of serious economic crises in the 1980s, in 1994 Mexico capped a decade of comprehensive economic reforms by signing the free trade agreement with the U.S. and Canada, and committing to opening its economy to exports and promising to limit government protections for local industries. In the decades since NAFTA came into effect certain pockets of the country have boomed and certain (affluent) segments of society have benefited greatly. But overall during the NAFTA era Mexico has become an even more deeply divided economy, a society that exemplifies the stratification of modern globalized capitalism.[7]

Mexico is still home to many of the poorest communities in the western hemisphere, but it also now hosts some of the most prominent examples of 21st century high-tech manufacturing hubs and successful urban economic development initiatives. Although its status as a migrant-sending country is diminishing and the flow of Mexican migration is now net zero, Mexico still pushes out thousands of desperate migrants searching for unsteady, but relatively lucrative work in the U.S. At the same time it draws in thousands of educated and skilled migrants from countries across the globe. Mexico is now the number one destination for professional migrants looking for work in Latin America.[8] Rife with paradoxes, Mexico is home to struggling rain-fed farms and bustling industrial agribusinesses. Mexico is Latin America's most globally connected economy yet it is also home to millions of rural residents who labor in local economies based on subsistence agriculture, government transfers, and remittances from migrant workers. Mexico has created modern police forces and improved security in cities such as Guadalajara and Tijuana, and yet in large swaths of the western coast state authorities have receded and citizen militias and cartel gunmen have established de facto control.

Over the last three decades a group of technocrats educated at Harvard, Yale, Columbia, and the University of Chicago followed the recommendations of multi-lateral development banks. The International Monetary Fund and World Bank helped craft reforms and draft laws that, on paper at least, make Mexico look like a global leader for implementing top quality, pro-business legislation. While working on this book I saw firsthand how this heavily marketed myth of a "modern," globalized Mexico doesn't accommodate the reality residents experience in many parts of the country.

Mexico is a perplexing and paradoxical country that perpetually seems to teeter between finally taking advantage of its geographic and demographic bounties and emerging as one of the world's great economic success stories, or collapsing under the weight of its problems of corruption, poverty, crime, and inequality. This book turns Mexico upside down, bringing readers deep into the unexplored territories of the country's south to explain the problems and paradoxes that define Modern Mexico. Working on this project I moved into the communities I write about and spent weeks living alongside the characters I describe.

The book introduces struggling entrepreneurs who are fighting to build businesses exporting truckloads of pungent, small-farm organic coffee, crates of crystalline, craft-made mezcal, and boxes of fresh avocados to the U.S. In the conclusion I move up to the U.S. border in Tijuana and discuss how we can understand the reality of inequality in Mexico through the lens of beer and tacos. I follow the example of the classic, but somewhat dated books *Mexican Lives* and *The Mexicans,* and introduce readers to a variety of characters from different parts of Mexico. Along the way readers can learn more about many of the most emblematic culinary products Mexico produces, but the book goes well beyond narrating the stories of small business owners and presents the concept of Modern Mexico, a country that often seems like it is careening towards crisis. *Searching for Modern Mexico* shows the challenges ordinary people face when trying to succeed in any environment characterized by extreme concentration of economic and political power.

No part of Modern Mexico is struggling more than the south.[9] In the pages ahead I bring readers to the states of Chiapas, Oaxaca, and Michoacan, places that are distant from the U.S. border and are experiencing unprecedented levels of social unrest after decades of government failure.

Throughout the first three sections of the book I explain how in these states activists, militant unions, and armed citizens are blockading highways and battling and sometimes overpowering battalions of heavily armed riot police. The state of Michoacan is confronting some particularly terrifying problems with organized crime. In the conclusion we touch on the nascent success seen in northern industrial cities such as Guadalajara and Tijuana. Each section of the book is short enough to be read in a single sitting, but I hope readers will treat each section like a separate meal and not try and gorge on more than one at a time.

I think that it's clear that Mexico's economy has grown in fits and bursts during the modern era of NAFTA and has produced a deeply divided society. In the U.S. some politicians criticize Mexico for robbing the U.S. of manufacturing jobs and investment. In Mexico, however, the modern era of industrialization since NAFTA came into effect in 1994 has not brought widespread benefits to the bulk of the population. Overall, during the NAFTA era people in Mexico have seen their country become a particularly extreme example of the lopsided style of capitalism that has emerged elsewhere in the world since the 1990s.[10]

In this book I bring readers to the front lines of some of the most inaccessible parts of the country and illustrate the deep-seated problems that are hindering Mexico's long term development. We see firsthand how the poverty in places like Chiapas and Oaxaca exists parallel to the emergence of clusters of "maquila" factories that pay workers just a few dollars a day to produce goods for companies such as Toyota, Boeing, and HP.

I first started forming the idea for this book in December 2012 during the first month of the administration of controversial Mexican President Enrique Peña Nieto's term in office. I came to Mexico believing myself to be pragmatic and intellectually allied with Mexico's new generation of technocrats. I had studied Economics and favored free trade and pro-market policies. I had worked on Wall Street and had seen countless reports and presentations touting Mexico's economic potential. Many of my Mexican friends from graduate school at Columbia worked on Peña Nieto's campaign and took jobs in his administration. At that time I was optimistic about Mexico's future and confident that a new package of reforms could finally kick-start a new era of meaningful economic development. Six years later I am finishing the final edits on this text in the days before Mexico's 2018 presidential election. Over the last six years I've watched firsthand as the Peña Nieto administration cynically permitted a disturbing level of corruption and flatly failed to control crime. This book was written during a challenging period for Mexico. I do focus on some current events in the text, but mainly I am trying to tell a bigger story about the myth and reality of Modern Mexico, and the challenges Mexico faces moving forward. While writing this book some of my naïve optimism about Mexico's economic potential has faded. But, I remain cautiously confident that Mexican intellectuals, civil society organizations, and business chambers may finally start collaborating to push their country's politicians to build and strengthen the institutions Mexico needs to function as a modern, democratic, capitalist society. But, overall I think the concept of a "modern" Mexico is still elusive.

When we sit down to eat and drink with residents in the forgotten and left behind stretches of places like Chiapas,

Oaxaca, and Michoacan, we come to a better understanding of Modern Mexico as a whole and the prominence of inequality in the 21st century global economy. There are still questions, however, about Mexico's future. The search for Modern Mexico continues.

Coffee in Chiapas

A worker loads a batch of freshly picked coffee cherries into the de-pulping machine behind Juan Carlos's house. This is the last batch of coffee the family harvested from their farm

Antonio uses a wooden paddle to arrange coffee beans to dry under the sun on the roof of the family's home

Workers hand-sort dried coffee beans

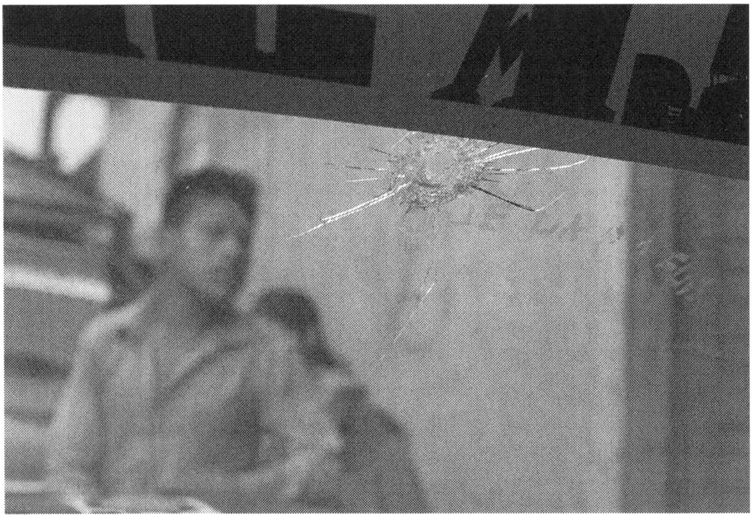

A bullet hole in the windshield of their neighbor's farm truck is a reminder of the most recent attack

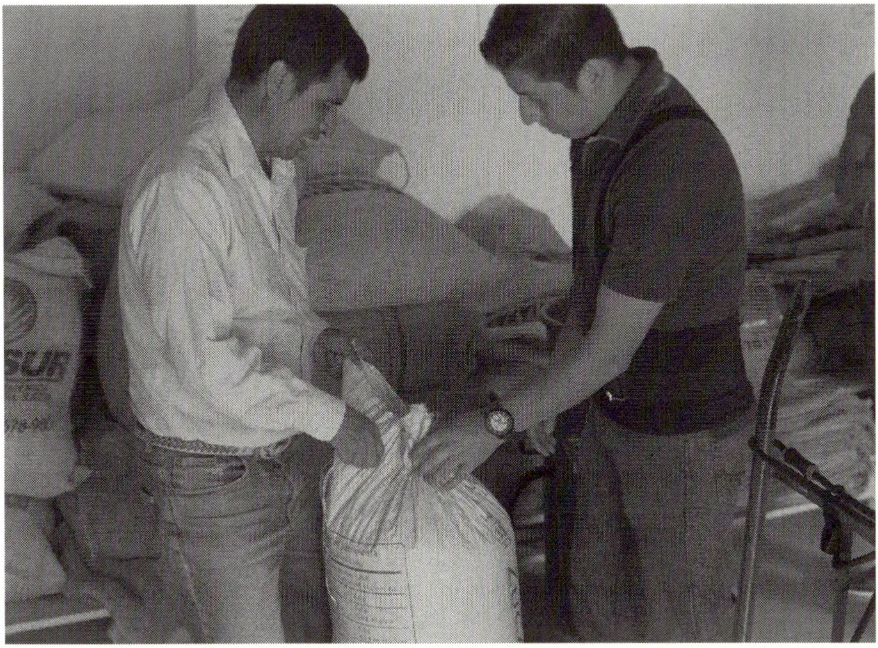

Antonio drops off a bag of coffee at a roaster in San Cristobal, Chiapas

A mural on the road leading towards Pantelho shows a masked Zapatista soldier with a gun tucked over her shoulder

A woman in traditional clothing walks past a hand-painted political advertisement in Pantelho

Pantelho, the village where Juan Carlos and Antonio live, is one of hundreds of small coffee growing hamlets in the broad expanse of mountains outside of San Cristobal

Antonio stands in front of his family's home

Juan Carlos stands in front of a model AK-47, a toy left-over from a childhood spent in the armed Zapatista movement

The speedometer stutters. With fog suffocating the narrow road, the motor wheezes fitfully in second gear as the rickety Nissan sedan strains up the hill, heaving around one tight curve after another. Juan Carlos grits his teeth. Sitting in the passenger seat, while his father's friend drives, he clenches his stomach and pushes his body against the seat. He scans the objects jutting out from the haze on the left side of the road. The precipitous drop into the valley on the right side of the road is obscured from view.

"I'm really scared," he tells me, speaking in Spanish, eyeing the shadows around the cement block houses that abut the road.[11]

There's no time to think about whether it was a mistake to leave so late. Juan Carlos and his father knew the type of danger they'd face on the open road, but they needed to deliver their coffee to clients. The constant threats they've faced from local gunmen have hampered their business and squeezed their family's finances. Now the heavy mist forces them to slow to a crawl on the last leg of their journey home from the city. In most sections of the road they can't see more than a few feet in front of them. The jagged hilltops and pine forests that flank the road are entirely obscured. Just a few days earlier he and his brother were ambushed while driving a load of coffee back from their farm. Juan Carlos knows the gunmen could be hiding anywhere. The car shudders as the driver downshifts to first gear. Tentatively, he eases around another corner and labors further up the steep incline.

Juan Carlos's mind races. The mundane details of the day's deliveries are pushed out. He is hyper-alert and focused on the details he sees with each passing second. In this isolated, but immense section of southern Mexico, their headlights fizzle in the darkness, only illuminating a tiny sliver of the long road in front of them. The high beams flash across a building painted with a woman's face. Long black braids frame her head and a red bandana covers her nose and mouth. There's a rifle slung over her back. "This is Zapatista territory," Juan Carlos blurts, straining to remain calm.

It's too dark to see if any masked men are posted inside the guard station at the Zapatista rebel town's entrance. The army's presence, however, is more visible. As the car presses forward, Juan Carlos can see the lamp in the watchtower, its light glowing dimly through the grey shroud of haze that hangs heavily over the street. "That's the military base," he explains. The presence of soldiers is unsettling. When a paramilitary group slaughtered four-dozen people in the town just down the ridge in 1996, the soldiers stationed there didn't intervene.[12] "They heard the shots and didn't do anything," Juan Carlos says, eyeing the barbed wire that surrounds the base. While the Zapatista rebel combatants who emerged in 1994 have mostly disappeared from view over the subsequent two decades, Juan Carlos is certain that the paramilitaries who were trained to fight the counter-revolution are still here.

In the mountain towns of Chiapas, in the rugged hills in the highlands just north of the Guatemalan border, justice is a scarce commodity. As his family has faced death threats over the past few years, the local police haven't done anything to help them. Juan Carlos knows he's facing the gunmen alone. "They are the threat," he repeats.

Dread is a uniquely tiring emotion. A racing mind exhausts the body, but Juan Carlos fights to stay alert. The last time he was attacked, the assailants dressed in black and wore ski masks. He wouldn't recognize the shooters if he saw their faces. Without their military-style attire the men could look like any other resident. So Juan Carlos scans for sudden movements; a raised arm, a rifle being aimed. In the shadows he can see two boys waiting by the side of the pavement. He scans their clothes, their faces, their movements. The boys peer in through the car's windshield and whistle as Juan Carlos passes. Is that a signal? Are the boys watchmen? Juan Carlos wants to be ready.

A few months shy of his thirtieth birthday, Juan Carlos still has a teenager's thin frame. He studies Economics in Mexico City. He hasn't trained to fight. He is not prepared for gun battles. His eyes dart from one side of the road to the other, examining, analyzing, looking for movement.

A week earlier, when the paramilitaries came for him he froze. He saw the muzzle flash. He heard the crash as a bullet smashed through the windshield's passenger-side corner. Juan Carlos didn't know how to respond. It seemed like a movie. It seemed like slow motion. The screams of his brother in the back of the truck caught his attention, but it was only when Juan Carlos saw his brother Alonso leap out that he was able to snap into action. He moved. He ducked. The second bullet tore through the windshield right in front of where he had been sitting. He could see the exploding star of thin cracks in the glass around the bullet hole. Peering above the dashboard he saw the men aiming and firing. His instinct was to stay low until the shooting stopped.

An attack leaves an imprint. When the tension fades there's a type of hollowness, an uneasiness that stays in its place. In the four days since the shooting Juan Carlos hasn't slept well. He isn't sure how he'll react if he's attacked again. His body tenses and surges with adrenaline. He thinks of the worst-case scenario. "The worst would be if they blocked the road and we couldn't pass and they pulled us out of the car," he says as he scans the shapes appearing in the illuminated space in front of the car's headlights. The heavy haze in the road limits visibility and Juan Carlos knows he probably won't see a roadblock until it's too late. In the fog ahead he sees the indistinct outlines of a dozen people. Shrouded by darkness in the shadows by the side of the road the shapes are hard to analyze. Juan Carlos squints. He can't see their hands. He can't tell if they are holding pistols. All he sees is that one of the figures holds a lantern. Juan Carlos clenches his teeth and tries to focus. As the car approaches the group his eyes flicker and flit, scrutinizing the scene for additional details. His thoughts accelerate, but the old car putters. Each passing second feels like an eternity. He sees a few of the shadowy shapes are wearing dresses. Still, he steadies himself for the unexpected. He waits for a sudden movement; a bang, a crash. Jittery, he braces for action.

Nobody moves out into the road to block the path. Nobody raises a gun. No muzzle blasts flare. Up ahead he can see the first few buildings in his village. Juan Carlos exhales. Speaking in Tzotzil, the one of two indigenous languages his family speaks, Juan Carlos turns to the driver, a friend of his father's, and stammers, *"La kuiha li bocho chopol xutzin wan-aye."* He thought they were the bad guys. He was wrong. Juan Carlos lets his breath out. His stomach softens. He's home.

Welcome to Chiapas.

§ § §

Chiapas, the southernmost state in Mexico, produces more organic coffee than any other province in the country.[13] Coffee farms lacerate the state's towering, chilly mountains and humid low-lying hills. On the big plantations, the coffee seedlings are cultivated in neat formations. In the highlands, the plants grow in tangles under the shade of the trees. Chiapas is overwhelmingly green. There's the vibrant, explosive green in the jungle in the south, and the drab military green of the Hummers from the army patrols that park near Juan Carlos's house. The Partido Verde party that backs the state's governor paints its political murals and messages a shade of florescent, optimistic green. The street-facing front wall of his house is a chalky shade of light lime green adorned with the hand-written letters "EZLN," the insignia of the Zapatista army. Dark, cucumber green splatters other parts of the town, appearing in the political ads for Mexico's dominant political party, the PRI, which uses the same colors as the Mexican flag. These different shades of green can help identify the different factions and groups fighting for local control in Chiapas.

From the peaks of the hills around Carlos' town, the verdant mountains fade into the distance. Carlos' village, Pantelho, is a tiny patch of white and grey cement homes scratched onto the top of a hill in the immense expanse of untouched, forest-covered peaks outside of the colonial city of San Cristobal. From the highest hill in Pantelho it's almost impossible to discern where the mountains end and the sky begins. In Tzotzil there is only one word that is used to describe both green and blue: *yox*.[14] The olive colored coffee leaves, the pale blue sky and the robust green of the Mexican flag are all tossed together under the same umbrella.

When the Zapatista army mobilized, they picked the attention-grabbing colors of red and black to symbolize their movement. On January 1, 1994, more than three thousand rebel soldiers, carrying old hunting rifles and a few machine guns, descended into the cobblestone streets of San Cristobal and advanced into the nearby city of Ocosingo. Aided by the alacrity of their attack, the Zapatistas scored a few ephemeral victories, but were quickly overwhelmed when Mexico's military finally scrambled to respond and launch a counter-offensive. The result was a negotiated truce, a détente that gave the insurgents an opportunity to voice their grievances. At a press conference in 1994 a masked rebel fighter outlined the Zapatistas' goals of land, liberty and regional autonomy. "This is what all the Indian *campesinos* of Mexico want. And until we get it we won't stop fighting," he said.[15]

In 2014, twenty years after their revolution fizzled, a few thousand Zapatistas staged a silent march in San Cristobal.[16] However, aside from a sporadic press conference, twenty years after their arrival the group has mostly faded from Mexico's national political arena. At their headquarters in the town of Oventic, the Zapatistas still operate a school, a cultural center and a community basketball court. While not exactly welcoming to outsiders, they do allow tourists to enter and take photos of their political murals. Visitors are greeted at the outside gate by men in balaclavas and then in a somewhat terrifying experience, led into a meeting room for a brief interview with a council of ski mask-wearing Zapatista leaders, where they are asked to explain the purpose of the visit. The council usually sends an escort to guide and guard any outsider who visits the compound. One mural shows a group of men, women, and children, a few of whom wear masks, standing in a corn field, under a brilliant orange sunset. The words "Dignified Rage," written in Spanish and Tzotzil, mark the top of the mural.[17] Another painting depicts a snail wearing a ski mask and a woman carrying a machine gun in one hand and her other fist raised high in resistance. The wooden slats on the backboards of the basketball court are painted black with red letters that spell out the words, "DEMOCRACY, LIBERTY AND JUSTICE!"

On some afternoons men in rubber work boots gleefully shuffle and sprint up and down the basketball court. Sometimes skinny teenage boys gather at the side of the court watching the action. Seeing a visitor, however, they recoil, startled, and pull their ski masks over their faces. The Zapatistas won't engage with outsiders. They stand as silently as the mural they have of a golden, god-like portrayal of their hero Emiliano Zapata. A hardy farmer from the state of Morelos, Zapata helped lead Mexico's early twentieth century revolution and rose up against the hermetic club of aristocratic industrialists who consolidated their control over the countryside in the late 1800s.[18] In the mural Zapata sits on a horse, holding up a banner that says "Land and Liberty!" They aren't welcoming hosts, but they do hope you'll stop by their gift shop where the rebels sell hand-sewn political banners and scarves decorated with snail-shaped designs. The twenty-first century group of Zapatista rebels is pushing forward with the most basic element of Zapata's cry to arms. They want land for farming and autonomy. Their hero, meanwhile, has become a pop culture icon. A stencil of his grizzled, bushy mustache and piercing stare has been pressed onto all sorts of consumer goods, a

Mexican version of Che Guevara. The gift shop at Oventic sells handkerchiefs embroidered with the outline of a mustachioed, sombrero-wearing gunman and the words, "ZAPATA LIVES THE FIGHT GOES ON."

In many ways, the Zapatistas' silence has become their defining characteristic. Following their uprising, the rebel fighters refused to engage in politics. They said they wanted to engage in dialogue in their arena. Even as paramilitaries hunted them, mostly they just disappeared from public view. Behind the walls of their communities the indigenous army that once galvanized support across the globe has faded into obscurity and political irrelevance. The Zapatistas failed to catalyze a major shift in Chiapas' longstanding economic and political dynamics.

Chiapas remains Mexico's poorest state. So far from the U.S. border, Chiapas is more disconnected from the global economy than any other state in the country. Despite a major influx of federal funds in the two decades since the Zapatista uprising, Chiapas continues to suffer. With the rebel army no longer leading the opposition, myriad groups of farmers, teachers, and other cliques from different towns have emerged to protest and advocate for their own narrow agendas.

§ § §

Gripping the sides of the wooden ladder that rests against the shipping container-sized cement block structure that Juan Carlos and his entire family share as a common bedroom, Juan Carlos methodically climbs the rungs, which are made from crudely chopped tree branches, and steps up onto a wooden platform. He glances out over the abandoned lot next door, a building that was once a campaign headquarters for the Mexico's historically dominant, but now struggling Institutional Revolutionary Party (PRI). Shifting his gaze out at the street, he scans the farm truck parked on the side of the road. As far as he can tell there are no assailants waiting today.

Juan Carlos walks out over the roof past the midsection above the space where his siblings sleep. Standing above the section of roof that sits over his grandfather's mosquito net-covered bed, he looks out in the direction of his coffee plot. "It's behind that hill. You can't see it because of the clouds," he says. He knows that the guayaba yellow and cranberry red berries are ripe and ready to be picked. But after he and his brothers were attacked, Juan Carlos figures that the year's harvest, and the bulk of his family's income, will be lost. Turning his attention to the town's center, Juan Carlos looks nervously past the strings of colorful plastic streamers fluttering in front of the town's pumpkin orange and cream-colored church and scrutinizes the hills on the other side of the plaza. "That big house—like five hundred meters from there—that's where they ambushed us," he says.

Juan Carlos warily surveys the scene. There's a haze of fog covering the mountains, but he can see the crosses and shrines in the cemetery that overlooks the town.

Up in the mountains, Juan Carlos is acutely aware of how alone he is. He knows he can't count on the local police or the state authorities to help him. He's not even sure if his father's friends who are affiliated with the Zapatistas will come to his rescue. He constantly worries about his family's safety. Seeing movement in the street, he glances over at a man walking up the sidewalk. "Up here I feel a little unsafe. If I go to the street I feel very unsafe. Somebody could be on the corner. They could shoot again. It scares me," he says quietly.

Juan Carlos knows that he and his brothers were lucky to escape when the gunmen came for them. If the assailants come back there's no guarantee his family will get away unscathed. Juan Carlos knows the *pistoleros* won't stop until his family flees and abandons their land.

The situation Juan Carlos and his family are confronting is not an anomaly. Internecine conflict roils Chiapas' villages. For centuries, the state's indigenous groups absorbed parts of Catholicism, creating a hybrid religion. The Catholic Church, for its part, worked to adapt to local conditions, training villagers such as Juan Carlos's father to work as catechists, translating the Church's message for the local audience. He's seen the ties that connect neighboring communities, fray and rupture. The villagers have become less flexible and less accommodating towards members of other languages, ethnicities, and religious affiliations. In some mountain towns political power brokers rally residents to drive out neighbors who are working to build support for a rival party. In other cases, Catholic residents have banded together to expel neighbors who have converted to evangelical Christianity. In one particularly jarring incident, the leader of a street vendor's association called the Emiliano Zapata Independent Proletarian Organization helped kidnap and shave the heads of a few teachers who earned the ire of local union bosses. When police detained the aggressors, their friends rallied and set fire to four cars, demanding justice, demanding impunity.

Juan Carlos thinks that his enemies are really just neighbors who are jealous of his family's moderate success and want to stymie their ambition and thwart their inchoate rise. He has become a target for some of the local political strongmen.

Nervously, he glances back at the street. "We don't know if the people who want to kill us are here. We don't know if they are the people passing in the street."

Nodding over towards the fifteen-foot-tall cinder-block wall that lines the back of his lot, Juan Carlos explains, "My father had to put that fence there so it wouldn't be so easy for somebody to enter. Before it was open. This fence they built five or six months ago because the rumors that they wanted to kill us were getting stronger."

The cement block barricade doesn't make him feel much safer. The fireworks that periodically blast throughout the day as part of the ongoing New Year's celebrations send tremors of panic pulsing through his body. From his perch on the roof Juan Carlos can keep an eye on the people passing in front of his house on the street. "I look to see if they have a gun. I keep watch for people passing on the street." It's a siege mentality that makes it hard to sleep at night. Sometimes Juan Carlos sees young men lounging, drinking beer by the 60-year-old farm truck in the street. He worries they might be *halcones*, scouts sent to let the gunmen know if he or his father leaves the house.

"We're scared. As a family we're scared. We don't have weapons. We work producing coffee. We aren't prepared for this type of stuff," he says bitterly. He isn't sure where he can look for help.

Around the corner from the house there's a small ice-cream shop and a tiny internet café. On the other side of the town square there's a street market where vendors sell bootleg CDs, dried beans and chiles, and fresh vegetables. Since the attack Juan Carlos hasn't ventured out to buy anything.

"The local government and the local police...they know what's happening and they don't do anything," he says.

All he wants from the government is the basic security to carry out his business. His family refuses to sign up for handouts through anti-poverty and anti-hunger programs. And, unlike most of his neighbors, his family didn't fill out the paperwork to receive a free flat screen TV as part of the New Year giveaway from the federal government.

A total of 4,295 families in Pantelho are participating in Prospera, Mexico's celebrated, but still controversial income subsidy program. The bulk of the town has signed up for the cash transfers. One of Juan Carlos's neighbors, a man named Fernando, came back from two years of working in the U.S. and bought a house, a car, and an old taxi in cash. He now works driving back and forth to San Cristobal and earns around six dollars a day after accounting for expenses. Like many of Juan Carlos' neighbors Fernando is happy to have his wife and children participate in Mexico's federal government's anti-poverty programs. The cash payments are a much-needed boost to the family's finances. Fernando also picked up one of the free TVs.

Unlike many of his neighbors, Juan Carlos vehemently opposes the handouts. He has a fervent anti-neoliberal ideology he absorbed as a youth during the Zapatista uprising and continued to develop at college in Mexico City, on a campus that is still one of the epicenters of Mexican leftism. However, he still harbors a libertarian idealist's expectation that hard work and individual industriousness should be enough to earn a living. He thinks the federal government should focus on guaranteeing public security and providing law and order rather than meddling in his community's affairs.

"We don't want government help. We just want them to leave us alone to let us do our work," Juan Carlos says. His eyes glare with tired, slow-simmering fury.

§ § §

Jorge Utrilla Robles, the director of Chiapas' state government's Coffee Institute sits behind his desk. Inside his air-conditioned office in Tuxtla Guitierrez, Chiapas' low-lying tropical capital city, he is protected from the hot mid-day sun. He wears jeans, boots, and a long sleeve work shirt, the comfortable clothes of a lifelong coffee grower. Brusque and self-assured, Jorge speaks animatedly, his sentences rolling out as if propelled by a belt-driven machine, with no pauses for air between syllables, words, or phrases. He inspires confidence and is equally comfortable talking to coffee workers and attending coffee trade fairs in the U.S.

Over the last half century he's seen Chiapas' coffee industry evolve. He grew up near the German-owned plantations near Ocosingo, a city that the Zapatista rebels seized during their uprising in 1994. Fifty-five years old, he saw the plantation owners in his town install the first electrical generators and build landing strips to export coffee. Rather than seeing the wealthy migrant farming families as colonizers or unwelcome interlopers, Jorge sees them as innovators who connected Chiapas to the global coffee market and created a potential path to prosperity for thousands of farming families. In the 1960s, Jorge's father owned a few small propeller planes, and the family loaded their bags onto single engine Cessna planes to bring the coffee to the city for export. At that time coffee was a relatively scarce and valuable commodity and many of the local growers drank expensive cognac and traveled between their villages and the city in private airplanes. The golden era of the Mexican coffee trade is long gone, but the struggles of the bad years during the coffee glut of the 1980s are also fading into the past.

Jorge's main focus is to build upon the progress Chiapas's coffee industry has made over the last thirty years. At the start of the NAFTA era Chiapas had 92,375 hectares of coffee farms.[19] At that time, nine out of ten coffee farms in the state were smaller than five acres.[20] Over the last two decades coffee production has expanded, but in a disjointed and mostly uncoordinated fashion. In the modern, free-market era the government hasn't taken on a centralized role in managing coffee production. Starbucks has come in and made a major investment in production in Chiapas and the amount of land dedicated to producing coffee in Chiapas has more than doubled, but overall the expansion has been driven by the proliferation of small, low-productivity plots. Across the state individual families are self-financing tiny, inefficient farms and make hardly any efforts to coordinate quality controls with their neighbors. Jorge, however, is optimistic.

"Coffee is now the most important agricultural activity in the state. We cultivate 253,000 hectares in eighty-eight towns in the state," he explains, rattling off a list of statistics about the business.

"Chiapas is the number one place in the world for organic coffee. There are 180,000 families here who directly depend on coffee. It's a source of employment," he explains.

The state's coffee industry, however, has not developed

optimally. Today Chiapas' coffee farms cover an area almost as big as the U.S. state of Rhode Island. There over eight hundred and fifty coffee plantations in Chiapas that are larger than ten hectares, but the overwhelming majority of the state's farms are a lot smaller. There are over sixty thousand coffee farms in the state that are under a half a hectare in size.[21] Overall, 64 percent of the state's coffee farms are smaller than five hectares and over 116,000 farms are smaller than a hectare.

"The immense majority are under five hectares. They are mainly indigenous farmers," Jorge explains.

The farms are small, scattered, and poorly coordinated. Chiapas state government and Mexico's federal Ministry of Agriculture aren't in contact with most of the state's farmers.

On the wall of Jorge's office there are a few photos of coffee berries and a large photo of the state's governor wearing a cowboy hat, jeans, and a freshly pressed lime green shirt with a crisp collar, leaning in for an awkward embrace with a coffee farmer who is cradling a seedling in one hand. The picture is supposed to be a sign of solidarity, but it also represents the distance that still divides the polished, urbanized figurehead of state government and most of Chiapas's humble small-plot coffee growers. For generations the state's politicians have ventured out of the capital and tried to foster ties with coffee producing communities, but there's still a vast cultural breach that is still yet to be overcome.

Jorge can confidently cite statistics. But, often his figures differ from the numbers in Mexico's Ministry of Agriculture reports, studies that rely on expansive surveys from Mexico's coffee growers' association. Overall, there's a major shortage of top-quality information about the micro-level details of coffee production in Chiapas. Mexico's agricultural agencies still don't fully survey or understand the local dynamics across the state's sprawling coffee industry. Part of the general problem in Mexico is that the federal government is disconnected from most of the country's small entrepreneurs.

Chiapas' small plot farms don't invest in technology or pesticides. By default due to their limited access to capital, they use organic production techniques. Jorge estimates that there are approximately sixty thousand acres of organic farms under cultivation in the state. The process for bringing these farms' beans to market, however, is largely informal and improvised.

Most producers in Chiapas end up selling their beans to companies that handle the logistics of trucking and bringing the coffee to consumers in the U.S. Farmers who sell to middle-men never see the same profits as growers who cooperate to create and promote their brands. Unsurprisingly, it's small farmers that have the most difficult time marketing and selling their beans at high prices. "There are some who don't know how to read or speak Spanish," Jorge explains. There are tens of thousands of coffee farmers who don't even seem interested in maximizing their profits. Many micro-scale farmers view coffee production as an easy source of supplementary income. They don't invest much in caring for their plants and they dry their beans on small tarps by the side of the road. Buyers of premium coffee demand quality and homogeneity.

Smaller farms are harder to manage. "Indigenous people have half a hectare. They are family plots," he explains. On a statewide scale, it is almost impossible for the Coffee Institute to coordinate production on nearly one hundred thousand small-plot farms. No government agency has even managed to put together a system to compile information about quality and production levels on the state's farms. Piecemeal outreach programs do exist, but participation is limited. On the smallest scale, coffee production is seen more as craft activity, not an integral part of the master plan for premium exports.

"When we look for specialized coffee we go to farms bigger than five hectares," Jorge repeats.

Small farms that don't join co-ops aren't a priority for the Coffee Institute. Jorge does, however, say that his team of technicians is always happy to help producers who seek guidance. "The doors of the institute are open," he says. He also points out that Mexico's federal government can offer support. "The federal government has a program called ProCafe through the Agricultural Ministry," he adds. Jorge isn't particularly concerned that most small-town producers might not be comfortable navigating their way through the state capital and many do not even know where to look for help.

"We go to them," he explains. "We have Tzotzil, Tzelzal…Ch'ol and Kaqchikel speakers. Our technicians all speak their languages," Jorge says as he enumerates the list of Chiapas's twelve main indigenous languages.

The institute's small team of technicians travel up into the highlands and deep into the jungle. The villages may be isolated, but Jorge thinks many indigenous communities have already found a good balance.

"They are involved in coffee, but they preserve their culture. They have their customs and we respect that," he adds.

Jorge says that many of the Coffee Institute's outreach efforts have been met with indifference. "We can help them if they have the will to do it. We can't force them. If they don't want to we can't obligate them," he says.

He doesn't seem to fully appreciate the fact that many indigenous producers might want help and support for their businesses, but aren't sure where to look. Many residents of the small towns in the highlands have never descended into the humid capital city and don't know how to navigate the state government bureaucracy. For Jorge, the coffee business is a simple affair that involves connecting top quality producers with discerning buyers. He doesn't seem to acknowledge how tenuous the connections are that link hilltop indigenous towns and the state and federal agencies.

"Coffee is one of the easiest products to sell. It's an export product. There are multinational corporations ready to buy coffee. They are buying all over the state," Jorge says.

Pausing briefly, Jorge taps on his smart phone's screen. "Today the market opened at 39.98 pesos. The coyote pays thirty nine," he says. It's good to know that a kilo of coffee is selling for about two dollars, but it isn't clear if Jorge understands the advantage his access to technology and familiarity with international buyers give him.

Data on market prices is readily available to producers who know how to look for it, but most rural residents don't have easy access to such information. Chiapas has the lowest rate of internet penetration in Mexico. Overall, nearly 87 percent of residents lack internet in their homes. Although over half of all households in Chiapas have a cell phone, many small communities lack both cell phone coverage and web access. Newspapers are usually only available in large and mid-size towns. Up-to-date information can be hard to acquire in many parts of the state. Overall, however, the prices paid by middlemen tend to be low, but stable. The real markup isn't seen as the coffee passes through the hands of the coyote. The price jumps most noticeably between the wholesale level and the final sale to the consumer.

Many small producers are happy to simply hand their beans over to itinerant buyers who sell them to aggregators who re-sell the beans to big multinational companies who mix the beans together into a branded, but rootless mix. The Coffee Institute is working to help business-oriented producers improve their production techniques, boost their harvests and create a brand for their product. Jorge thinks coffee from Chiapas should be recognized as some of the world's best.

"Our coffee is shade-grown. It compares to the best Colombian coffee," Jorge explains.

Jorge wants Chiapas' farmers to follow the example Colombian producers have set. "Colombia has specialty coffees that sell for twelve-hundred dollars for a fifty-pound bag. Like Colombia we have the right soil conditions to make high quality coffee," he says. Jorge is confident that over the next few years as marketing and outreach efforts continue Chiapas will be recognized across the globe as a source for premium coffee.

Colombia's annual harvest is still ten times larger than Chiapas'. The small and medium sized farms in Chiapas will never rival the scale and output of the massive plantations in Colombia, but Jorge thinks that Chiapas' best managed farms can compete with the top producers in the world for the upper niche of the market.

"The idea is going for niche markets for specialty coffees," Jorge explains.

Chiapas' most savvy producers have had success targeting wealthy buyers with exacting standards in the U.S.,

Japan, and Germany. Right now around 80 percent of the state's coffee is sent to the U.S. It is packed onto pallets, loaded into trucks, and shipped over the state's winding highways up from southern Mexico to *El Norte*.

Jorge thinks there's a big opportunity to connect Chiapas' producers with coffee aficionados who demand the highest quality beans. He believes there's a role for the state government to play in helping producers and consumers overcome a classic case of imperfect information in the market. There are tens of thousands of small producers in Chiapas and a scattered global market of consumers of top quality coffee. The only challenge is the producers don't know who the consumers are or how to access them. Consumers as far away as Norway and Japan might be interested in Chiapas's coffee, but aren't sure where to buy the best beans.

Most small producers struggle to brand and market their beans locally, let alone in Mexico City or abroad. Many independent coffee farmers need to rely on certification programs to signal quality to buyers. Small-farm producers slowly and meticulously sort through their beans to remove the damaged coffee kernels. At a store or market, however, consumers looking at bags of coffee have no way to differentiate between good and bad products. Starbucks sells bags of coffee, and consumers across the world can see the white and green logo and know that they are getting a standardized, quality controlled product. Buying bags from smaller operations is more of a blind endeavor. Looking at a bag of Chiapas coffee, a buyer doesn't know anything about the quality of the beans, or the flavor profile of the roast. This obstacle of imperfect information between buyers and sellers inspired a group of local entrepreneurs to work with Chiapas' state-level Ministry of Economy to create a regulatory council called Brand Chiapas. The council reviews the production facility and product quality and sees its seal as an indicator that assures quality. Jorge sees the regulatory council at Brand Chiapas as playing a similar role to the business group that oversees the companies making tequila. Their seal is a market indicator that signals quality. When buyers see the pink logo they have a guarantee.

The Brand Chiapas initiative alone, however, isn't enough to overcome the geographical and cultural barriers that isolate indigenous communities. The state government has yet to create a single consolidated database that includes information on the characteristics and quality of each farmer's coffee. Even the Coffee Institute is still working to find the best producers.

Jorge understands the market and knows that to boost profits the state's producers need to do to standardize their production techniques and find new ways to more effectively market their beans. "The focus is on working with farms larger than five hectares and finding ways to maximize productivity," he says. The state's small farms, by contrast, have fewer options for technical assistance.

On his family's farm, Jorge has implemented many of the techniques he is promoting and says that he now sells his beans for 240 dollars a bag. With his own farming, Jorge is shifting to ultra-premium production. He'd like to see more of the state's farmers get a similar return for their work.

Few producers in Chiapas, however, can match his finesse for deal-making. Jorge enjoys a position of privilege and is well connected with government agencies, business chambers, and industry groups. His upbringing and education differentiate him from the indigenous growers in the mountain villages around the city. Small-plot growers aren't a priority for Mexico's agricultural agencies. Family-farm operators like Juan Carlos and his father have to define their strategy.

The most successful model for small farms is aggregation into collectives. It's a business strategy that Juan Carlos and his father are still trying to emulate. Other groups have already found success building up co-ops. On the outskirts of Tuxtla there's a facility owned by Ecological Indigenous Federation, an organization that brings together nineteen smaller cooperatives that span twenty-six different villages. The compound has a dormitory for members visiting from far-away towns, a large garage filled with tractor trailer trucks, SUVs, and delivery vans, a laboratory for testing the quality of samples of coffee, and an airplane hangar-sized warehouse filled with twelve-foot-tall stacks of fifty-pound bags of coffee as well as modern machinery for sorting and processing the beans. The Federation exports between 1 and 1.5 million pounds of coffee a year, and earns revenues of around 3.3 million dollars. The group sells some beans to premium brands, but also markets beans produced by the Federation's 2,500 families under their own logo. The co-op educates members on best growing practices to maintain a uniform standard of quality. The scale and scope of the operation also allows the organization to re-invest some profits in branding and marketing, activities outside of the range of possibilities for most individual farmers. The co-op's size also gives it economic relevance and extra support and attention from state government agencies. Co-ops have the resources to seek out help from initiatives such as Brand Chiapas.

Overall, however, the state's scattered and poorly managed coffee sector will struggle to modernize and increase productivity and profitability. Moving forward, Jorge hopes that more producers will seek out certifications to show that they are organic producers and follow fair trade guidelines. He knows that it can be hard for cooperatives to coordinate groups of small producers, but he also thinks that standardizing production and seeking out certifications are steps that are utterly essential to success. It isn't going to be easy, but he hopes that over time Chiapas' disparate group of coffee growers will find a way to consolidate their production into a more modern business structure, connect with premium buyers, and earn more.

To Jorge the strategy for developing Chiapas' coffee industry seems clear. He wants the state's growers to get higher prices for their beans. "What does the government want? That this coffee is priced right. That it pays," he says.

§ § §

Unlike the British colonies in New England, which were settled by tenacious middle-class farmers who traded Britain for bleak, snowy winters, rocky soil, and the promise of democratic institutions, Mexico has always been ruled by an oligarchy and defined by immense class divisions.[22] Even in the pre-colonial era Mexico's major civilizations were highly stratified.[23] Starting around 200 AD and finishing some four hundred years later, the Mayans, the ancestors of the Tzotzil and Tzelzal groups that now live in the hills near Juan Carlos's house, built an impressive limestone city in the humid jungle in the lowlands near the modern village of Palenque. Before the Mayans abandoned the city, the royal family lived in decadence and documented their exploits in elaborate hieroglyphic murals. Leaders such as Pacal The Great were buried in tombs like Egyptian pharaohs. Peons, on the other hand, were expected to eke out an existence growing corn and supporting the empire. Their subservience was exchanged for protection from raiders from rival societies.

When they arrived in 1519 the Spanish didn't have to impose the foundation for a hierarchical order; they just manipulated and built upon existing social structures. While colonists in New England built public schools and formed community-level governments that were considered to be egalitarian by contemporary standards, the Spanish constructed massive haciendas designed to produce and export cash crops. Like the mines in other parts of Mexico, the haciendas in Chiapas relied on the brutal exploitation of indigenous labor to extract wealth from the land. Wealthy Spanish landowners had few incentives to invest in quality public education and social services for their workers.

Thomas Cage, a British traveler who visited Chiapas in 1626, was not particularly impressed with the local elites. "Though they say they are great in blood and birth…they are, but rich graziers, for most of their wealth consisteth in farms of cattle and mules," he wrote in his travel journal.[24] The real source of wealth was not the plantations themselves, but the taxes that could be levied on locals. "Some indeed have towns of Indians subject unto them…and receive yearly from every Indian a certain poll tribute of fowls and money," Cage explained.

The relationship between governors and governed was predatory and exploitative. Forced labor was a valuable component of the colonial economy in Chiapas. Deriving so few benefits from colonial rule, indigenous villages in Chiapas rose up in rebellion in 1712.[25] Armed uprising, it seemed, was the only way to end the heavy-handed system of enforced inequality.

§ § §

Antonio, Juan Carlos' 47-year-old father, sits at the head of the long table at the back of the lot behind the house his family shares with another family who helps them sort and process their coffee. At five and half feet tall, Antonio has a sturdy frame, wide shoulders, and strong hands. He has neatly-trimmed black hair and no beard or mustache. Juan Carlos' mother, Petrona, who speaks only a few words of Spanish, works in the wood slat shed the family uses as a kitchen, heating water. Most days she wears a t-shirt and a skirt. On special occasions she puts on an elaborately embroidered red and white blouse, with a black skirt and a sash around her waist. Antonio's oldest daughter, who is also named Petrona, sets down a bowl full of beans.

"It's an indigenous breakfast," Antonio says, smiling. Picking up a thin, fire-blackened CD-size disk made from yellow corn meal, he adds, "these are real tortillas, made at home." The younger Petrona mills the dry corn kernels to make the dough. In Tuxtla, the city is filled with restaurants serving roasted shredded pork *cochito* tacos, a local delicacy, as well as more typical Mexican fare such as spit-roasted, shawarma-style tacos al pastor, a dish imported from Mexico City, and other regional dishes brought in from other parts of the country. The one small café near the main plaza in Pantelho has a more limited menu. The owner serves up simple scrambled eggs and tortillas. She also has a refrigerator full of bottles of beer and a row full of plastic gasoline jugs to make sales to customers who don't want to eat.

Antonio prefers wearing simple, utilitarian farmer's clothes. Today he picked a sun-faded maroon work-shirt. He never dons the white, thigh-length cotton tunic that some men in town still sport. Antonio sips a bowl full of black coffee and starts eating his breakfast. There are no spoons or serving utensils on the table. Antonio simply dips his tortillas into the bowl, scooping the stewed black beans into the fold.

Most days Antonio and his family just eat tortillas and beans, but sometimes they add greens. When the local farmers bring back their harvests they also collect some of the plants that grow in their fields. "Yerba morra—it grows in the farmland with the corn and the beans. It's good when its young, it's not bitter, but how do you say it? When it's not so young it's bitter," he explains, speaking slowly and deliberately pulling his words together.

Antonio also grows squash. He points to the broad flat leaves on a squash plant next to patio. "You can boil it or fry it—it's really good fried."

Turning to one of his workers, he speaks in Tzotzil, spitting out a string of rapid-fire, consonant-heavy syllables punctuated by a few words in Spanish.

Looking back down at his food, he explains that because of the security troubles his family is facing, he can't visit his farm to tend to his crops. "We can't enter the community. It's a difficult situation," he says.

As he looks down at his plate, a flicker of sadness flashes across his eyes. The food didn't come from his own farm. "We bought it from growers," he says.

While Antonio finishes eating, one of his workers loads freshly harvested coffee fruits that look like yellow and red cherries into a de-pulping machine. The electric, belt-driven machine draws the coffee in through a funnel and spits out the meaty fruit of the cherry, dropping raw coffee beans that look like golden peanuts into a small pile, and leaving a slightly sour smell in the air. The fruits have already started to decompose. They were left unattended while Antonio and Juan Carlos hid behind closed doors after the shooting. Antonio isn't sure when or if he'll be able to return to his land to harvest his coffee.

"It's impossible because of this difficult situation- we can't go in – it will go to waste. There's already spoiled coffee there that wasn't harvested," he says.

Antonio is considering his options. The bulk of his yearly income is in danger of being eaten away as his coffee fruits fall to the ground and rot. Antonio, however, is worried about his workers. He doesn't want to see somebody killed while collecting his crop, but he's also not sure that the local police can help him. "We'll see if the police can send a patrol, but coffee season won't wait for us. We'll see what they think," he says. The business world is full of battle-worn metaphors for violence. Cut-throat mercenaries can eviscerate their rivals through a series of hostile takeovers, put a tourniquet on bleeding profits, slice away fat and lop heads. Ruthless entrepreneurs can make a killing.

Antonio doesn't have much inclination for rhetorical flourishes. He hasn't thought about arming his workers with machetes or rallying local hunters to join together and help him protect his harvest. He just wants to make sure that his friends and family are safe.

"I'm thinking to let the coffee go to waste to avoid incidents. That's my idea. But we'll keep thinking," he says softly.

While he talks, he flattens out a pile of dry coffee beans on the table. Inspecting carefully, he pulls out white beans that are still covered by a thin husk. In a separate bowl he collects the small misshapen ones. It's a painstaking process to separate the bad from the good. The best quality coffee beans have a nice round shape and their colors fade from white to grey on the sides like tiny seashells. Speaking over the jangle of the pulley on the de-pulper, Antonio watches the machine spit out a small mountain of husks in back.

After the pits of the coffee cherries are collected and washed, the next step is air-drying. "When it's cleaned then it's laid out on the patio to be dried," Antonio explains. Antonio has thought about trying to certify his operation as Fair Trade or organic, but he isn't sure what office he needs to visit to start the process. He hasn't heard of Brand Chiapas. "I don't know which forms to fill out," he says. He's heard of the Coffee Institute, but says he hasn't heard of the group's technicians visiting any producers he knows recently. "They came to the community, but about twenty-five, thirty years ago," he says.

Antonio pulls a blue round-brim fisherman's hat over his head for protection. He climbs up the ladder onto the roof and sweeps away dust. He strains to pick up a heavy bag of coffee and dumps the beans into a pile on the cement. Using a wooden shovel that looks like a signpost, he flattens the beans out so they rest side by side. "I'm laying it out to dry. It has to be thin to dry evenly. If it's tall some will dry and some won't," he explains. The mid-day sun breaks through a thin layer of wispy clouds that hangs just over the hills on the outskirts of the town.

Depending on how much sun the beans get, it can take five or six days to dry. In hamlets all over Chiapas residents can be seen during harvest season drying out small batches of coffee on tarps by the side of the road or on the flat surface of their municipal basketball court. In the 1940s, Mexico's revered populist President Lázaro Cárdenas built basketball courts in Chiapas to help create a new secular culture in the state. Subsequent Mexican governments have continued to fund the construction of basketball courts as multi-use spaces that can be used to host tournaments, meetings, and for drying coffee. Absent the introduction of major industry or infrastructure, a basketball court is a small, but tangible sign that local politicians can point at to show their work for the community.

Balancing carefully, Antonio drags the rake over the beans, spreading the pile out evenly along the rooftop. Barefoot and moving adroitly, Antonio pushes the mound of beans with graceful, deliberate movements, leaving a uniform layer of hard coffee beans in his wake.

Once a week, after the beans are dry, Antonio passes them through another machine that shaves off the thin husk that clings to the dry bean. In twelve hours he can de-husk a full bag of dried beans. He then collects the shavings, which look like brittle slices of pistachio shell, and mixes them with the pulpy fruit from the coffee cherry to make organic fertilizer. The by-products of the production process are put back in to the soil, helping to ensure the success of future harvests.

The coffee operation is a long-term investment. It took Antonio ninety-five days to clear out the brush and ready his land for planting. The coffee plants he bought took several years to mature and begin to produce fruit. But now, just as he's starting to collect his coffee, security problems have made harvesting impossible.

Listening to the jangle of de-pulper Antonio pauses and looks over at the machine.

"That could be the last time this year we use it because of the incident," he says softly.

He doesn't think it is likely that the police will send patrol trucks to stand vigil while he collects his harvest. He doubts the soldiers that stand guard in the town center would come with him either.

Standing still, Antonio's eyes flicker in a brief moment of sadness. "For me," he pauses, "it'll be the last time."

§ § §

In Mexico the fight against entrenched inequality has been long and complicated. In the U.S., the American Revolution represents the end of the era of colonial exploitation. In Mexico, history unfolded differently. The 1810 uprising that severed ties with the Spanish ushered in a new era of national independence, but preserved the same crushingly unequal social structure. The majority of Mexicans simply saw their Spanish oppressors replaced by homegrown despots. In Chiapas, European-descended elites in San Cristobal launched a brutal Caste War against poor indigenous farmers from the surrounding communities in 1869. More than fifty years after the end of Spanish rule, the dynamic in Chiapas had hardly changed. By the start of the twentieth century, many landless peasants in Chiapas were still being forced to work on large plantations for a few pesos a month.

In Mexico, the civil war of 1910-1920 is called the Revolution.[26] It was the Revolution that aimed to replace the heavy-handed and highly elitist political structure that persisted throughout the eighteenth century with something more democratic. The men who fought to consolidate the country during the Revolution are today viewed as the most important hands behind the formation of Modern Mexico.

The early days after the Revolution, however, were a difficult time in Mexico. As rival rebels and generals killed off potential presidents one after another, a political movement emerged to pull all of the disparate and dysfunctional factions together under one umbrella party. The group, today known as the Institutional Revolutionary Party, or PRI for its initials in Spanish, consolidated Mexico's political life into one mercilessly well-organized machine and governed Mexico uninterrupted from 1929 until 2000.[27]

The PRI was built to bridge the extreme gap that has always existed between Mexico's classes. Today the party's name seems like a paradox. Some political parties such as the Christian Democrats in Chile or the Workers Party in Brazil choose names that hint at their ideals and loyalties. In the twenty-first century the concept of an institutionalized revolution is oxymoronic and almost entirely meaningless. Right now the PRI is far from revolutionary and also not much of a champion for creating strong, independent institutions.

In its early days however, the PRI party brought together industrialists and unions, urban elites and illiterate farmhands, the working class and the intelligentsia, disparate groups that shared few policy priorities. Over the first few decades of its existence Mexico's PRI-led government carried out perhaps the most audacious public relations coup of the twentieth century, employing globally recognized cultural luminaries to create high profile works mythologizing and manufacturing Mexico's new national identity. Diego Rivera splashed the walls of the stately National Palace in Mexico City with a bold and beautiful mural documenting the socialist roots behind Modern Mexico's rise. The mural shows a peaceful and dignified representation of Mexico's pre-colonial past and depicts an Aztec emperor and Hernan Cortes the conqueror standing side by side. It is Mexico's more recent fight against elitism and exploitation that Rivera paints as a violent struggle. He shows workers striking and protesting, Zapata holding a sign that says "Land and Liberty" and Karl Marx holding up a banner that says, "It is not a question of reforming the society of today, but rather of forming a new society."

Like Rivera, the Nobel Prize-winning writer Octavio Paz helped shape the world's opinion of Mexico's twentieth century identity. In his venerated work *Labyrinth of Solitude* Paz writes, "Propaganda and totalitarian political action...follow the same rules. Propaganda defends incomplete truths...later these fragments are organized and converted into absolute truths for the masses."[28] He then goes on to argue that, "the habitual reactions of the Mexican aren't exclusive to a class, race, or isolated group."[29] In post-revolutionary Mexico, Paz saw a common identity that cut across class lines. Rich and poor, multi-racial and European-descended, college graduates and uneducated day laborers all had to fight to forge their own identity looking towards the future and fighting against the "vestiges of the past."[30] But Paz also hinted that the ideal of an equitable society might not yet correspond with reality. In Modern Mexico, Paz says, "We lie not just to fool others, but also ourselves. Our lies reflect...what we aren't and what we want to be…At every moment one has to re-make, re-create, modify the personality we fake, until the moment arrives when, appearance and reality, lie and truth, are confused."[31]

In the first few years after the Revolution, Mexico's new federal government worked to turn its ideals into reality. The PRI's early origins were progressive and in many ways socialist. President Lázaro Cárdenas, the Mexican hero of the twentieth century, is lionized in Mexico for standing up to Standard Oil and nationalizing Mexico's oil industry. In Chiapas, however, many Cardenas' other initiatives are remembered as his true legacy. Expanding on work he started as governor of the state of Michoacan, Cardenas built up a massive public education system, and established schools in isolated communities throughout the country, sending in educated teachers from cities and setting a precedent for the policy initiative Fidel Castro would carry out two decades later in Cuba. Cardenas built a policy platform that is still alive today in Mexico. Within Latin America, Mexico's students trail only their peers in Chile in terms of performance on standardized tests. (In more recent decades, Mexico has not, however, pushed for a second wave of investment to match gains made by emerging economies in Europe and Asia.) In Chiapas, Cardenas is perhaps best remembered for his efforts to divide up the old haciendas and give many former plantation peons their own small farms.

A wide-shouldered veteran of the battles of the revolution, Cardenas had a serious demeanor. His short dark hair and bushy mustache framed his rectangular face, making him look pensive and intimidating. Cardenas is still remembered as the paternal founding father of Modern Mexico, a devoted leader with good intentions who cared deeply about the wellbeing of the residents in the mountain communities in places like Chiapas.[32] He stands out in Mexican history in the same way that Franklin Delano Roosevelt does in the U.S. His policies were transformative and still have an impact today.

Few of Cardenas' successors came close to matching his ambition and prestige. In the latter half of the twentieth century Mexico quickly became defined by the divide between the lucky club of politically connected patriarchs and a wider swath of the public that lacked profitable ties to government elites. As the revolution faded to memory, the PRI became the Institutional Party. The state built up the economy and created powerful allies to help keep the PRI in power. The worlds of politics and business were inextricably intertwined. Postwar governments abandoned many of Cardenas' most progressive outreach programs and focused more exclusively on industrial development. In the 1960s, seventies and early eighties, while Japan and South Korea emerged as strong industrial juggernauts, politicians in Mexico built up an inefficient state-controlled empire, connecting an expansive collection of government-owned companies to the PRI-controlled bureaucracy. While Mexico's mid-century PRI politicians succeeded in padding their own pockets, they never built any companies that were globally competitive in producing machines or electronic goods. Borrowing and negative trade balances financed the entire economy. The employment boom was unsustainable. During the mirage of the postwar bonanza, Mexico's government created more than a thousand state-owned companies and a complicated mess of price supports for farmers and food subsidies for urban consumers. The system didn't make economic sense, but it was profitable for politicians. It is telling that one of the most successful men in Mexico during the postwar era was Jorge Lopez Portillo, who pocketed an estimated 1 billion dollars during his term as president, building an ostentatious compound on the outskirts of Mexico City.[33] By the end of the 1970s this flawed, protectionist economic development model was failing, not just in Mexico, but across Latin America.

At the start of the 1980s, the mirage of Modern Mexico was already falling apart and the existing class divisions became even more entrenched. While elites shuttled their money overseas, the middle class went bankrupt when the economy finally collapsed in 1982. The country's federal government was forced to slash support for agricultural subsidies and let inefficient state-owned companies fail. By 1988 the Mexican Coffee Institute, a now-defunct federal agency that was tasked with buying coffee and providing technical support for coffee growers, had accumulated 90 million dollars of debt.[34] With the whole state-led development apparatus in trouble, Salinas' administration shifted away from the model of using the government to finance and support coffee production. The new generation of neoliberal PRI technocrats also put an end to Cardenas' land reform and created new rules to allow community farms like the ones in Chiapas to be broken up or sold and merged into larger estates. Factory workers lost their jobs and millions of small farmers saw their way of life upended. For much of the 1980s Mexico reeled like post-Hugo Chavez Venezuela, struggling with hyper-inflation, a series of severe recessions, and private sector bankruptcies.

In 1984, a U.S. Central Intelligence Agency analyst drafted a report warning about political instability in Mexico.[35] The American intelligence officers looking at Mexico saw the federal government's lack of control of many rural areas, surging inequality, poverty, unrest, and guerrilla activity in the countryside and sounded an alarm bell.[36] The report included an estimate that Mexico faced a 20 percent chance of collapsing into another period of revolution.[37] Mexico, however, has defied these pessimistic expectations.

The only good news of the era was that the breakdown of Mexico's monolithic state-controlled economy led to a new spurt of inspiring, but insubstantial democratic competition. With the PRI no longer able to deliver guaranteed economic growth, opposition parties gained strength. As the PRI shifted towards a more neoliberal, pro-trade agenda, the hardcore left wing of the party, led by Cuauhtémoc Cárdenas, the son of the former president, broke off to form the Democratic Revolution Party, or PRD for its initials in Spanish. At the same time, the longstanding opposition party, the National Action Party, or PAN, a group mostly composed of wealthy Catholic industrialists from northern Mexico, gained strength.

Throughout the 1980s, the PRI's untenable umbrella structure continued to buckle and break. The country's right wing, long frustrated with the government's misguided interventions in the economy, rallied behind the PAN. Mexico's left wing, dismayed by the disintegration of the PRI's most ambitious social projects, backed the PRD. In 1988, the PRI had to resort to outright electoral fraud to defeat the PRD's Cardenas, bringing a Harvard-educated economist named Carlos Salinas de Gortari to power. Salinas oversaw the final stage of the transition away from Mexico's hermetic, state-centered past towards a more open and trade-centered outlook.[38] Through a series of privatizations, he dismantled much of the state-owned economy and created Mexico's modern generation of billionaires. He signed a decree that gave Carlos Slim his telecom empire.

If Cardenas is remembered for the populist policies that helped the PRI consolidate power, Salinas is known as the architect of Mexico's modern, neoliberal policy framework. It wasn't the Zapatista uprising that toppled the PRI. It was Salinas's successor, a technocratic Yale-educated economist named Ernesto Zedillo who graciously oversaw the end of the PRI's "perfect dictatorship."[39]

As Mexico's public steadily pushed away from the 70-year-old Institutional Revolution, the country's center and right wing coalesced in 2000 around a tall, brash former Coca-Cola executive named Vicente Fox. And, on December 1, 2000 in a historic ceremony, Zedillo decorously passed a rolled-up Mexican flag to Fox. The world watched as power transitioned peacefully from the PRI to the PAN.[40]

The politicians from the PAN, however, never carried out any game-changing economic initiatives; mostly they stuck to the same strategies designed during the Salinas era. As was the case after the War for Independence, the people in power changed, but the policies and social structure remained the same.

In the 21st century, the overall focus of Mexico's national development agenda is still overwhelmingly concentrated in the industrial export hubs in northern Mexico. As was the case during the lead-up to the Zapatista revolution, during the first eighteen years of the 21st century, the well-being of isolated communities in places like Chiapas has not been in any way a policy priority, but rather a secondary concern handled by social workers. Independent, rural, entrepreneurs like Juan Carlos and his father feel like they can't count on anybody in the government to help them build and protect their business.

§ § §

Antonio squeezes into the back seat of the white Nissan taxicab. Juan Carlos climbs in front. "We're going to a local roaster. They buy green coffee," Antonio says. The cab winds through the mountain road, passing signs that advertise the purchase of coffee and the sale of chicken, corn, and medicinal plants and in hamlet after hamlet, hand-painted billboards advertising Coca-Cola. The world's most famous soda sells for five pesos a bottle in the Chiapas highlands, a substantial markdown from the twelve-peso bottles sold in cities. Selling soda for around twenty-five cents a bottle has helped Coca-Cola establish a foothold in Chiapas. More than any other global brand, Coca-Cola has succeeded in ingratiating itself into the insular, isolated, indigenous communities in the Chiapas highlands. During the five centuries since the conquest by the Spanish, the priests at the Catholic Church in the town of San Juan Chamula never fully embraced Christianity or abandoned their traditional beliefs. They instead embraced a form of *sincretismo,* a mix. The shamans, however, had no flexibility when it comes to their rituals. For the past few decades when performing rituals such as cleansings or sacrificing chickens, they used only Coca-Cola, never Pepsi.[41] Now there's a Pepsi distributor in San Juan Chamula and the shamans have started to use some of the brand's products inside the church. Pepsi also paid to paint over one of the main Coca-Cola murals near the plaza by Juan Carlos' house. In Mexico the balance of power between different cartels is always shifting. But on weekday evenings when the men in the town gather for pick-up basketball tournaments, they buy two-liter "jumbo" bottles of Coke to use as currency to bet on the games.

Juan Carlos is irked by the success Coca-Cola has had in the highlands. "They distribute to the communities. They have ads in Tzeltal and Tzotzil. Now that the communities get income from the government the businesses know they have money. This didn't happen before," he says. In the past, he says, soft drink companies didn't target the mountain towns. "It wasn't a profitable market for them. Now it is profitable because people have money from the government. They spend it on soda," he scoffs. By not charging the bottlers more for hundreds of thousands of gallons of water they pull from the ground every year, Mexico's federal government is indirectly subsidizing the soda industry.[42]

Descending through the final chicanes on the access road to the city, Juan Carlos looks out at the colonial cityscape, over the narrow roads and red-tile roofs. It's a conservative, Catholic, colonial enclave that has been infused with new energy from entrepreneurs who cater to the Mexican tourists and foreign backpackers who pass through. Through his window, Juan Carlos sees a spray-painted message. "Never forget October 2," the graffiti reads. "That's about the massacre in 1968 in Tlatelolco in Mexico City," he says, referencing the most brutal and overt instance of political repression during the 71-year rule of the PRI party, an incident that continues to resonate with a younger generation of protesters.[43] "Without justice there is no democracy," says another hastily spray-painted message. Juan Carlos looks out at a tourist with dyed blonde hair and a tongue ring taking a selfie on a cobble-stone side-street.

At the roaster, Antonio pours one bag into another as a worker inspects the beans as they cascade out. They adjust the bag on the scale and weigh it. "It's just short a little," the man says, scooping in a few extra handfuls of beans.

Working together, they load the next heavy sack onto the scale. The numbers 50.56 flash across the scale's digital screen, indicating the bag is half a kilo overweight.

"From this we'll take a little out," the man says.

Just by making the hour and half drive from Pantelho to San Cristobal, Antonio and Juan Carlos can charge higher prices. Buyers in their town center pay forty pesos per kilo. The roaster offers more than twice as much. "It's at ninety pesos per kilo right?" the man asks. It's a price that the roaster and his customers are happy to pay.

Rather than mixing the beans together with coffee from other producers into a faceless, undifferentiated mix, the roaster separates the beans by their place of origin and sells them to up-market customers looking for distinctive flavor profiles. Pointing to the bags on the wall the man lists the provenance of each bag. "There's coffee from different producers. It's Pantelho, Montecristo, Traiche," he explains. "Pantelho is a fruity, sweet coffee. It's balanced. It has a strong flavor, but the sweetness balances the acidity."

It's a business that caters to local consumers, but hasn't yet begun to export. "We have a restaurant and we have the roaster and we have a coffee shop too. But it's local. It's just sold locally," he adds.

With their bulk order of raw beans delivered, Juan Carlos and Antonio hand-carry bags of roasted, milled, and packaged coffee to other clients. They walk down main the pedestrian road and pass two light-skinned women in flowing luxury travel apparel who look like they are ready to do a photo shoot for *Vogue* magazine. The first stop is a vegan restaurant. Although a few high-end restaurants and cafes in San Cristobal have begun actively working to foster ties with indigenous suppliers from the mountain communities around the city, the state government hasn't launched a program to educate hotel owners and help place ultra-premium local coffee in front of the wealthy tourists visiting the city. Most hotels still serve watery, bland *café Americano.* If Juan Carlos and his father want to make inroads in San Cristobal, they have to do it on their own.

Antonio, who has changed into a long-sleeve button down work shirt for his business trip to San Cristobal, walks past two Mexican hipsters dressed in black. The couple's grey and white husky eyes him as he passes. On the sidewalk there's a black sign with playful white letters advertising "Jugo" and "Ensaladas" in Spanish and "Sandwich" and "burgers" in English. The couple by the door chats in Spanish while three blonde-haired, English speaking tourists hunch over a corner table under a mural of Emiliano Zapata. The Revolutionary leader's emblematic shotgun shell-holding harness has been painted as a vegetable carrier stuffed with carrots and instead of holding a rifle he grips a leafy, presumably vegan burger. Antonio smiles and greets the manager and hands over a stack of silver submarine sandwich-sized packages of milled coffee. "We charge one hundred and eighty pesos per kilo for roasted coffee," he says. It's about eight dollars more than he'd receive if he sold the coffee un-roasted to a buyer in the highlands.

Walking through the main plaza Antonio and Juan Carlos pass by the city's ancient cathedral towards a narrow side street that is home to many new high-end establishments, the types of restaurants and cafes that they want to connect with both in Mexico and abroad.

They walk past an artisan bread-maker with a sign says in English "Traditional bakers since 2015" and a restaurant called Bagel Station. It has a sign explaining that it's a multi-use bakery, art gallery, hostel, bar and cinema. They also stop at a restaurant called Bilil and talk to Ricardo Hernandez, the establishment's owner, a 47-year-old community development worker who left a job at the St. John the Divine Cathedral in Manhattan to return to Chiapas. In addition to serving food, Bilil also has display shelves that highlight products such as sausage, coffee, dark chocolate, and honey that are made by small producers.

"Tourists might just want to visit the city. But when they come here they get information," Hernandez says. "We focus on the local economy. If somebody wants coffee we sell it, but if they want to know the story behind the product we tell them," he says, eying two elegant, light-skinned Mexican tourists who settle down at a table in the middle of the restaurant and huddle together to take a selfie. The secret to helping small-time producers such as Antonio connect with consumers, he thinks, is to explain the history behind their products.

"There's a story behind every product. We bet on the local economy. The global economy doesn't let money stay in the community."

With the day's deliveries complete, Juan Carlos walks back to the main plaza to stop at a French bakery that sells flaky, fruit-covered pastries and croissants in addition to locally produced coffee. A hand-painted sign explains the prices. A *cargado* coffee made with a double shot of espresso costs twenty-one pesos, four times the cost of a bottle of Coca-Cola in the highlands. A *café Americano con leche* costs nineteen pesos. Each cup costs about a dollar, the same price that producers in the sierra receive for a pound of coffee when they sell wholesale to opportunistic middlemen.

For Juan Carlos, enjoying the privilege of sitting down for a coffee in such a posh café is something of an achievement.

When he was in high school he never came down from the mountains to visit San Cristobal's restaurants and bars with his friends.

Settling into a chair on the restaurant's second floor, he looks out at the urban Mexican tourists passing on the street wearing expensive, puffy, down jackets from brands such as North Face and Patagonia. "Things were more difficult then. My family had very little money. I didn't come here. For us this is the zone for rich people. You can pass through, but you can't enter the restaurants because it's so expensive. Now we have some income," he explains.

The first time he stepped into one of the coffee shops in San Cristobal was in 2008 when a co-worker, an engineer who didn't grow up in the hills, invited him to come for a coffee.

A few months away from receiving his bachelor's degree from one of Latin America's most prestigious universities, Juan Carlos feels more comfortable rubbing shoulders with Mexican and foreign professionals. "Now there's more tolerance and acceptance. In the nineties a Mexican from San Cristobal would say that the life of an Indian was worth a lot less than the life of a *ladino*," he explains.

He thinks that relations between Chiapas' Spanish-descended urban communities and the indigenous mountain people have improved, there are still divisions. Inter-marriage between the communities is still uncommon.

But, even the French pastry shop hasn't proved to be a particularly welcoming place. "An indigenous graduate student wanted to come in and they thought she was a street seller and they denied her entry because of her traditional way of dressing," Juan Carlos says. It's a story that was picked up by local newspapers.[44]

Still, things have improved from the heyday of Mexican nation-building during the economic boom years that followed the end of World War II. "My grandfather says that in the sixties and seventies, an Indian walking on the sidewalk had to step down to the street to let the ladino pass. The discrimination was really bad," Juan Carlos says.

"In the sixties and seventies they wanted to get rid of the indigenous communities. They tried to teach us mestizo ways because they said if we stayed indigenous we'd always be an underdeveloped country," he adds.

"My grandfather says that when he was young, the teachers came to school and brought kids to school by force. They taught the kids that they had to change. They tried to erase their identity. So parents hid their children," he explains.

Some of Juan Carlos' neighbors are equally skeptical about the federal government's conditional cash transfer program. Some men are happy to accept the money as a boost to their income, but others refuse to join. They are unwilling to let their wives participate in the mandatory health check-ups conducted by out-of-town doctors.

"Now, my generation has the awareness that they don't have to change what they are and submit to a way of life that exploits them. People are rescuing the ways of living that our ancestors had," Juan Carlos explains.

Selling in bulk at higher prices has boosted the incomes for the families participating in Juan Carlos' father's collective. "They're happy. It's collective work and because we're in the cooperative we get paid better for our coffee. Working alone we couldn't get that price. So, people are happy. They get better incomes. They can buy the things they need," Juan Carlos says.

As the waiter sets down a chocolate croissant and an almond pastry and a cappuccino, Juan Carlos turns to the waiter. "Where's the coffee from?" he asks.

"San Fernando," the waiter replies.

"Is it a cooperative?" Juan Carlos asks.

The waiter isn't sure. Juan Carlos nods. Maybe he'll come back a different day with some samples for the manager to try. Juan Carlos looks down over the balcony at a strikingly beautiful light skinned woman with dark hair and a baggy cashmere sweater. Listening to the jazz music wafting from the café's speakers, Juan Carlos settles into a comfortable pose on his stool. His current position in life is a long way from the hard years of economic isolation during the Zapatista uprising. Juan Carlos thinks the Zapatistas were too closed-minded. They ex-communicated him from their social circle when he decided to attend college in Mexico City. Their insular dogmatism makes no room for outside ideas. Juan Carlos is more pragmatic.

"We look for modes of co-existence with the capitalist economic system," he says. He wants to bring together a large group of small-time producers and form a collective that has the scale and revenues require to invest in machinery and marketing and help individual families connect with a wider array of buyers.

He's sure that in spite of the challenges his family faces, the coffee cooperative will be a success in the long run. "People taste our coffee, they say it's the best they've tried," he says.

He's confident that the cooperative will help connect his producers with better paying customers. "It's complicated, with coffee some people produce coffee and for being a small individual producer they get a very low price. They produce a small quantity and sell at a low price. It's unequal in the sense that the income for small producers who sell locally—the prices are low. They work that goes in, the fact that it is organic, isn't valued by the buyer," he says.

"There's an absence of vision by producers to bring their products to informed consumers like upper middle-class people in Mexico City who are prepared to pay higher prices for products that are gourmet, organic. They want organic products from small local producers," he adds. In his mind, productive enterprise will pull his community from poverty, not small-scale government programs.

"Mexico is a very unequal country. It has to do with the policies of the government. For whom are the policies designed? They aren't designed for the indigenous communities." Carlos Slim, Mexico's wealthiest man, has a diversified business empire that spans from telecoms, to construction, to retail. At his Sanborns restaurant chain, which has locations in cities throughout Mexico, Carlos Slim serves cheap, un-branded coffee. The absence of links between urban economies and rural communities is still one of the defining characteristics of Modern Mexico, nearly two centuries after the end of the Revolution. Mexico continues to be defined by immense class divisions. In the two decades after NAFTA came into effect Mexico's economy grew by an anemic average rate of 0.6 percent. Mexico's sixteen wealthiest families, however, saw their fortunes increase fivefold over the same period.[45] Mexico's wealthiest 1 percent controls almost half of the country's wealth. In 2012, the year Mexican President Enrique Peña Nieto entered office, Carlos Slim had a personal treasure chest of assets worth 69 billion dollars.[46] During the two decades after NAFTA Mexico's government spent a nearly equivalent amount on anti-poverty programs in Chiapas, but today nearly eight out of every ten of the state's residents live in poverty.[47] The dream of broad based middle-class economy in Mexico hasn't materialized. The NAFTA era has corresponded with an immense surge in inequality within Mexico, (as well as within the U.S. and other countries around the globe.) Chiapas is the most unequal state in Mexico.

"There are a few very rich people and a lot of very poor people," Juan Carlos says.

§ § §

The sun is still low in the sky, but already the asphalt on the road to the airport that sits between San Cristobal and Tuxtla Gutierrez is baking. Inside a late-model Volkswagen pickup truck a stocky driver named Otoniel sits fitfully in the morass of traffic clogging the avenue. The air conditioning is blasting. Most of Chiapas has been brought to a standstill by a group of farmers who have blocked off the key highways in the state. The state police are sitting by idly, allowing the protesters to prevent the capital's residents from leaving the city. Otoniel, who crossed over into the U.S. to look for work, came home and found a job as a driver in the state where he was born. He now works chauffeuring bureaucrats from Mexico's flagship anti-poverty program, Prospera. Otoniel makes his way slowly towards a back road that leads towards the airport. He knows not to try to force his way past the protester's barricade. "They are a bunch of *cabrones*," he says, using the utilitarian Mexican slang that is used to describe hardheaded tough guys.

Otoniel and his boss Fernando are often stymied in their work for Mexico's main anti-poverty agency, the Ministry of Social Development, by protests and demonstrations by angry groups of residents. Fernando is a friendly 26-year-old who studied civil engineering. He rose up quickly in the Social Development Ministry in his native state of Nayarit, midway up Mexico's Pacific Coast, north of Chiapas. Fernando has the delicate features of a Huichol Indian from his home state, but considers himself to be Mexican, not indigenous. "My family, we're *mestizos*," he explains, using the Spanish word for multiracial. "I consider myself to be *mestizo*, a cross between pure Indian and Spanish. Most Mexicans are *mestizos*," he adds. He lives a different lifestyle from the people he's visited in isolated, rural areas, but considers himself to be a good ambassador to help Mexico's federal government bridge the immense cultural gap and connect with indigenous communities. Through Prospera Mexico's federal government transfers cash income subsidy payments to the country's poorest residents, helping to alleviate the worst effects of extreme poverty.

This type of outreach program is no longer unique to Mexico. If any democratic country's economy fails to create mass employment the government eventually has to intervene. In the U.S., as Silicon Valley has surged back after the great recession in 2008 and the bulk of the economy sputters, a few tech billionaires have taken to promoting the idea of universal basic income, an automatic cash transfer to people whose jobs have been replaced by software and robots.[48] As the U.S. struggles to adjust to its twenty-first century economic reality and automated processes are replacing many service jobs, the idea of universal basic income has found proponents on both the left and right of the political spectrum. In Chiapas, the idea is already a reality.

Former Mexican President Carlos Salinas, a Harvard-educated economist once touted as Mexico's savior and now reviled as the architect who implemented NAFTA and eviscerated Mexico's inefficient old factories, provided early support for what is now Latin America's most ambitious anti-poverty program. Today Salinas' effigy is burned every year at religious festivals throughout Mexico as a stand-in for Judas.

The oft-maligned former president is mostly blamed for the deep recession that followed his presidency and singled out as the catalyst for Mexico's current economic struggles. What is forgotten, however, is that Salinas devoted his time at Harvard not to studying arcane macro-economic policy topics or industrial development strategy, but rather to analyzing the best techniques for building community-level organizations and addressing the poverty in under-developed rural areas.[49] The program connects the federal government with the country's most marginalized families and encourages poor parents to keep their kids in school.

Fernando has worked to build up a career helping to implement and orchestrate the cash transfer program. He started off giving surveys to residents in hundreds of small communities in Nayarit. He sometimes saw residents run into the hills abandoning their homes at the sight of approaching outsiders. Some towns were only accessible by foot or horse, a long way from paved roads. Still, Fernando has seen some success stories. He thinks Prospera can help pull isolated communities into contact with Mexico's broader economy. The program, however, often seems like a palliative measure. The cash transfer program doesn't seem sufficient to offset the other effects of opening Mexico's economy or compensate for the failure of the NAFTA-era economy to create enough well-paid, formal sector jobs.

Fernando and Otoniel are driving to the airport to pick up a Prospera's senior director. The only problem is, the protest might keep them from even getting to the airport. Fernando isn't sure that they'll be able to drive up into the highlands to visit the mountain communities. The blockades have become a frustrating, but unavoidable part of life in Chiapas.

"It's been difficult. The protests are constant and lately they've been aggressive. If you don't stop they can beat you. They destroy stores. It's vandalism," Otoniel says. In one recent case a group of protesters refused to let an ambulance pass. Two injured boys died inside the ambulance, unable to make it to the hospital.[50] In any case, sending a few officers often isn't enough. On a few occasions the Federal Police have sent in battalions of riot police to clear roads or protect government buildings. They have been met with fierce resistance.[51]

"The state government doesn't act. The demonstrators have become more aggressive. They fight," Otoniel says, inching his way forward in traffic. The tense dynamic in the surrounding community contrasts uncomfortably with the optimistic political slogans that plaster the side of the road. The truck passes a political ad for Chiapas' governor. "In Chiapas we achieve," the hand-painted message proclaims, a message that few residents in the state still believe.

Manuel Velasco, Chiapas's governor, is a young politician. Born in 1980, he was thirty-one years old when he was elected in 2012. He has brown hair, a thin frame, and paste colored skin. His nickname is El Güero, or "The Blonde." Like a courteous, but unpopular schoolboy whose mother still picks out his clothes for him in the morning, El Güero seems to be present at a never-ending string of public events, but is nevertheless disparaged as a failure. Since being elected, Velasco has decorated state government offices across Chiapas with large photos that show him wearing brilliant white shirts and standing, messiah-like, over crowds of dark-skinned indigenous people in colorful outfits. When he ventures out into rural communities El Güero dresses up in uncomfortably clean and starched rancher's clothes that look like they've never been broken in with a day's work. He shows up to shake hands for photo shoots and often flies away by helicopter. He isn't jumping into the middle of the disputes rocking the state to try to foster dialogue and try and resolve conflicts. El Güero disdains the dirt of local politics. He has bigger ambitions.[52]

As the traffic grinds to a halt, Fernando looks out the window and grimaces. "The governor wants to be president and he can't govern his state," he snarls.

There's a growing sense of frustration in Chiapas at the state and federal government's failures to govern effectively or catalyze any meaningful economic development. The coordinators at Prospera are facing a difficult operating environment.

Finally the traffic frees up, and the men arrive at the airport, a modern two-story steel-and-glass facility surrounded by a flat valley and ringed by mountains. The airport was opened in 2006 and is operated by the state government. It serves more than a million customers a year, most of whom fly in from Mexico City. There still isn't a lot of demand for flights that connect Chiapas to the rest of the country.

Celestino Calderon, a 57-year-old career public servant who now works as Prospera's National Coordinating Director climbs up into a passenger seat in the back of the truck's cabin. He closes the door with a muted clunk, locking the cold air inside the vehicle. Celestino has a disarming demeanor and an ingenuous, cheerful smile. He believes in his work and is proud to oversee public policy in action. Like Otoniel and Fernando, he wears a long sleeve button-up cotton shirt, opened at the collar with no tie. Even as social unrest and violence rise across Mexico, Celestino works hard to bring enthusiasm to his daily tasks.

Fernando delivers the bad news. "We'll have to go back to Tuxtla. The other highway is taken over," he says. "They are saying that nobody will get in or out of Tuxtla."

"It's like guerillas. *Chingue*!" Celestino exclaims, spitting out a Mexican curse word in disgust.

"Here in Chiapas it's complicated," he adds.

Frustrated over the protests and the cancelation of the itinerary of site visits, Celestino resigns himself to explaining the Prospera program's operations in the state.

"You have to attempt to understand the characteristics. In the state there are different regions. The south isn't the same as the north. We have thirty-eight coordinators who speak Spanish and a mother tongue. They can give presentations and surveys in Spanish and Tzelzal, Ttzotzil, and Ch'ol," he says, rattling off a list of local languages.

In Chiapas and other parts of southern Mexico communities are divided by language, ethnicity, and religion. Local political strongmen still govern many hamlets. In many towns, the local leaders, political bosses called *caciques*, are the de facto authority.[53] Because of laws granting indigenous communities high levels of autonomy, the federal government enters these areas as a humble guest rather than an absolute authority. The locals solve their problems. One of the towns near Pantelho has a large sign posted in front of it. "Welcome to the Autonomous Zapatista Rebel Town of San Pedro Polho, Chiapas… Where The *Pueblo* Rules And The Government Obeys."

Most of the time this improvised and informal dynamic appears to function moderately well, but in many communities conflicts are constant, sometimes igniting along ethnic lines, and other times because of religious differences or inter-party politics.

"There are confrontations," Celestino acknowledges.

Prospera agents have become accustomed to hearing about fights and murders arising from these village conflicts. In the mountains the local leaders decide how far the federal government can extend its influence. "Towns have their authorities. They have *caciques*," Celestino explains. "In the whole state there are social and political conflicts, but you see it more in the highlands," he adds, referencing the hills around Juan Carlos' town. Celestino sees Prospera as being implemented effectively in a very difficult context.

"The important point is to break the trans-generational chain where poverty is passed from generation to generation," Celestino explains as the truck rolls by a neglected adobe brick building.

Its roof, which is made from weather blackened red clay tiles, has partially collapsed. On the other side of the street there's a small restaurant post with a corrugated metal roof held up by a tree branch and a few slats of wood.

"All their lives they lived that way. They see it as normal. That's one of the biggest problems we've faced," Celestino explains.

Despite the massive investment the federal government has made in Chiapas, the tangible impact of the social programs has been minimal.[54] In 1990, 75 percent of the state's population didn't earn enough to meet its basic needs. Today that figure is 78 percent.[55] At the national level poverty has fallen in Mexico since 1990. Chiapas is one of only four states in the entire country that saw poverty increase during the post-Cold War era.[56] Today, over 38 percent of the state's residents suffer from food insecurity, the third highest rate in all of Mexico.[57] Whatever economic development has happened in Chiapas has been extremely concentrated. Chiapas is now the most unequal state in Mexico.[58]

Otoniel eases the truck past another billboard for Chiapas' governor. "In Chiapas we achieve," the sign declares.

Fernando has visited a handful of tiny hamlets in different parts of the state. He tries to be patient with the protests. "It's logical they demand more. For a long time they didn't get enough. Now that the government is offering programs, they demand it. Before they viewed it as a bonus, now they see it as obligatory," Fernando explains.

Still, Celestino is confident that the program can help. "At the national level we are helping seven million families, approximately thirty million Mexicans," he says enthusiastically. "In Chiapas we're in the whole state. We go to the mountains. Our coverage is really wide. We're helping

761,000 families. We're talking close to three million people," he explains.

Every year the program disperses more than 43 million dollars to people in Chiapas. To receive the payments, the families have to agree to make sure their children attend school and also come in for regular doctor's visits. There are also voluntary programs designed to teach financial literacy. Prospera offers the mothers who participate in the programs help opening bank accounts and also provides access to small loans. "There are successful cases of women who want to get out of the situation they're in. I think in Latin America we're the best program of this kind," he adds.

In the U.S. some critics complain that government agencies establish strict standards for child welfare, but don't do enough to assist low income families. Conditional cash transfer programs like Prospera are an alternative policy option, an anti-poverty program for an environment in which well-paid private sector employment isn't a viable or accessible option for most parents.

Overall, however, the impact of the program has been hard to measure. The percentage of the state's residents who failed to complete elementary school increased from 34 percent in 1990 to 37 percent in 2010.[59] As was the case at the outset of the Zapatista uprising, Chiapas still has the highest illiteracy rate in Mexico.[60] More than 21 percent of the state's residents can't read or write, a figure that is more than double Mexico's national average.[61]

Over the last few years Prospera has shifted from being a simple cash transfer program to trying to better address the country's social imbalances by fostering micro-scale entrepreneurialism.

"The supply of jobs is low. Monetary transfers aren't enough to pull people out of poverty. What's missing? That they start to produce," Celestino explains.

In the hamlets around the town of San Juan Chamula, Prospera has connected with almost 21,000 families and is working to help residents create businesses producing wool and handicrafts. Prospera also offers programs designed to help small coffee producers. *Ceterus paribus,* on a family-by-family basis, the initiative probably does have a positive impact, but in a marginal, incremental way.

It's not a game changer.

Critics, Juan Carlos included, say that Chiapas doesn't need more cottage industry, it needs a massive investment in infrastructure and an ambitious program to attract new industries and create more jobs. Prospera is a sedative designed to alleviate the worst effects of poverty. Chiapas needs a more intense intervention to fix its malignant structural problems. Absent supplementary economic development programs Prospera has the perverse effect of encouraging millions of residents to stay in the most isolated and least economically productive communities in the country. Juan Carlos sees the program as a means of creating a farm-system for loyal voters.

Celestino acknowledges that there have been challenges, but refutes claims that the program is designed to foster political alliances at the local level.

"In general terms, as a program we don't force the families to vote for a party. We don't say they have to vote. It's a social program. We don't do political activity," he says. In theory the program isn't politicized, but each presidential administration re-brands it and uses it for partisan advantage instead of building it up as trustworthy and independent institution.

As President, Salinas implemented his program under the name Solidarity. He quickly put it to use to undermine the swelling ranks of the revolutionary Zapatista army in Chiapas. Many prominent scholars believe that the Zapatistas launched their uprising prematurely, because they were worried about losing supporters as locals abandoned the movement to join Solidarity. Absent any real efforts to build up export industries and create jobs, the conditional cash transfer program no longer seems like a sufficient solution for social unrest.

Unfortunately for the people who live in the highlands around Juan Carlos's village, Mexico's federal government has concentrated expenditure for its national development agenda in other parts of the country. In southern Mexico economic development has been relegated to the micro scale. Chiapas has many basketball courts with uneven, unpaved dirt playing surfaces and backboards made from scraps of wood. The federal government seems to be just trying to teach the locals to subsist with what they have. Prospera's expanded ambitions are something of a paradox, an explicit acknowledgement that cash transfers aren't enough. The truck passes two small roadside stands selling "CARNE ASADAS" and "QUESADILLAS" in large, hand-written letters.

Fernando looks out the window eyeing the tall, parched grass and dry patches of dirt in the farmland next to the road and speaks into his phone. "Can you look for a project that we can get to?" he pleads. With the protest barricades in place, however, it looks like the day's itinerary will be canceled.

The line of cars creeps forward, inch-by-inch.

It's a frustrating end to the day, but Fernando, Otoniel, and Celestino are all grateful that the protest is peaceful. A few months earlier a group of indigenous protesters from San Juan Chamula, Chalchihuitan, and Mitontic, three towns near Juan Carlos's village, blocked the highway at the entrance to Tuxtla. When the police came to push them out of the street, the villagers attacked with stones and clubs. They beat one officer to death and injured five more.[62] In Chiapas, the protest blockades aren't just a form of free speech, they are also an open invitation to battle. Social unrest has become a major security threat.

As the serpentine line of cars pulls up next to two policemen standing next to a row of orange cones, Fernando eyes them with contempt. "When the protesters come they run!" he seethes.

In Chiapas local political factions have learned how to challenge and undermine the state authorities. Even the federal government can't manage to establish complete control over the state. A few days later a group of protesters tried to block the highway again. This time Federal Police in riot gear showed up and pushed the blockade out of the street. A separate demonstration in San Cristobal was less well contained. Protesters stormed the mayor's office and set it on fire.[63] In response the federal government sent in nine thousand federal police with riot gear to help impose order on the streets.[64] Less than a week after the reinforcements arrived, however, Tzotzil protesters from Chenalho, a village near Pantehlo, kidnapped the president of the state congress and demanded that their town's mayor resign immediately.[65] In San Juan Chamula residents shot and killed their mayor.[66] Following the Zapatistas example, the villagers in the mountains outside of

San Cristobal have learned to take drastic actions and demand that their grievances be heard.

In the hills around San Cristobal power respects power and the Tzotzils know how to get what they want. It's clear that Prospera alone isn't enough to contain the social tension rising in Chiapas.

§ § §

The highlands of Chiapas are a difficult place to do business without a knack for forging convenient alliances and a frigid, calculating appreciation for the value of *realpolitik*. Juan Carlos and his father are idealists who are being pulped and spit out by the brutal machinery of Mexican power politics. While Juan Carlos and his family are seeking pacifistic solutions to their problems, residents in the nearby town of Oxchuc stormed into action to solve their own problems. They set up protest marches, burned tires in the street, and kidnapped several dozen police officers and public servants. After several months of conflict, the town's mayor finally resigned, ending one *cacique* family's hold on the town's political leadership.[67] Juan Carlos and his father flatly reject the option of using violence to achieve their goals. They don't want to lose their dignity. They don't want to become like their enemies.

Sometimes before eating Antonio will gather his family around the table. *"Das bil te dios datil de dios niche nil das sol soktechu espirtu santo,"* he says solemnly, reciting the Lord's Prayer in Tzelzal. The prayer itself is a testament to the amalgamated nature of indigenous identity in Chiapas. *Datil* is father and *nich a nil* is son. Both concepts translate directly. But for the "holy spirit" no similar concept exists in Tzeltal, so the locals simply absorbed the Spanish *espiritu santo,* holy spirit.

Over the last five hundred years the Tzotzils and Tzeltales have found ways to accommodate foreign concepts. Although cocoa is a pre-Hispanic crop produced and harvests by the Aztecs, coffee is a more recent import. The Spanish word is café and in tzeltal it's *kah-pay*, a rough approximation of the Spanish pronunciation. Coffee might not be a traditional crop, but it's been embraced by traditional indigenous families. Antonio and Juan Carlos see it as their ticket out of poverty.

"The consumption of coffee in a lot of countries is growing. It's growing in Mexico. Finland, Denmark, Holland too. In general in the world coffee consumption is growing," Juan Carlos says.

With breakfast over, Antonio stands at the cement sink that his wife uses to hand wash the family's dishes and clothes. He fills up small jugs with honey, a gift he'll bring to a meeting with leaders from the Zapatista-affiliated community in Acteal, just down the road later in the day. Antonio is still looking for help. There's a crude wooden model of an AK-47 sitting in the window of the family's sleeping quarters, but it's just a home-made toy, a relic from a childhood spent living among the rebels. None of Juan Carlos's brothers have any real interest in going to war. Antonio and his family have always been committed to non-violence. When local politicians made a plan to build a sewer line that crossed through the family's orchard they sent workers to chop down a swathe of productive fruit trees. Juan Carlos and his grandfather went to videotape the scene and try and dissuade the workers and prevent the destruction. The men were undeterred. They beat Juan Carlos and his grandfather and took their camera. Antonio believes firmly in justice and sought help in San Cristobal. State authorities imposed a fine on the aggressors. The local politicians imposed a fine of their own on Antonio. They also started making threats. Faced with violent opposition, Antonio moved his family to the neighboring village of Pantelho, but he still has plenty of enemies among the local club of *caciques*.

As the threats against his family have become more frequent, Antonio has stopped attending the local church. He hasn't seen the sanctuary decorated with a nativity scene built from giant paper palm trees and a mismatched set of plastic animal toys. He no longer attends the church services, which are delivered in Tzotzil with a bit of Spanish mixed in. Antonio has suffered in silence, behind the security wall he built to cordon off his house. He thinks about the years he spent clearing away the brush and caring for his coffee trees. A flash of sadness sparks in his eyes. "Little by little we planted more coffee. Every year two hundred seedlings," he explains. He tended the plants diligently, waiting for them to mature, a process that took years, one he'll have to repeat if he's forced to abandoned his land.

As Antonio tries to explain his current struggles, his voice breaks into loud, heaving sobs. Seated on a chair next to the shed that holds his coffee roaster, Antonio is unashamed. He lets the tears streak down his cheeks. His voice strains. "I'm really sad... We lost our production.... I ask sometimes where is the word of God?" he seethes, heaving his words out in forceful bursts. Both Petronas cry quietly as they see Antonio suffer. Juan Carlos listens attentively.

The sun-bleached cow skull nailed on the wall of the shed watches over the scene.

While his father continues to talk outside, Juan Carlos ducks into the wood-slat shed on his back patio, and takes a seat alongside his grandfather on child size wooden chairs in the center of the loose dirt floor. The late morning sun glares through between the cracks of the boards in the building's walls. On one side of the floor there are a few empty coffee sacks, an old ax, and a circular disc of wood from a spool of electrical wire left over from a recent repair to the town's frail and often damaged electricity network.

In three generations, Juan Carlos' family has gone from being coffee plantation workers to independent entrepreneurs. Juan Carlos' grandfather used to travel down to the lowlands in Tapachula. He'd leave the family and go work on the plantations for three months at a time. In his limited Spanish, Juan Carlos' grandfather explains that he didn't earn much as a coffee picker. "*Muy poquito*," very little, he labors to say. Seeing the coffee business gave Juan Carlos's grandfather the idea of starting his own farm. Together with other families they bought an inexpensive stretch of property in the steep hills just outside Pantelho. They planted fruit trees and coffee seedlings. But in the eighties and nineties during the doldrums of the global coffee market, coffee was not a lucrative activity.

At the start of the NAFTA era they started to believe that coffee could become a good source of income. "We thought it was a good business because at the time we didn't have income. Our corn and beans were for our own consumption," Juan Carlos explains. The family embraced coffee as a way to try to engage the global economy without losing their community's values. Juan Carlos's brother Alonso drew a mural on the wall behind the coffee roaster. It's the face of an Aztec worker blowing on a hot cup of coffee. Next to the drawing there are depictions of giant coffee beans and the letters "EZLN."

From the beginning Juan Carlos and his family have believed that organizing a producers' cooperative would be the key to success. But it hasn't been easy to coordinate with other growers. They ended up abandoning a previous collective after bickering between members made collaboration impossible. But now, just when they think they are starting to get some momentum and find clients for their coffee, they fear that they might lose their farm.

"For the last three years it's been very hard to harvest. My dad can't go because of the death threats. My mom went in 2012. She was threatened," he adds.

Like stoic frontiersmen they hacked into the forest and built a small farm. Now, they fear they are going to lose it all. In a land where power respects power and justice is scarce Juan Carlos knows his family has few options for recourse. He and his family exist on the absolute margin of Mexican society, but he's still frustrated about how hard it is to move forward. "There's no justice in Chiapas," he says.[68] When the local authorities tasked with resolving community problems are the protagonists stoking the conflict, there is no one else in town that Juan Carlos can turn to for help. Juan Carlos and his father certainly don't think they can look for any allies at state or federal government agencies and they haven't thought about trying to align themselves with any local political parties.

Antonio has also lost faith in the efficacy of the Zapatista movement. "The armed uprising in '94 was supposed to end corruption. But it didn't happen. It's still the same. It was just some families who benefited," he says. He doesn't think his old friends who trained in the Zapatista army will come to his aid.

So far, the family's attempt to embrace Mexico's export-oriented development strategy and build a small business has been a string of successive disappointments. The

NAFTA era has mostly just been a boon for large corporations, billionaires, and wealthy urban professionals, but Juan Carlos and his family haven't yet given up hope on their dream of building a successful coffee export collective.

Antonio has a long-term view and a lot of patience. One of the most important symbols painted in the murals at the Zapatista headquarters in Oventic is the snail. The EZLN advocates gradual change. Bit by bit the family is moving forward. Juan Carlos studies Economics and focuses on community organization. His younger brother studies law. Maybe his younger sister will study marketing and English and work to better connect the cooperative to customers in the U.S. and other parts of the world.

Saying good-bye to his family and heading out towards Acteal, Antonio says that his goals are simple.

"Keep working. Keep fighting. I hope in three or four years it will be better," he says.

Mezcal in Oaxaca

A pile of raw agave hearts sits next to Pedro's distillery

Pedro stands in front of the barrels he uses to ferment the roasted and milled agave

Workers load agave on top of smoldering coals that have been covered with wet agave husks

After a day spent making mezcal, Pedro's workers dismantle the copper still

A wheel barrel sits in front of a pile of roasted agave

Alvaro stands in front of a truck filled with agave husks, the waste product of the mezcal-making process

The men stand next to the smoldering oven, watching the agave roast

The horse Pedro uses to pull the heavy stone grinding wheel pauses from mashing the roasted agave in the distillery's circular mill

School children stand in front of the basketball hoop at San Baltazar's bilingual elementary school

Pedro's daughter Flavia walks through an early morning haze of smoke to school

Carlos sips a small glass of mezcal after work

One of Pedro's workers stands with his family in front of their home in San Baltazar

Boys play soccer on a patch of dirt in front of the bilingual school

It's 6 a.m. on a chilly morning in mid-autumn, in the town of San Baltazar, high in the hills, an hour-and-half drive beyond the wide, colonial streets of Oaxaca City. Eduardo and Armando are already working, filling the still's copper pot with soft, soggy, pumpkin-orange, agave husks and thick coffee-colored water from the distillery's fermentation barrels. Their boss, Pedro, who lives next door, hasn't yet walked over to check on the operation. Down the hill in the town, the basketball court next to the village's centuries-old church sits empty, and the narrow dirt roads that wind between the cement block and adobe brick houses are silent. The schoolchildren, who attend the town's one-story middle school wearing white and navy blue uniforms, are still at home.

Climbing up onto a bench next to the six-foot wide, four-and-half foot tall barrels, Armando, a 22-year-old who grew up tending goats before transitioning to making mezcal explains, "It's been here for six days, because of the cold. When it's hot it doesn't take as long." A few yards away, the *palenque*'s dirt-covered underground oven emanates dull heat as a fresh batch of agave hearts finishes roasting. The sky, which on clear nights ignites in a blazing display of bright stars, is shrouded by a heavy layer of clouds, the culprits behind the previous night's rainstorm.

Using a pitchfork to load up a wheelbarrow with fermented agave, Armando explains quietly, "This is what the work is like every day." Armando and his friend Eduardo labor in insulated isolation. Their town is tucked into a valley behind a tall mountain out of sight from the nearest city, far from the coast, and farther still from the major highways that connect Mexico City to the U.S. border. When Armando climbed the peak he was able to see a long way off into the distance. "You see just mountains. Mountains and more mountains," he explains.

On most days Armando and Eduardo, a 24-year-old who returned to Oaxaca from California after earning enough money to build a house, start work by five. Before the sun comes up, the only light at the work site is the red glow of the hot coals from the wood fires used to heat the site's copper distillation equipment. During the cold mornings, they work diligently to a soundtrack composed of a cacophonous mix of braying horses, mooing cows, and screaming roosters, a chorus that mostly drowns out the tinny ranchero music blaring from the small speakers on Armando's cell phone.

Eduardo, a broad shouldered young man with pudgy cheeks, pushes wide, four-foot long logs of dried pine into the open ovens under the stills. To help get the fire started, he splashes pure ethanol, a waste product from a previous batch of mezcal, onto the logs and drops a match on. He sloshes in more ethanol from a green two-liter Fresca bottle and the heavy logs erupt in neon blue flames. He knows how long the agave juice will take to heat up and boil. "It takes about forty minutes, sometimes maybe half an hour," he says.

The two then load in two heaping wheelbarrows full of *vagaso* agave paste and eight knee-high white plastic buckets full of *tapache* syrup to each pot. The dark caramel brown sugar-water froths as Armando pours it into the belly of the still. With the fire now crackling and popping, Armando works to connect the copper tube that runs from the cooking pot to the condensation tank. He packs in natural putty made from the mud-like paste that forms on the tops of the distillation barrels to seal the joints. His breath is visible in the light from the red embers of the fire.

By 7:20 a.m. the night sky fades to a muted light blue, and by the time the fire in the third oven is lit, the first still is already operating at full boil, sending a trickling stream of clear, raw mezcal pitter-pattering out of the still into a plastic jug. "Look, it's ready," Armando says. He flicks a plastic cup under the trickling stream and brings it up to his lips for a taste. "It's really sweet because it's the first distillation. The second is more alcohol flavor," he adds.

§ § §

Oaxaca, Mexico's second most southern and second poorest state, has not fared particularly well over the past two centuries. In many towns, despite the introduction of a few superficial signs of modernity, life is in many ways the same today as it was two hundred years ago. Clustered in small villages, residents farm tiny plots of land and make simple products at home for sale in the city. Oaxaca enjoys the distinction of being the birthplace of the two most important Mexican leaders of the nineteenth century. Benito Juarez, one of the founding fathers of the modern Mexican state, was born in a small Zapotec town and served as president for five terms in the mid 1800s. Mexico's most famous dictator, Porfirio Diaz, another denizen of Oaxaca, formed strong alliances with Zapotec fighters and took power in 1876, serving as Mexico's iron-fisted president for six terms in office.

Diaz is remembered for successfully spurring industrial development in many other parts of Mexico during his time in office, but despite his deep personal interest in his home state, was unable to encourage much investment in Oaxaca.[69] Then as now, the principal problem is the absence of adequate infrastructure and the difficulty of shipping goods produced in Oaxaca to other parts of the country and world.

In the decades since World War II, during Mexico's modern era of industrial transformation, Oaxaca has continued to struggle. Highways built to better connect the state to Mexico City had the paradoxical effect of de-industrializing the state, as local factories that were unable to compete with less expensive goods imported from other parts of the country and world were forced to close. At the same time, Oaxaca's small farmers, like their counterparts in Chiapas, saw their traditional livelihoods squeezed as Mexico dismantled its complicated mix of agricultural supports.

Today, over eight out of ten of the state's 3.8 million residents work in the informal sector of the economy, running small roadside stores, picking up odd jobs on farms, and tending to their small patches of corn and beans.[70] But, despite all of its challenges, Oaxaca is also emerging as one of rural Mexico's few success stories, as the makers of mezcal, the smoky, rustic cousin of tequila, win new customers and a boost to their incomes as the state's traditional spirit finds favor with a new generation of consumers in Mexico's major cities. While the mezcal boom has encouraged many young men to stick around their home communities rather than migrate north to the U.S. to look for work, it also presents new challenges for indigenous groups looking to preserve their traditional way of life. Mezcal makers like Eduardo and Armando and their boss Pedro want to see their children receive an education that provides them with the option to go to college and become professionals while also conserving their Zapotec language and customs. At the same time, efforts to improve the thousands of schools that dot the mountain towns of Oaxaca have become one of the fiercest battles of President Enrique Peña Nieto's term in office. The reform effort is pitting parents against teachers and representatives from the state's notoriously militant teaching union. Across the country, the SNTE, the national teaching union has earned the ire of residents. The largest union in Latin America, the SNTE has come to exert a mafia-like control over Mexico's public education system and has violently resisted efforts to reform the system and reduce the graft and nepotism that define the currently reality of day-to-day operations.[71] Rather than present proposals and engage in public dialogue, the union's tactics involve violent protests that take over streets and enrage drivers and residents. The hardball tactics bring entire cities to a standstill and force the government to agree to concessions. The union doesn't care about the public's perception. Their principal field of operation lies at the negotiation table, behind closed doors and away from the political process. Teachers from southern Mexico have formed their own dissident, sub-section of the SNTE, the CNTE, that is even more belligerent and ready for conflict.[72] Teachers in Oaxaca along with their counterparts in Chiapas, have earned the reputation for being the most bellicose and battle-ready union members in Mexico. For Pedro and many other residents the teachers' union is seen as an obstacle rather than an ally.

In towns all over Oaxaca residents are working to find the balance between preserving their traditions and preparing for the future. The union, rather than emerging as a champion for one side of the debate or the other, has literally lodged itself in the middle of the street, tirelessly fighting to preserve its privileged position as the undemocratic arbiter of public education policy and payroll.

§ § §

With the stills now up and running Armando takes a seat and mixes up a cupful of bland instant Nescafe. "*Lac Ne-oh*?" [How old are you?] he calls out in Zapotec to Eduardo. "*Veinte-cuatro*, twenty-four!" Eduardo shouts back, using a mix of the Spanglish he picked up while washing cars in L.A.

"We're used to speaking Zapotec every day," Armando explains. For five centuries after Europeans first arrived in Mexico, Oaxaca's pre-Hispanic languages and traditions flourished. The start of the twenty-first century, however, has been challenging. The state is still home to communities who speak at least one of the fifteen indigenous languages recognized in Mexico's constitution. Around half the Oaxaca's population, just under two million people, identify as indigenous. Only around 400,000 of the state's residents speak Zapotec, a number that seems to decline decade by decade. Zapotec culture is just one of Mexico's distinct indigenous sub-groups, but it is known throughout Mexico for the intricately woven and embroidered blouses and dresses that women throughout the state continue to wear to festivals on religious holidays. The Zapotec people are an entirely different nation from the Tzotzils and Tzeltals in Chiapas, their language branched off and formed on its own sometime around 1500 BC. "Now a lot of people speak Spanish, but there are still a lot of residents who speak Zapotec," he adds. Armando, Eduardo, and the still's other workers speak Zapotec among themselves, but speak Spanish with visitors and customers.

"We mix Zapotec and Spanish," Eduardo explains. "*Wenca* is *bien* [good] and *Zac si* is *buenos días* [good morning]," Armando says. They worry, though, that the younger generation of kids growing up in San Baltazar is not learning Zapotec. Many can understand when their relatives speak it, but prefer to converse in Spanish when talking to peers.

§ § §

After a morning spent dumping dried, boiled agave husks in a compost heap by an agave field on the outskirts of the town, Alvaro, one of the still's workers, a slight-framed 46-year-old with a friendly demeanor and a bushy black mustache, stops by to visit the town's locally-financed bilingual elementary school. Hermelando Hernandez Garcia, a stocky, athletic 40-year-old teacher who works at the school that Armando and Eduardo's boss Pedro helped build, takes a break from teaching and stands outside the Corona-logo stamped sheets of corrugated steel that the residents used to cobble together the three-room building. The school doesn't have electricity or plumbing. The walls are held together with wire cable. The students share a small outhouse and a giant jug of drinking water that is trucked in from a nearby spring.

"We have a lot of needs, but the kids have a desire to learn," Hermelando says. "Here the parents speak the Zapotec language, but the kids don't. We think that's bad. We're promoting the rescue of the traditional language so it won't get lost," he adds. Still, despite the school's noble intentions, the teachers have faced challenges. "Their parents speak to them in Spanish. We speak Zaptotec here 5 percent of the time," he explains. Nodding towards a kindergarten-age girl he says, "For example she doesn't speak it." Pointing out a different boy, he adds, "But him he's older, he does."

The diminished importance of indigenous languages in Mexico is part of the legacy of the country's early efforts with rural education. In addition to dividing up big estates and handing land to small farmers, Mexico's fondly remembered president, Lázaro Cárdenas, invested heavily in rural schools, trying to bring Mexico's disparate countryside communities into the national fold. His policies may have helped forge a new national identity, but they also eroded community traditions. Alvaro remembers his own brief experience at the town's schools. "Teachers got mad at us for speaking Zapotec. They'd pull your ear," he says, smiling. The younger generation faces a different challenge. "They don't know what *zac si* means, how to say *buenos días*. They are missing out," Alvaro adds.

The men sometimes worry their Zapotec traditions are being erased. "Little by little it's dying," Hermelando explains. "Before we called oranges *ndrax* [a word he pronounces as gn-drahj]. Now, the kids call them [the Spanish word] *naranjas*. The language is being lost," Alvaro adds.

Hernandez rounds up his class from the dirt lot in front of the schoolhouse and corrals the students into the dark classroom. The kids take their seats at a mismatched collection of small desks and chairs. Hermelando writes on the board in blocky print the words *beku*, *xob*, *xil*, and *xuan*. "Sshhh, zhhh," Hernandez hisses, enunciating the Mandarin Chinese-like sounds of the words he's written. "*Xuan, Xop, Xibia,*" the kids repeat in unison, smiling enthusiastically and following the lesson attentively. The students also learn science, Spanish, history, and math just like the town's other schools, but most enjoy getting the chance to learn the language of their ancestors.

A few minutes later, the lesson ends and Hernandez and the kids climb up to the school's basketball court, a cliff-top patch of dirt sandwiched between two wooden posts adorned with comically small wooden backboards and tilted metal hoops. One of the school's other teachers leads the students through a song, first in Zapotec then in Spanish. Then she asks the kids to try shooting at the basketball hoop. A tiny girl holds a deflated blue ball behind her head and heaves it up towards the hoop. As the class watches, the ball rises only a few feet into the air before flopping into the dusty dirt with an empty thud. "OK, we need to get a smaller ball," the teacher says.

Hermelando looks on from the sideline. "This is the face of education in Mexico," he says. "Mexico needs to spend more of our GDP on education. Schools lack water, electricity, bathrooms, and computers." Although nearly nine out of ten schools in the state are now connected to the electrical grid, only one in ten schools has access to the internet.[73] More than 80 percent of the state's schools lack even one computer, a fact that makes the Oaxaca's public education system seem woefully underprepared to educate students to compete with peers from countries such as Finland and South Korea for jobs in engineering and industrial management.[74] Although he's seen changes in Oaxaca over the last two decades, Hermelando hasn't seen much improvement to rural education. Fifteen years ago to get to his school he walked for up to eight hours through the mountains after being dropped off after a 14-hour drive on the state's serpentine roads. Most of the students in Oaxaca's small mountain schools will probably find work in the state's massive informal economy. A few might go and look for entry-level jobs in factories closer to the border. Others might still want to try their luck crossing into *El Norte* and working in the U.S. for a few years. It's unlikely that many of the students will go on to attend college and break into Mexico's professional class. Stable, secure jobs in the formal economy seem like a distant possibility. "In this area the towns are very far apart," Hermelando explains. "But it's getting better, there's electricity and highways now."

§ § §

Easing his giant farm truck around a tight corner in the narrow road, Pedro peers through the windshield at the silhouettes of two men and a herd of sheep in the road ahead. "I started making mezcal when I was twelve," he says. It's a trade he acquired while working alongside his father, a fourth-generation master distiller. Pedro learned to grow and harvest agave and passed his days at his family's work site, a place that mezcal-makers refer to as their *palenque*. With each batch he produced, he watched weeks' worth of labor and several thousand pounds of agave turn into a few dozen bottles of clear mezcal—a product he then carried by horse to nearby villages to sell or trade.

Even today some producers continue to try and sell unbranded bottles of mezcal at roadside stands for as little as three dollars a bottle. As Mexico's economy convulsed in the 1980s and 1990s, Pedro didn't see much of a future in the mezcal business. "I wanted to work in *El Norte*, but I didn't want to leave my wife and kids behind," he says. He looked for opportunities to create a differentiated product and increase his profits. "I went up to the sierra to work with wild agaves," he says. Pedro learned to search for wild and rare strains of agave, identifying the plants by their shape and height and carting the plants' heavy hearts back to a tiny still that he rented.

Slowing his truck to a near crawl Pedro passes the men and their sheep. "Take a picture of me with my dog!" one of the men shouts out in staccato, accented English. Pedro, laughs and responds in Zapotec. He finishes with the utilitarian Mexican Spanish slang affirmation "¡*Órale*!" and accelerates up the rutted road.

The truck's headlights pierce through the low dusk light, illuminating tall cactuses and plants by the side of the road. Pedro cautiously passes a man with a donkey laden with bowling ball sized agave hearts, a product the men call *piñas,* the Spanish word for pineapple (with their leaves clipped off, the green and white balls resemble giant pineapples). The town's life centers around mezcal production—it's one of the only links that residents have to Mexico's modern economy. For Pedro and his workers, every day involves different tasks related to production. One day they might climb up into the hills looking for wild agaves. Another, they might cart a truckload of spent agave husks from the still out to their agave fields to use as compost. Although the hills around San Baltazar have been scraped by tilling of small, precariously terraced farms, mezcal is the only agriculture-based product that residents produce to sell. "The corn, beans, squash and chiles are just to eat at home," Pedro explains.

Mexico's Europe-enamored elites once ridiculed mezcal as the boorish swill of day laborers and *rancheros.* Now, ultra-premium artisan-produced mezcals like Pedro's are being embraced by Mexico's new generation of chefs and introduced to a new group of wealthy consumers across the globe. Just as Oaxaca's most traditional dish, the mole sauce, is celebrated for its complicated production process and complex layers of flavor, mezcal is starting to be recognized as a spirit that merits consideration along with the world's best whiskies and cognacs.

"The mezcal business is better now, but the agave is more expensive. The agave growers are earning well, but it's more expensive for mezcal producers," Pedro adds.

He's confident that his business will continue to grow. "I think it will get even better. Mezcal is better known and people like it." With high-end mezcals, Oaxacans finally have a product they can export.

Over the last twenty years Oaxaca has built new highways and Mexico has opened itself up to global trade and commerce. "Before it was different. There weren't a lot of cars and there were fewer highways. Fifty years ago they just took horses to go to the city. It's an hour and a half by car and on a horse it's five. Ten hours to go there and back," he explains. The truck bounces over the ruts in the road, its massive tires straining for grip as Pedro coaxes his way up a steep hill at 15 miles per hour. With darkness falling over the valley, Pedro eases the truck down through a canyon lined with steep cliffs and towering cactus plants, splashing across a narrow streambed.

"What I want is a life-long business," he explains. He's seen success through his partnership with a group of entrepreneurs from Oaxaca City. "They handle the management and I handle production," Pedro says. Steady sales over the last few years has made him confident that he'll be able to buy his children houses and keep the business going for another generation. Pedro has been able to move his family down from a small house in the hills to a brick home next to the still. The house has three bedrooms, simple cement floors, and a large plastic table on the covered porch where his family and workers can gather for meals. "All my ancestors were mezcal makers," he says proudly. Stopping to think, he adds, "We want to live better."

With his truck parked next to a giant pile of raw agave *piñas*, some of which are two-and-a-half feet tall, Pedro walks down the steep, rocky driveway to his distillery. Standing next to his oven, a massive pile of dirt girded by a waist-level fence made from heavy tree trunks, Pedro explains, "It's an underground, conical oven. It's four meters wide and just under two meters deep."[75] The agaves Pedro's workers haul down to the *palenque* have a color and texture similar to jicama, but are rock hard and filled with caustic juices that can burn the skin of the men who cut them. The roasting process, which is similar to a New Zealand-style *Hangi* or a New England clambake, caramelizes the agave. After lighting the fire in the center of the pit, "we load in tree trunks and rocks from the river. When the rocks get red hot we load in the *piñas*," he says.[76] They then cover the agave with sacks made from agave fibers and then pile on dirt, leaving the *piñas* to roast for seventy-two hours. It's a slow-going process that imparts the finished mezcal with a deep, earthy, smoky flavor, right out of the still. Industrial mezcal and tequila companies, by contrast, cook massive quantities of agave in steam ovens, and then impart the smoky flavor later through barrel-aging. "Tequilas are good, but they aren't 100 percent [craft-made]. They're industrial. There are industrial mezcals, but it's a different product. It's not 100 percent [mezcal]," Pedro says.[77]

After the roasting process is complete, Pedro and his men carry the agave to a pile underneath the roof of an adjacent shed to let the baked *piñas* cool. Pedro picks up a chunk of roasted agave, its color turned coffee brown and its flesh now soft and pliant. He hacks one of the large agave bulbs in half and plunges the machete into the heart's center, watching a stream of sweet brown nectar bleed from the wound. "Each agave has its own flavor," he explains, picking up a piece of the caramel-colored *piña* and popping it into his mouth. "It tastes like candied squash," he says, smiling. The next step is the milling process. At tequila factories milling is done by noisy machines that pass the agave on a conveyer belt through an industrial size grinder or an even more modern machine called a diffuser which extracts the juices directly. Pedro's team, like the other family-owned mezcal stills in Oaxaca, still uses a horse drawn stone called a *tahona* to slowly mill the roasted agave. "We pass it through the *tahona*, the mill," Pedro explains. "The horse pulls the stone wheel and does laps."

The next step is fermentation. While industrial tequila producers may use three-story-tall stainless steel vats, Pedro uses four chest-high wooden barrels. His workers use pitchforks to load in the dry milled husks and soupy, sugary pulp into the barrels. Pedro adds water from a nearby spring and waits for the pulp to ferment. It can take several days, depending on the temperature. "To see when it's fermented we use our five senses," Pedro says. In addition to running their hands over the pulpy brown paste that rises to the top of the barrels, "we look, we smell, we taste it, and we listen." Holding his ear next to the barrel he takes note of subtle hissing, crackling, and popping of the yeast at work. When the sounds stop, the fermentation is finished. Pedro also acknowledges the color and odor. "This one is blacker and smells less sweet. This one is almost ready for tomorrow. We'll pass it to the distillation area."

Under the roof of the shed that houses the stills, Pedro oversees Eduardo and Armando's work, watching the fermented agave paste boil and condense into sparkling, crystalline mezcal. As sales have increased Pedro has installed two additional stills in the shed. "There's a lot of demand right now. It's grown a lot. Sales have doubled in the last three years," he says, watching the steam rise from the condensation tank, the mezcal trickling out into a storage jug.

§ § §

With the wind picking up, Pedro watches Armando and Eduardo work. He runs a brisk business, but one that is facing critical constraints. As demand has grown, Oaxaca's supply of wild agaves is coming under stress. Every year Pedro and his employees have to push farther into the mountains to find plants to use for production. "Every ton of agave gives us 180 liters of mezcal," he explains. One of his favorite varieties is Arroqueño, a gigantic agave which imparts a complex, pungent flavor into the mezcal made from it. "Arroqueño is farm raised, but it takes fifteen to eighteen years to mature," he says. The mathematics of the production process create problems for the longevity of the business. It might take a week to produce a batch of mezcal, but ten to twenty years to grow the agave used to make it. Wine makers and vodka producers, by contrast, use inputs that grow in a single season.

It's a complicated business environment and Pedro isn't exactly sure of the plan for the future. He completed only four years of elementary school. Although he thinks in Zapotec and is more comfortable speaking his native language, he did pick up some Spanish during his brief experience in the classroom and learned a little bit more when he visited nearby cities. "I went to go sell my mezcal at restaurants and hotels and doing that I learned more because they just speak Spanish," he explains.

After dismantling the copper tubes in the still, Pedro watches the steam rise from the open boiling chamber, and pulls his jacket tighter. The cold night air gusts through the valley and Pedro eyes the last few electric red embers in the fire fading to dull grey. He has a 68-year-old father who hardly speaks any Spanish and two teenage daughters who study at the local school and almost never speak any Zapotec with their friends.

"My other daughter is six. She wants to be a mezcal master, a mezcal producer," Pedro says proudly.

He knows his bottling operation has upset some people in the town because he's hired women to package, label, and box the mezcal for sale and export, breaking a local taboo about women joining the workforce, but Pedro wants to see his daughters succeed.

"I've asked them what they want to do. They say they want to study," Pedro says. He thinks that formal education is the best option. "The six-year-old wants to help work. She doesn't want to study but I think it's better for her to study. If they study chemistry—we need chemists, they could work here," he explains.

Pedro sees education as providing the means to a better set of options than the ones he and his peers faced—choosing between making mezcal or migrating to the U.S. He says he tells his kids, "There's a lot you could do. If you want to do business administration you can do that. If you want to be an accountant you can do that too. Or you can be an agricultural scientist and study the soil." He's certain that the jobs available to people with a formal education are better work than hacking open agaves or bottling and boxing mezcal. "You don't need an education for this, but it's harder," he says.

He's happy with Hermelando's bilingual elementary school and is proud that his youngest daughter is a student there. "This school is really important because people [who graduate from there] can speak and work in Spanish and Zapotec," he adds. He's less confident in the overall situation with public schools in Oaxaca. "Here in Oaxaca there's a lot of corruption with the teachers. They are earning good salaries. They work five hours and earn [fourteen dollars] a day. Farm workers earn [eight dollars] and labor for ten hours a day." He is also frustrated with the teachers' political agenda. "Teachers prefer to go and protest. There's a group that's behind this, the Sección 22. They protest and ask for what they want and the kids miss out on their classes. The students suffer. They miss their classes and don't learn," he says. In recent years it's been common for students in Oaxaca to miss two to three months of school due to teacher protests. Pedro has a negative opinion of the teacher's union in Oaxaca. "Some are good people, but others just wait for their payday. They don't see to it that their students get a good education," he adds. In recent years the teachers' union in Oaxaca has blocked the federal Ministry of Education from administering exams to evaluate students' academic proficiency.[78] In 2009 Oaxaca participated in the global Program for Student Assessment (PISA) exam. In comparison to a group of the world's leading economies, Mexico comes in last place in student performance in Math, Science, and Reading.

Although overall Mexico performed better than Brazil,

Colombia, Peru, and Argentina, Mexican students lag far behind their peers in Europe and Asia. In Math, Mexico scored 419, ahead of Kazakhstan and Albania, but behind some late-blooming economies such as Singapore (562), Finland (541), and Serbia (442).[79] Overall, Mexico ranked 51st in PISA's ranking for student aptitude in math. (The U.S. performed marginally better, achieving a math score of 487 and a ranking of 31 in the list.) Within Mexico, Oaxaca stands out for the poor performance of its students. The state sits second to last within Mexico, behind only Chiapas, in terms of total number of years of schooling completed by residents. On average, Oaxacans have completed less than nine years of formal education.[80] Students who took the PISA exam in 2009 performed poorly. One third of all test-takers in Oaxaca showed insufficient math skills. Overall the state posted the fifth worst math scores of any state in Mexico.[81]

Still, despite the problems he and his family confront, Pedro feels at home in the hills of Oaxaca. He prefers life in San Baltazar. "I like to live in the village. I don't like cities," he says. By touch, feel, and practice he's become one of the best mezcal producers in Mexico. Today his mezcal, which is marketed under the brands Mezcal Union and Mezcal Koch, sell for as much as eighty dollars a bottle.

As the heat from the still's fires fades and the evening chill sets in, Pedro pours a cup of mezcal from a plastic barrel. "It's good for the cold and good for your dreams," he says. Considering the changes he's seen in his life, he says, "My grandfather, he knew more about the natural world." Zapotec elders have rituals to predict the weather for the upcoming year. "They watch the moon," Pedro says. As early as 1500 BC, Zapotec communities had already built impressive cities and satellite villages in the hills of Oaxaca, along with a rigid caste system that predated the hierarchical colonial government imposed by the Spanish conquistadores in the 1500s. Even though the Spanish were terrified by the Zapotec's penchant for sacrificing their enemies and destroyed whatever religious records they found, they did marvel over the complexities of the Zapotec language. In the late 1500s, one priest wrote a report in which he speculated that the Zapotecs might even have a more expansive vocabulary than their Spanish colonizers.[82]

Even without written records, however, the Zapotecs used stories to pass their language and traditions from one generation to the next. Village wise men trained their protégés to learn to interpret the dreams of residents, filtering their experiences through the lens of Zapotec theology. Like their neighbors in Chiapas, people in the Zapotec sierra continued to sacrifice animals, ignoring the prohibitions of the church. Local traditions survived three hundred years of Spanish colonialism and another two-hundred years of nation-building under Mexican governments. Pedro and his brothers laugh about their traditional courtship rituals which involve delivering firewood to a girl's father and waiting to see if he burns it or lets it sit unused. A few centuries ago, the Zapotecs switched from drinking fermented agave juice to adopting copper distillation equipment to make mezcal. More recently they have also picked up a penchant for blue jeans, basketball sneakers, and northern Mexican *corrido* music, but at least until the last decade they have also done a remarkable job of preserving their language and many aspects of their traditional way of life.

Pedro has seen his life improve as his mezcal sells to a wider base of consumers, but he is also aware that his community's traditions are slowly being eroded. "We can count in Zapotec. I can just count to thirty, but older people can count to two hundred. Only some people can count to one thousand." Unlike the modern Hindu-Arabic numerical systems used by all Spanish and English speaking countries, which is based on ten digits, the Zapotec numbers system requires an extensive vocabulary, words that most young people in Oaxaca aren't taking the time to learn.

Enjoying the evening unaccompanied by any of his workers or family members, Pedro sits and thinks. The only sounds around the *palenque* are the chorus of crickets in the surrounding hills and the intermittent pop from the logs in the dying embers in the oven. Pedro slowly sips his third cup of mezcal and reflects on how his business has evolved. He's now more successful than he imagined he might become as a child, but he knows his daughters will have to study new areas of expertise to bring their product to more consumers and carry the trade on for another generation. Rather than industrializing and shifting to a wage-based economy, Pedro wants to preserve his traditional, family-style, artisan production techniques while also looking for consumers in new markets who are willing to pay better prices for his bottles. "We ask God that the job will pay so that we can keep working," he says.

§ § §

November 28, 2015: As an army of federal police officers stand guard, cordoning off the streets surrounding a government office hosting a day-long test for student teachers, several thousand teachers gather in the center of Oaxaca's capital city. Oaxaca's teachers are notorious for their militancy and aggressive protests. Learning the autocratic style of *caciquismo* – or strongman politics – over the last twenty years, they have consolidated control over Oaxaca's education system. The Peña Nieto administration has seen constant protest from Oaxaca's teachers who have set up campsites in public areas both in Oaxaca and Mexico City, staged marches, and blocked roads.

In the process, they've drawn the ire of the public. Nearly nine in ten people in Oaxaca say they oppose the teachers' extreme tactics.[83] In Mexico City, economists and political analysts pillory the teachers, saying they want to protect their racket-like control of hiring and payroll and are the number one enemy of efforts to improve education in Mexico.[84] In 2015, however, after two-and-a-half years of appeasing the teachers, the federal government began to take a harder line, arresting teachers when protest tactics extended beyond the realm of free speech and took the form of kidnapping, destruction of property, or assault. In the first major success story of the education reform, the national Ministry of Education seized control of the Oaxacan Education Institute, effectively retaking control of promotion and retention and distributing salaries from the union.[85] Never a group that shies from conflict, however, several thousand teachers gathered in Oaxaca City to denounce the government's efforts to meddle with the existing system for managing public education.

Marching along with thousands other protesters, Julio Arias, a 27-year-old teacher, holds up a sign and nods towards the crowd stretching off into the distance on the road ahead.

"This is what happens when the government imposes a repressive reform. They want to give us temporary contracts, fire teachers, and lower salaries. Anyone who doesn't get evaluated will be fired," he says. "I have colleagues who are here because they know they'll lose rights," he adds.

He teaches in Juxtlahuaca, a small town that sits a six-hour drive away from Oaxaca City. "It's a community with a lot of needs. A lot of people go to the U.S. to work. There are no upper level schools nearby."

Passing graffiti that spells out, "No to the Evaluation," Arias explains, "In Oaxaca there's a lot of corruption. It's not transparent."

While Arias does acknowledge that Mexico's education system faces problems, he doesn't see Peña Nieto's reform as an adequate solution. "In Oaxaca and the whole country, education needs to be improved, but the reform isn't the way to do it. We need equality. We need to improve the working conditions for the whole country. We have a lot of natural resources and a few people control all the wealth while others have to work all day long to bring food home. That's not fair. Some kids come to school without eating."

Arias, whose parents are both teachers, says that he joined the profession because he enjoys seeing kids from disadvantaged backgrounds grow and develop. The school where he teaches is in an isolated town where students have little contact with outsiders. "It's a community with a lot of needs," he repeats.

Mexico's national teachers' union, the SNTE, has developed a bad reputation in part because of the cynical corruption and ostentatious displays of wealth that characterized the group's former leader Esther Gordillo before she was arrested at the start of the Peña Nieto administration in 2012.[86] At the time of her arrest, Gordillo had developed a taste for collecting real estate both in Mexico and the U.S.

Her flashy designer clothes and gaunt, surgically enhanced face became an indelible visual reminder of the profligacy of the union leadership. Gordillo's greed and the increasingly militant practices of the union members, who block roads and trap drivers in bumper-to-bumper traffic for hours on end, have earned the teachers a great deal of public contempt.

While many teachers see their fight against education reform as a battle against privatization and (misguidedly) claim that the government wants to charge families fees for public education and force schools to cover their own costs, Arias sees a more complex picture.

"We have to root out corruption. It can be corruption with the teachers too. We have to talk about it. That's what we need. There's no communication," he says.

The crowd chants, shouting in unison, "Section 22. There's only one!"

"They're saying there's only one [legitimate] teachers' union," Arias says.

Section 22 is actually just one part of the CNTE, an offshoot of the national SNTE union. The self-aggrandizing chant is one more sign of the Section 22 union members' view of their importance within Mexico's political system. But, perhaps such rhetoric is useful when formal methods of interacting with government representatives have broken down. "Marching is the only way to be heard," Arias says.

On many occasions after teachers from Section 22 have abandoned their posts to attend protests, parents and government officials call in teachers from a rival union group the Section 59, another part of the CNTE. In towns where the economy hasn't evolved much since the middle ages, Section 22 teachers have adopted medieval battle tactics, attacking en masse to drive out interlopers from Section 59 and re-take physical control of schools, hurling rocks with slingshots and using home-made bazookas to launch fireworks at the invaders.[87] Most of Oaxaca's indigenous communities have communal property structures that grant control of particular parcels to the residents who take the effort to till and farm them. The teachers seem to have a similar view of the control of the schools. "There's an ideological fight that can turn violent. We need to communicate and work together. We need to be united," Arias says.

"We need to improve education. It's not just evaluations of teachers. We need better books. We need a lot of things. Teachers need professional training programs," he adds.

The teachers rightly criticize Peña Nieto's education reform as being more of a labor reform than an education reform. The policy overhaul, after all, is also designed to wrest control back from the militant union members who have hijacked the education apparatus from the state and federal governments. "If you miss three days in a month it's grounds to be fired. The law creates a lot of rules that can result in firing. It's total control," Arias says. The new rules, however, are also designed to combat the chronic absenteeism that has characterized education in southern Mexico. Students who lose three months of classes per year when teachers leave campus to attend protests miss out on a lot.

The new rules are designed to hold teachers accountable and will be almost impossible for the teachers to overturn. They are part of a broader package of reforms Mexico is implementing to improve its economic competitiveness. Over the first few months of his term in office President Peña Nieto's PRI party tried to promote itself as a technocratic, pragmatic, and powerful party that combines Ronald Reagan's enthusiasm for slick public relations, Lyndon B. Johnson's ability to corral political support for political initiatives, and an old-school Tammany Hall style taste for (often corrupt) behind-closed-doors deal making. Early on Peña Nieto's administration did succeed in pushing through a series of economic reforms were celebrated by many Mexico analysts and economists in the U.S. In addition to the education reform, Nieto's government also squeezed through controversial tax-code reforms and an energy reform bill that most Wall Street analysts say should help boost tax revenues and attract investment in the long term. The education reform, however, has quickly become a major point of controversy. As more accusations emerge about corruption scandals relating to senior members of the PRI it's becoming harder for Peña Nieto and his team to lecture the CNTE about the need to eliminate graft, fraud, and nepotism and increase the efficiency of government spending.

But, despite heavy opposition from teachers, the education reform in Mexico continues to be one of the most popular reforms of the Peña Nieto era.[88] In many respects, the teachers are pushing against the popular will when they work to disrupt it. "It won't be easy, we know that. But as teachers we have to defend what's right and face the consequences," Arias explains.

As a rule, Mexico spends a higher percentage of its education budget on teacher salaries than any other country in the Organization for Economic Co-operation and Development, a club of thirty-four industrial countries. But, in terms of test scores, Mexican students fare the worst of any country in the group. "It's not that salaries are high, it's that there's a shortage of infrastructure," Arias explains. The challenge is that the perseverance of traditional community lifestyles in southern Mexico has meant that the states of Chiapas and Oaxaca, as well as many other parts of the country, have largely bucked the worldwide trend of urbanization. In a largely agrarian pre-industrial economy, many Zapotec and other indigenous communities prefer to continue to live in tiny hamlets in the mountains rather than consolidating into larger, urban centers. A total of 5,600 primary schools serve over 529,000 students spread out across the state's mountain villages.[89] To put this in perspective, the U.S. state of Connecticut has a similar population size and body of elementary school age students, but barely over 1,000 elementary schools.[90] Oaxaca also has 2,510 high schools that serve an additional 231,000 students. Providing quality education for such a dispersed population is a nearly impossible task.

The fact that Mexico's rural schools face problems doesn't diminish the fact that over the last half century Mexico's government has invested massively in public education. Within the Latin American context, Mexico's schools compare favorably when stacked up against institutions in Brazil, Venezuela, or Colombia. But, by global standards, Mexico is lagging.

In Oaxaca even students who graduate from high school face bleak options in the labor market. "We need more jobs. Oaxaca is one of the states where people leave to look for work. Jobs here don't pay well. We need more employment. Some communities make hats, pottery, fabrics, mezcal. They need help marketing their products," Arias says. What Oaxaca needs, he thinks, is a better way to connect producers to consumers. Mezcal might sell for two dollars in unmarked bottles at stands by the side of the road in the sierra and for several hundred pesos in Mexico City. The difference is that the entrepreneurs who sell in Mexico City or abroad know how to brand and market the product.

"The earnings don't stay in the community. Producers sell cheaply and middlemen sell for more in other places." The problem is, for local people to market and sell their goods to a broader market, they need to be able to hire people who know how to run businesses, speak English, and promote sales online and in social media. Students at schools with no computers who miss out on classes and abandon their studies after a few years aren't likely to acquire the skills that the artisans in their communities need to connect with customers in big cities. Overall, in Oaxaca most young people still have little hope that they will find work outside of the precarious informal economy.

"We need to do a lot to improve Oaxaca. But it can happen if poor people stick together. We can make something positive happen. There's hunger for justice," Arias says.

Walking past men wearing Kentucky Football and Rolling Stone sweatshirts, Arias explains why he is upset. "Politicians earn really high salaries. Congressmen earn[nearly six thousand dollars] a month. A teacher earns [nearly five hundred dollars] a month and we have a university education. That's not fair," he says.

As the crowd swarms up, over, under, and around an elevated overpass in the road, a woman yells into a megaphone. "Who loves the political class?" she screams.

"Nobody!" the crowd roars back.

With the marchers now approaching the cordon of police, their energy starts to build. The police, eyeing the demonstrators, stand in tight formation behind a heavy metal security fence, holding their riot shields in front of their bodies. "It's over, it's over, your reform is done for," the crowd taunts. Frequent violent clashes in Oaxaca have marked Peña Nieto's presidency. In one of the worst instances civilian gunmen started a shoot-out with the Federal Police and also assassinated a photojournalist. Arias knows that teacher's rallies can turn violent quickly.

The teachers in the front row lock arms, restraining the mass of people choking the highway behind them. "Don't let them provoke you!" a woman on a megaphone yells. Young men in sweatshirts wearing t-shirts over their faces jockey for position, hurling insults at the police.

At a separate event in Chiapas during the same month, teachers attacked a testing site and after the conflict with local police escalated, one group of protesters tried to use a bus loaded with Molotov cocktails to break through police lines. When the homemade bombs exploded prematurely, the bus caught fire and the driver lost control and ran over and killed a teacher.[91] That protest then devolved into a protracted street battle in which teachers carrying sticks and wearing masks hurled Molotov cocktails at the police who maintained their positions, letting the bombs explode against their shields, sending bursts of flames into the air.[92]

"We're peaceful. We don't look for conflict, but we have to defend ourselves," Arias says.

As the tension in the crowd boils, a few rocks whiz out up into the air from the crowd and crash down into the phalanx of police in riot gear. A few organizers try and fail to assuage the crowd. "Calm down! Calm down!" a middle-aged man yells, holding his hands up towards the men pushing towards the security fence. Out of the police lines rocks fly back, smashing on the ground in the middle of the street by the protesters. One of the men calling for order jumps out of the way as mango-sized hunk of stone explodes on the tarmac next to him. As people shout, a group of young men in masks runs into the street, shaking the fence, trying to knock it down. Like a violent storm-wave crashing into the beach, the police rush forward. As officers fire tear gas grenades into the panicking crowd, baseball sized rocks fly over the fence in both directions crashing into metal posts with frightening clangs. While a few young men wearing masks seek shelter behind a wall and fire rocks with slingshots, the police up the ante, firing a self-propelled tear gas missile that hits ground in front of the teachers and continues whizzing in circles before flying up into the air. The teachers look up, running in panic, not sure where the grenade will land. The projectile rises again into the air and instead of crashing down again near the crowd, lands innocuously on the roof of a building.

A few men seek cover by the edge of a wall, hurling rocks over into the adjacent street where the cops stand. The avenue, however, is already filled with noxious gas, and the protesters are feeling the effects. A young woman pours Coca-Cola over a pudgy man's face. Tears stream down his cheeks while he squeezes his eyes shut and stumbles forward blindly. Another man walks away splashing water on his face. His eyes burn red. He wipes his face and blows his nose, blinking blankly and walking forward, stumbling away from the melee. One block away from the confrontation, a group of teachers belittles the police stationed on a side street. "Sons of whores! Go take care of your families. Go take care of your wives!" The officers hold their positions. “We’re here to take care of your wife,” one of the police retorts.

Seeking safety a block away from the fracas, one protester explains, “We hope that’ll be it, that there will be no more confrontations,” As the tear gas lingers in a white haze near the security fence the crowd began to dissipate. A teacher wearing a motorcycle helmet and sunglasses who had previously been pontificating about fighting privatization surveys the scene. “That’s it, the show’s over,” he says.

§ § §

By 7:30 a.m. Pedro’s 15-year-old daughter is ready to walk down the hill to the town’s public middle school. In Oaxaca many students walk for more than an hour to get to class. Flavia has it relatively easy. “If I go fast it takes me twenty minutes. If I go slow, half an hour,” she says. Flavia, who is heavyset and wears a navy sweater, knee-high white socks, and black dress shoes to school, says her favorite classes are Spanish and Science. Walking through a heavy haze from a neighbor’s charcoal bonfire Flavia explains that she likes reading chemistry books. She doesn’t read much literature. She’s heard of *Romeo and Juliet*, but she doesn’t know who wrote it. She wants to learn more about the world.

Unlike her neighbors who work burning firewood to make charcoal to sell, roasting agave to produce mezcal, or making simple garments on wooden looms, Flavia thinks she wants to leave San Baltazar to look for work. She plans to attend high school in a nearby city and wants to go to college in Oaxaca’s capital city. She thinks there are other opportunities beyond the border of San Baltazar. She prefers to study Chemistry, a subject area her father supports. But, she also has to study English, a subject she practices for an hour a week along with the other students in her classroom.

In terms of English education, Mexico's public school system is failing students.[93] Studies show that despite being the southern neighbor of the world's largest English-speaking economy, Mexico ranks behind forty-three countries including Finland, Estonia, Poland, Argentina, Spain, South Korea, Peru, Chile, and Ecuador when it comes to English language proficiency.[94] During English-hour her teacher leads the class in repetition exercises, dictating phrases from an English textbook published by Mexico's Ministry of Education. The book is choked with errors and on the nights that Flavia has to complete her English homework, she struggles to comprehend anything beyond the most basic words. She recognizes some phrases, but struggles to remember the meaning of words that don't have Latin roots and often confuses words that sound like Spanish words. "I don't really understand English," she admits. She has an illustrated Spanish-English dictionary, but she says, "I don't really use it because at school our teacher helps us translate." Her book is filled with awkward phrases such as "My mother was cooking meal" and "It looked as a common day." Flavia needs to look up the meaning of even the most basic words such as "because" and "when." She isn't even sure about how to use the Spanish-English dictionary and flips back and forth between sections, aimlessly searching for a particular word at random rather than scanning alphabetically through the list.

By contrast, the teachers at San Baltazar's bilingual elementary school help the students learn incrementally with assignments that involve clear explanations of the words involved. Both of Flavia's younger sisters communicate fluidly in Zapotec. English is more of a struggle for Flavia. She knows simple words like "father," but labors to read directions. She can't understand simple commands such as, "Answer the following questions." She estimates that she understands around 15 percent of the words in the passages she is tasked with translating. "I don't get it. I don't understand English," she says. Partly her struggles have to do with the limited time her school dedicates to English instruction, but she also misses class when her teachers leave to attend meetings or protests. She estimates that she loses three days of school per month when her teacher doesn't show up to teach.

Still, learning English is not her top priority. She doesn't plan to follow the example of her uncles and travel north to look for work in the U.S. "Our parents don't want us to go. They say it's far," she says. Walking past the adobe brick houses that line the narrow street leading to her school she explains that many of her classmates want to study. "Some want to be teachers. Others want to be architects or scientists."

Walking through the main entrance to her middle school, she passes the small, dimly lit classroom where she and her twenty classmates study. "It's one teacher in the same room all day," she explains. She walks towards the basketball court behind her school. The court has a massive Chicago Bulls logo painted in the center and additional Bulls logos on the backboards. Flavia isn't sure of what the drawings represent. She hasn't heard of Michael Jordan. Even though her cousins wear basketball jerseys and Jordan brand sneakers, she and her friends don't watch the NBA. "People here don't have cable. Some people might like to watch, but they don't have the equipment," she says, taking a break from heaving two-handed set shots towards the rim. Flavia plays on her middle school basketball team and practices two times a week with her squad.

At 8 a.m., the school's director calls the students towards the basketball hoops. As the students form neat rows around the four edges of the court, a skinny student wearing a dark blue sweater yells out, "The military band will now honor the national flag." A group of female students in purple and brown outfits that look like girl scout uniforms carry the flag towards the Chicago Bulls logo painted in the center of the court, walking in a stiff-legged march, moving forward with military precision, an homage to the Zapotec army units that fought during Mexico's nineteenth century civil wars.

A few students playing horns provide a squawking backdrop and skinny boys play snare drums, shattering the morning silence with their military rat-a-tat-tat drum rolls. The students sing together.

"Mexicans, at the cry of war prepare the steel and the steed and may the earth shake at its core to the resounding roar of the cannon," the sixty students sing with muted enthusiasm. The song, written in 1854, is a call to action that the students' ancestors heeded during the country's nineteenth century conflicts.

"I want to commend the students I've seen who have stood still with their hands in their pockets for the whole presentation. You can now break formation," the school's principal, speaking in a friendly, encouraging tone says. With their Monday morning ceremony over, the students file off of the court and walk up the hill to their classrooms.

§ § §

A few hours after the teacher's protest ended, a wedding party moves past the cathedral in the center of Oaxaca. Isidoro Yescas, an elderly professor wearing a grey suit and frameless glasses, settles into a seat at a restaurant on a quiet side street. By now traffic has resumed in the highway and the teachers have all dispersed from the street. The confrontation, however, is not an event that Yescas will forget. In the absence of dialogue and deal-making, the battles on public roads have defined the interactions between the teachers and the state's political apparatus.

"It's a mistake by the Section 22 to use methods that alienate society such as leaving the schools, but the government also makes mistakes. Today the state government let the Federal Police take control of the city of Oaxaca. The reform has been carried out in a context of police control. It shouldn't be a threat. It wasn't right to have the Federal Police here." Yescas explains. Sipping a cup of black coffee, he jokes, "I'm not from any party. I'm a sociologist, a political analyst; a Oaxacologist. Oaxaca is so complicated that we need Oaxacologists to understand it."

He thinks that the education problem in Oaxaca needs a Oaxacan solution. "The problems with education in Mexico are focused on the problems of indigenous people in southwestern Mexico—the problems of nutrition, food." The root problem in Oaxaca, Yescas says, is poverty. "It's holistic. You can't solve the education problem without solving the poverty problem," he says.

The challenge is that the public debate has almost entirely ignored the details of the reform and focused on the confrontation between teachers and the police. Newspaper articles focus on politicians promising to push their reform through despite any opposition from teachers. In the absence of policy debate, teachers warn parents that their schools may be privatized. In reality, the reform will increase local control of the education budget, helping make sure that schools get the money earmarked for them.

At the heart of the issue is the insane amount of money being handed out to individuals on the payroll who aren't really teachers at all. The fraud has been well documented by respected media outlets such as *The Economist*. According to studies conducted by prominent Mexican think tanks, there are tens of thousands of people on the payroll who never show up to teach anywhere. There is another equally large group of teachers who are either retired or dead, but remain on the payroll as active teachers. Likewise, there are tens of thousands of teachers working at union offices or in other capacities who are still collecting salaries from the Ministry of Education even though they aren't working in the classroom. While the federal government has tried to conduct headcounts and verify the names on the payroll, the Section 22 has blocked these efforts and demanded the government honor the current arrangements. Mexico's Ministry of Education calculates that there are over forty-four thousand "ghost teachers" illegally collecting salaries as educators even though they don't teach in classrooms.[95] By some estimates, corrupt teachers (and the politicians who help them) may be pillaging the education budget for as much as 262 million dollars per year.[96] It's a fraud of massive proportions that the teacher's union has made no effort to fix. The teachers' rhetoric does not mention the problem. It's an issue that is swept out of the union's bellicose dialogue in favor of a focus on privatization, a buzzword designed to spark public outrage.

Meanwhile, the teachers continue to draw the public's ire. In Oaxaca, drivers can download an app called S-22 to warn them about blockades from the union.[97] "Oaxaca has the most radical union. People get upset when they go on strike. People get upset when they block highways and take over buildings and disrupt life," Yescas says. Over the last decade, the use of home-made bazookas during protests has defined the Section 22's violent struggle to protect their jobs and power.[98]

"Those bazookas are urban warfare weapons," Yescas says.

The battle lines have been drawn and many people feel that the teachers are fighting against the public's interests. "The problem I see with the social movements in the region is that they push for their private interests," Yescas says. The teachers are putting their labor struggle ahead of the education of the students. Like the peaceful protesters standing near the front lines of the march, the students who miss months of classes are unfairly being caught in the middle of the dispute. On average students in Mexico spend just nine years of their childhood in school.[99] In the U.S. the average is more than four years higher.

Individual teachers might not notice much difference from the movement of payroll allocation being shifted from the state level to the Federal government. But, for corrupt union leaders siphoning off the salaries paid to fictitious ghost-workers, it's the end of an empire and a cause for rioting.[100]

Teachers in Mexico have fought for and won the right to be paid salaries that sometimes pay them for up to five hundred days of work even though they only work two hundred days a year.[101] They can still expect these salaries to be paid by the federal government. Union officials, however, can't openly admit that they fear losing control of payroll and rally teachers from humble backgrounds to join them in the (entirely made up) fight against privatization. Many of the claims the teachers make about the potential effects of the reform seem designed by union leaders to cloud and confuse the policy debate. No real discussion can take place when the two sides are not even talking about the same reform. In Oaxaca, rather than sifting through the truckload of details, the debate has been distilled to a discussion of the teachers' methods.

"In Oaxaca we can no longer tolerate the suspension of classes. That can't be a tactic. We have to prioritize the students," Yescas says.

Instead of being a discussion of policy details, the war over education reform has turned into a polarized *lucha libre* free-for-all wrestling match. Depending on who you talk to, the dispute is either a fight of Mexican nationalists against a corrupt class of neoliberal technocrats or a struggle by federal bureaucrats to wrest control of Oaxaca's schools from a nepotistic and self-serving union of power-hungry pedagogues. "Each side set its conditions and neither is willing to look for middle ground," Yescas says.

He also thinks that while both the police and commentators in the media have moved in to attack the union they are ignoring the role that corrupt politicians have played in ransacking the education budget. "They hide the massive corruption at Oaxaca's education ministry of the PRIista governments from 1992 until now. Former Oaxacan state governors Ulises Ruiz and Jorge Murat—they used the Oaxaca's education ministry as their piggy bank for political campaigns—they had ghost workers. If they accuse the union of corruption they have to admit they participated," he seethes.

Oaxaca's governor Jorge Murat has also faced his fair share of scandals. A lifetime politician, Murat faced down heavy criticism after a newspaper report revealed that he owns a luxury condo in New York.[102] While the teachers are lambasted as corrupt and self-serving, the public debate in Mexico has largely avoided the topic of grab-and-go state-level politicians who have helped facilitate the graft and fraud that is draining the education system of its resources.

Growing animated, Yescas shouts, "How many ghost teachers have there been between 1992 and 2015? How many? It's a ton!" He slams his hand down on the table. Nobody in the restaurant hears him or looks over.

§ § §

In the early afternoon, while Pedro's cousin, a former migrant worker named Leo who played pick-up basketball after work in California and still has a few pairs of basketball shoes from the U.S., finishes dumping the last load of milled agave into the fermentation barrels, Pedro sits down to savor a glass of mezcal with his business partners Carlos, a Oaxaca-based entrepreneur of Zapotec descent and Andres, a Mexico City-based executive who started working as the Chief Operating Officer of a mezcal company two months earlier. Andres previously worked as a business development manager at some companies including Proctor & Gamble, Diageo (the company that produces Johnnie Walker whiskey), and the tequila company Don Julio.

Andres has the relentlessly analytical mind of a business consultant. While Pedro speaks in simple terms about his production process and Carlos gushes about the unique characteristics and almost spiritual benefits of the artisan techniques, Andres looks at the underground oven and horse-drawn mill and sees a bottleneck with the process. "It's not scalable," he says.

Andres, who wears spotless clothes and an iWatch, saw different forms of production when he worked for Don Julio, a company that distills industrial-sized quantities using high-tech automated production techniques. He's the sort of well-educated Mexican professional who is equally comfortable meeting for a business lunch at a fancy bistro in Mexico City or a trendy hotel in Brooklyn, the types of places that have started serving boutique brands of mezcal as the spirit has garnered acclaim in the last few years. Andres knows the small-batch production that defines ultra-premium mezcal brands is essential for imparting unique flavors. However, the outdated machinery also makes it difficult for him to create a global brand the size of Jose Cuervo or Herradura.

"The *palenques* have limitations. If it stays artisan there are limits on production. It doesn't support growth. There are three big bottlenecks. One is the fragmentation of suppliers, the second is long-term planning of the supply of agave, and third is the process; you can't expand production by growing a plant and putting in 30 ovens. You have to form alliances with more families. We need to have Pedro too, but also his cousins," Andres explains, rattling off rapid-fire sentences filled with business jargon. Unlike other spirits which can be scaled up into global brands and made profitable through mass marketing and economies of scale, mezcal production is still tied to its artisan roots and hard to scale up.

Pedro listens to Carlos and Andres talk. He wraps his wide fingers around the glass. His fingernails are stained with agave juice. He relaxes in his seat and soaks in the conversation, letting his feet hang limp, resting on the sides of his dusty, leather huarache sandals. He represents the old generation of farmworkers who both produced and consumed mezcal. For now, he's happy to let Carlos and Andres promote his mezcal to wealthy young consumers and handle the complicated paperwork to get permits for exporting. Mostly, he is just proud to see his mezcal winning approval and find steady buyers for his bottles. Three different varieties of his mezcal have won gold medals in different competitions over the last few years.

Carlos explains that as the public both within Mexico and abroad embraces mezcal, "People judge more. They question more. Where is it from? Who makes it? Bartenders are interested in knowing."

Carlos is a hipster who wears trendy leather bracelets and might fit in well at Burning Man. He is the bridge between the worlds of the rural residents making mezcal and the urban elites who drink it. He speaks Zapotec and jokes around with Pedro's children when he sees them. He dresses a lot like the leftist, anti-establishment intellectuals who first brought mezcal to popularity in grungy, punk rock dive bars in Mexico City's bohemian Coyoacan neighborhood.

"It's growing, it's a trend. People who don't know about mezcal are trying it. Its flavors are complicated," Carlos says enthusiastically. Presenting the brand to bartenders and foreigners is a time-consuming job, one that is well suited for Carlos's gregarious and tireless personality. Pedro, who tends to be shy around people he doesn't know, once tagged along with Carlos on a business trip to Spain, but he declined an invitation to give a presentation in Spanish in front of a room filled with strangers. Walking through the sierra, Pedro can identify several dozen varieties of wild agaves by the size and shape of their leaves. But without Carlos, Pedro knows that he'd be just like the other local mezcal-makers who hope to sell their bottles to passing motorists and tourists.

The impact of the mezcal trade goes beyond the employees who work at the stills. The mezcal boom has also created a surge in demand for agave, a boon for the area's family farmers. Rather than trying to buy land, Carlos has embraced the communal *ejido* property structure and signed deals for fifty-fifty profit sharing arrangements with landowners who agree to plant agave on their properties. "In four years we've planted seventy hectares," he says. A farm that produces 160,000 kilos of agave might garner more than fifty thousand dollars for the crop at today's prices.

Carlos is also proud to see his bottles selling for market-leading prices at boutiques in Mexico City. "Our bottles cost up to eighty dollars and they are respected," he says.

Andres adds, "Mezcal is now the most expensive product category. It's more expensive than cognac."

Carlos sees additional opportunities to foment economic growth in rural Oaxaca. "The development of agave could be a business. But nobody has developed the farmland in Oaxaca—because there's no private property. The property here is communal. You need permission from the community."

The still's workers also see opportunities for growth. Eduardo, Armando, and Pedro's cousin Leo earn less than ten dollars a day working at the still. "It's not enough," Leo says. Eduardo wants to build his own still in his backyard, but hasn't been able to find a partner to front him the money to build it. "I could earn more producing," he says. If sales continue to grow in coming years, more brands may start combining mezcal from multiple stills to create a single umbrella company. If this happens, more small producers will be able to sell their mezcal to foreign consumers and the economic impact of the mezcal boom will start to be felt in places such as San Baltazar. When that happens, Eduardo and his co-workers will build new stills and become managers and mezcal masters in their own right.

With the bright morning sun already flashing over the mountains in the distance, Pedro looks down at the smoking pile of rocks in the open pit oven. Leo and the others work to stack up a truckload of agave to roast for the next batch of mezcal. As a billowing plume of smoke rises, Pedro reflects on the evolving nature of his mezcal business. Thinking about whether it is better for his daughters to study English, Spanish, or Zapotec, he says, "For me it would be all three. They speak Zapotec. They need to speak Spanish too and English too. People come here to visit who speak English and we need to be able to speak English."

Pedro's primary concerns are about his daughters getting a comprehensive education that will allow them to achieve professional success. He sees the young generation of residents in the town growing up speaking Spanish, but isn't worried that Zapotec culture is being destroyed. He's already seen the cultural disruptions caused by several generations of cyclical migration to and from California. He wants to make sure that his children find jobs closer to home. As a neighbor leads a pack of horses past the still up into the dry hills behind the *palenque* to look for sparse greens to eat, Pedro says, "It's not necessary for them to speak Zapotec to understand the traditions." Thinking about what life in San Baltazar will be like by the time his children are grandparents he says, "By then [the Zapotec language] will be lost. Here in the town just 40 percent speak Zapotec. The rest speak Spanish. For me that's bad because they are losing their roots. The kids feel ashamed to speak Zapotec. They are losing their language." But, even though the change saddens him, he thinks the benefits may outweigh the costs. He says that most of the town's elders agree with his perspective. "The elders they also think it's good and bad," he says. It's true that some traditions are being lost, but if young people from the town can speak Spanish, "they won't be scared to leave to go work," Pedro says.

Pedro sees his limitations. "There are a lot of words that I can't explain in Spanish," he says. He sees the changes in his community as the evolution of Mexico's national character. Since its formation as an independent country, he says, Mexico has been an amalgamation of "a lot of different cultures and different languages." But, he thinks that the preservation of indigenous languages can't take precedent over the creation of education and employment opportunities. "There are still people who are closed off. They still don't speak Spanish and they are scared of people who speak Spanish. There it's so isolated the teachers can't get there. [The residents] don't know how to read or write. The life there is different. They produce everything they eat."

But, Pedro doesn't want to see his kids struggle to earn a living in the informal economy. He hopes that they can join Mexico's professional class and find careers at formal sector companies or help him finally produce and market his brand. Rather than feeling a tremor of nostalgia for the village life of his youth, Pedro, who sometimes struggles to express himself in Spanish, sees the restrictions that isolation engenders. "It's not easy for them to learn. The kids there don't have the option [of going to college.] For me wide options [are better.]," he says. Thinking about his children, Pedro says, "They can leave to get to know other parts of the country." Young people who don't learn to speak Spanish, by contrast, might be more scared to leave. "If they can take advantage [of their education] and do what they want, that's good," Pedro adds. He sees what his business partners in Oaxaca and Mexico City bring to the business and he wants his children to acquire those skills. "We want to access different markets in other countries. They can be ambassadors for the brand." Pausing and thinking about his own children's interests, he says, "Or they can be chemists." For Pedro, the changes do have an upside.

"There's good and bad, but if they can speak both languages they can carry on the traditions of the *pueblo*," he says.

Avocados in Michoacan

Javier eats avocado and birria beef stew before starting work at his avocado orchard

Former autodefensa vigilante fighters patrol with the newly formed Fuerza Rural police force

Avocados inside a packing plant in Tancitaro

A volunteer community police gunman guards a checkpoint on the outskirts of Tancitaro

A Fuerza Rural officer stands guard on the road leading into Tancitaro

A worker loads in cases of avocado to a US-bound truck at the JBR packing facility in Tancitaro

An old man watches police and pedestrians pass through the main plaza in Tancitaro

A new truck parked in front of a row of traditional houses in Tancitaro

A white SUV drives in front of a castle-like security checkpoint on the road leading out of Tancitaro

Two volunteer citizen police stand guard in Tancitaro

Citizen gunmen standing guard in Tancitaro

Javier brings his horse out of the stable after a day spent overseeing operations on his avocado orchard

Members of the CUSEPT police patrol in front of an avocado orchard in Tancitaro

It's Super Bowl Sunday and Michoacan is at war. Over the last few weeks of 2014 residents have seen major shootouts almost every week, but it's still not clear which side is winning. When a vigilante leader named Estanislao "Papa Pitufo" Beltran rolls into the town of Tancitaro, leading a caravan of eighteen trucks from inside a massive black Hummer with bulletproof, tinted windows, locals are on edge. The cross over the church in Tancitaro's center glows bright neon red at night, but residents still aren't sure if it's safe to walk around after dark. They know that cartel gunmen have killed heavily armed federal police in ambushes. The locals feel like they've been left unprotected as the state's crime bosses slowly weave their organizations' tentacles around the mechanisms of control of local political institutions and police forces. In Tancitaro, residents have become tired of the threats, the demands for "protection money," and the mutilated bodies they find dumped in the street.

Over the last few months residents in the town and other parts of Michoacan have been fighting back, forming militia groups and taking over cartel-controlled towns one at a time. The real battle in the sleepy farm-town of Tancitaro had come three months earlier when a charismatic doctor named Jose Manuel Mireles led an offensive against the cartel enforcers who had taken up residency in the village. The tall, gregarious doctor quickly won the respect of the people in Tancitaro. He uploaded a YouTube video of his gun brigade crouching behind pickup trucks advancing on the community of Pareo on the outskirts of town.[103] While a military helicopter hovered overhead, watching, but not intervening, Mireles and his men braved machine gun fire and a grenade attack. By the end of that day they killed two gunmen and showed that the vicious Caballeros Templarios cartel isn't invincible. The militiamen have achieved other important victories, but cells of cartel gunmen remain and many of the small hamlets in the area are still under the control of organized crime.

On Super Bowl Sunday, the vigilante gunmen are ready for action. One of the mercenary army's leaders, Estanislao Beltran, whose nickname means Papa Smurf in English, is calm.[104] Dressed in a grey and blue plaid shirt, dark jeans and rancher's boots, Beltran effuses a quiet sense of resolve. With his long and carefully combed grey beard flowing down in front of his shirt, Beltran seems like he's more likely to throw on a Santa Claus costume to entertain a room full of children than lead a few dozen hard-looking gunmen on an anti-cartel assault. But Beltran's amiable nature and stoic confidence have won the respect of his fighters.

While people in the U.S. mix up bowls of guacamole in preparation for the football game, Beltran leads his caravan of one hundred and fifty so-called *"autodefensa"* (self-defense) gunmen roaring through the roads that wind through Tancitaro, passing the neat rows of trees in the orchards of Michoacan's avocado territory.

Many locals are unsure of how to react. In the town of Tancitaro, the world capital of avocado production, many residents choose to stay in their houses. Over the previous few years, during the worst days of the era of cartel control, residents learned to seek comfort in the ephemeral security they felt behind the locked doors of their houses. Javier, a charismatic avocado grower, has watched the rise of the civilian rebellion with a mixture of respect and trepidation. He's happy to see the vigilantes push out the cartel *sicarios*, but he's worried about the potential repercussions if the movement fails and only angers the cartel gunmen who have been squeezing the life out of the state's avocado industry. Javier is cautious. He even built a basketball court on the patio behind the wall around his house so his kids don't have to venture out to the park to play. So, when Beltran's gunmen pass along the road through Tancitaro, the streets are mostly empty. Javier doesn't leave his house to see them drive by.

Over the first few weeks of 2014, the army and Federal Police sent extra patrols to Tancitaro, imposing a tense sort of military rule. Residents feel temporarily safer, but aren't sure what will happen when the soldiers leave. The November 2013 uprising has been embraced as a tentative success and residents have strung up a banner with the word *"AUTODEFENSA"* written on it near the entrance to the town. But it's still not clear if the vigilantes will be successful.

Only a few men from Tancitaro decide to join Beltran's gun squad. The town supports the cartel-fighting *autodefensa* movement, but local men haven't rushed to join the offensive. So, somewhat paradoxically, the "self-defense" force liberating the hamlets around Tancitaro is mostly composed of gunmen from towns from neighboring sections of the state. The Caballeros Templarios are still entrenched in their stronghold of the neighboring city of Apatzingan and although the vigilantes have had some success in outlying towns, it remains to be seen if the rough group of gunmen can take on the highly trained cartel killers posted up in Apatzingan.

Beltran's caravan pulls off the highway at a pit-stop store in Los Reyes, another avocado town just outside of Tancitaro. The men chug cans of Red Bull and beer. Beltran walks among his trucks, surveying his fighters. He eyes an athletic-looking young *autodefensa* fighter carrying an M-16 who is standing near a big pickup truck adorned with a hand-written message, "For a free Los Reyes." The man's physical appearance, tactical vest, military boots, and kneepads differentiate him from the skinny old men manning the trenches behind the walls of sandbags at the security checkpoints on the road outside of Tancitaro and the citizen police patrols in small towns in other parts of southern Mexico. These gunmen are intimidating.

Beltran is confident in his army. He nods at a light-skinned man with broad shoulders who is wearing a gray shirt, jeans, and a U.S. Army hat, holding a shotgun in one hand and a Modelo Especial beer in the other. To some residents in Tancitaro the gunmen seem to have the same sort of quasi-military presence of the enforcers who work for the new generation of militarized cartels in Michoacan. The provenance of the weapons the men use and the wads of cash Beltran's men pull out to pay the bill at the pit-stop store is unclear. The gun squad might be receiving money from frustrated and terrified avocado growers, but there are rumors that the group has ties to a drug cartel from the neighboring state of Jalisco.

Near the exit of Tancitaro on the way to Los Reyes, there's a sun-faded sign with a picture of a uniformed police officer that says, "Tancitaro is a clean city!" Another billboard says, "Don't get involved! Police and public servants…who engage in…kidnapping, extortion and robbery [can get] up to 45 years in prison."

Beltran's gunmen are always ready to react if they are attacked. Rolling one-hundred-and-fifty deep, they know they aren't likely to encounter a cartel squad with similar firepower. Still, there's a risk that they could face sniper fire or be hit by a roadside bomb. As Beltran walks through the assembled squadron, he nods at a young man carrying a heavy machine gun in front of a white Lincoln Navigator SUV. He is coy about the origins of his weapons and vehicles. "We take the guns and the trucks from the criminals," he says.[105] He looks up at a man wearing an Armani Exchange T-shirt, gripping a pistol in one hand and an AK-47 assault rifle in the other. "We've found arsenals with twenty, fifty, even seventy guns," he adds.

Although the hardened men in his brigade look more like battle-tested gangbangers and former soldiers than country boys raised riding horses and stalking game in the hills, Beltran has a simple explanation for their fighting skills. "We're hunters," he says, "We had shotguns and rifles."

"Some had machine guns," he adds.

Beltran's breezy openness and seemingly ingenuous nature are other characteristics that have helped him win the role of spokesman for the *autodefensa* movement. "We scavenge for our weapons. We find [cartel] caches with eighty guns and bullets. [People] ask us about our trucks. They're the criminals' trucks," he affirms.

As the Seattle Seahawks prepare to face off against the Denver Broncos at MetLife Stadium in New Jersey, the vigilantes have already established a presence in about a fifth of the state, an impressive feat given that Michoacan is larger than New York State and contains some of Mexico's most rugged territory. The *autodefensas'* offensive drive has been successful, but they still haven't broken through the pockets of cartel defense in many parts of the state. There are still many small towns that lie behind the defensive lines of the mafia, outside of their control. Slowly though, yard by yard, the citizen militia is advancing. On the side of the highway outside of the city of Los Reyes, Beltran and his men prepare to blitz into the town of Santa Clara. "Come on," he says, "We're going to take back another town and give a speech for the people there."

The men clamber up into the trucks, holding their guns. One by one the trucks pull onto the highway. Out on the road, the caravan of trucks moves deliberately, wending its way slowly through the side streets of residential neighborhoods. One gunman waves at residents. "For the people!" a vigilante shouts. A woman on the sidewalk smiles and nods, waving back. "Peace and tranquility! That's what we want," another man in one of the squadron's trucks yells as the brigade slowly presses its way down a narrow street.

So far, the *autodefensas* are enjoying a type of success that the federal government was never able to achieve. During former Mexican President Felipe Calderon's six years in office soldiers and federal police killed and arrested a few cartel bosses, but they never eradicated the lower levels of the criminal networks. Between the start of Calderon's offensive in 2006 and the end his term in office over one hundred thousand people were killed in Mexico.[106] During that period some big groups were broken up, but overall criminals, especially lower level henchmen, just learned to adapt and form smaller gangs. The emerging problems in Michoacan are a worrisome omen about the Peña Nieto administration's handle on security issues. As a new wave of violent crime is crashing through states across the country there's already a risk that Peña Nieto's term in office could be the most violent six-year presidential *sexenio* term in Mexican history.

The trucks' mufflers warble and rumble as they accelerate for the final push into Santa Clara. "A free Michoacan, let's go for it comrades," another gunman screams. "Goodbye, Templarios!" another man yells. Outside of a cement-block house, a family cheers in support as the caravan passes by.

As the caravan approaches the town square in Santa Clara the tension builds. "Brap-Brap-Brap-Brap!" a burst of rapid-fire explosions breaks the silence. A split second of panic ensues before the men can discern where the blasts are coming from. The sound is too sharp, too soft. It's not gunfire. The men relax. It was just a string of firecrackers. It might be a warning or it might be a celebration. But it's not a mortal threat. Not yet.

Alert and scanning for movement, the men hold their weapons ready and leap from their trucks. The gunmen fan out to form a perimeter around the main plaza and post sentries along the entrances to the square. They park a black SUV that has bulletproof metal plates welded over its windows and a machine gunner's roost in the roof. "It's been Mexicanized," one of the gunmen explains. The homemade tactical vehicle could serve as a refuge for Beltran in the event of a Templario attack.

While the militia members post up around the plaza, Beltran finds a seat on a metal bench. Confident that his men have secured the area, he's already preparing to give a speech for residents. "Sometimes they shoot at us, but organized crime is getting weaker. We're cleaning up," he says.

"We have a cause. We fight with courage. We all have experience hunting. We've got practice shooting," he adds. Banded together, the men have found a way to put their skills to use. The Templario *sicarios* have given them ample reason to fight back.

"They extort us. Taco sellers, cattle owners, avocado farmers, lime growers... everybody has to pay," Beltran says. Just three months after Tancitaro rose up, the *autodefensas* still seem like the best option for fighting the cartels.

In many towns, "the municipal police were the armed wing of the Caballeros. Instead of protecting the people they kidnapped people and turned them over."

Beltran has found that some locals have been wary of his outreach efforts. The *autodefensas* still haven't managed to capture or kill Nazario "The Craziest One" Moreno, the Templario's founder. Moreno, a shrewd maniac, returned to Mexico after a stint working in the U.S. He was inspired by some of the evangelical preachers he learned about in *El Norte*.[107] He planned to turn his gang into the most feared cartel in Mexico. Moreno quickly built up a fearsome reputation. In addition to sending caravans of gunmen to attack mayors' offices and federal police patrols Moreno published a 101-page book titled *They Call me 'El Más Loco.'* Moreno was born in 1979 in a destitute town called Guanajuatillo in a desolate stretch of Michoacan known as the Tierra Caliente, or Hot Land. He claimed to have never attended a day of school during his childhood and instead went north to the U.S. at age sixteen to look for work. In his book, Moreno asks the reader, "is the government not guilty for betraying the people and allowing extreme wealth in the hands of the few and extreme poverty in others?"

As a child Moreno had worked harvesting corn and limes and in the U.S., he found work as a gardener. He quickly found out, however, that he had a knack for drug dealing and a flair for protecting his nickel and dime bag operation. One time he overpowered two rival dealers who attacked him and stabbed them with their knife. After that he was re-baptized as "The Craziest One." In the 1990s Moreno set up shop in the border city of McAllen, Texas, one of the main crossing points for Michoacan's avocado, and ran a small-time marijuana smuggling operation. In the 1990s Michoacan was still just a base for minor league drug runners and pot growers. By the turn of the millennium, however, the big cartels from Mexico's north were starting to muscle their way in. In 2003 Moreno was indicted by a federal grand jury in Texas.

Around the same time, he turned his attention back to Michoacan. With stories circulating about gunmen from the terrifying, militarized Zetas cartel strong-arming and extorting Michoacan's businessmen, Moreno had a chance to build up his base. While the Zetas instilled fear, Moreno sought to inspire loyalty. At first the gang called itself "La Familia Michoacana" and took out ads in local newspapers, where they declared their love for their home state and promised to eradicate extortion, kidnapping, and murder. He infused his gang with a sense of purpose, a duty to protect their homeland. As time passed Moreno started associating the crew with imagery of Catholic knights. The shields and suits of armor were the accouterments of the real Knights Templar, a medieval order of religious warriors. Moreno followed the teachings of John Eldredge, a macho evangelical preacher from the U.S. who urges his followers to think of themselves as Christian warriors. Moreno taught his gunmen to not just join the gang, but to also buy into its cult of personality. This inculcation proved useful. federal police supposedly killed Moreno in 2010, but his body was never found, and his fame only grew. The gang built shrines to honor Moreno and some locals even reported seeing him in person, apparently back from the dead. With Moreno rumored to be running the Templario's operations and other cartel leaders still loose, many small-town residents are wary of showing too much support for the *autodefensas*.

While Beltran prepares his speech for the residents gathering in front of the gazebo in the plaza's center, Arturo, a wiry 25-year-old fighter from Tepalcatepec, a city near the state border with Jalisco, stands guard near the edge of the square. "I joined [the vigilantes] because the Templarios disappeared four of my family members…my dad, two uncles and a cousin," he says. "[The Templario members] have robbed houses, stolen cows, trucks. They kidnap, rape. Everything that's bad, they do."

Gripping the handle of his AR-15 assault rifle, Arturo explains the complicated local dynamics. At least three of his family members joined the Caballeros Templarios' cartel. Another uncle served time in jail in the U.S. for drug trafficking. Despite his proximity to organized crime he can't forgive the Templario killers. His father was brutally tortured and burned alive. He and his cousins joined the vigilante group in part to seek revenge and end the Templario's reign.

"If we detain somebody suspected of working with the cartel, we turn them over to the police," Arturo says. "But, when it comes to shootouts, we've never detained anybody. They fight until the end," he says, clenching his jaw remembering the gun battles, the adrenaline. As he speaks, a tall and heavyset gunman wearing hunting camouflage and carrying a machine gun with a circular ammo wheel attached walks by. It's a gun that's ready to spray big-bore bullets that can smash through most bulletproof windows. The men are battle-tested and ready to fight if they need to.

Arturo, like the other vigilantes, is hunting the Templario kingpins. The *autodefensas* are focused on capturing or killing men such as Moreno, who have imposed a reign of terror on Apatzingan, Tancitaro and the surrounding communities. Arturo isn't satisfied with the low-level gunmen he's taken out. "The bosses hide while the *pistoleros* die. They don't have numbers, but they shoot until they die," he says. Maybe the Templarios most skilled and highly trained cartel assassins have fled the state or are now hiding out in the mountains. Arturo hasn't exchanged gunfire with any of the Guatemalan Special Forces fighters rumored to be working for Moreno's cartel.

Within the towns, so far at least, the vigilante fighters are being embraced. "At first people are scared. But then later they help us. Yesterday and today people brought us drinks and helped us take care of the barricades," Arturo says. "People wave, it makes them happy to see us advance. We treat them with respect."

Arturo is also pleased to see the *autodefensas* being recognized for their success. Before the Tancitaro uprising, Mexico's president devoted part of his state of the union address to condemning military action by civilians. In early 2014 soldiers even killed a few *autodefensa* members while trying to disarm them. But by Super Bowl Sunday the *autodefensas* have been afforded a sort of tacit acceptance and de jure status. Vigilantes now stand alongside federal police officers at security checkpoints on the roads around Tancitaro. "The federal government, the Federal Police, they're with us 100 percent," he says.

Arturo turns to watch Beltran address the crowd. Standing on a stage with several gunmen behind him in the center of the plaza, Beltran speaks into a microphone to a group of a few dozen locals who have ventured into the plaza to hear what he has to say. "We're not killers. We just want the pueblo to defend itself," he booms. Standing by the railing on the stage flanked by two gunmen with machine guns draped over their backs Beltran looks like a revolutionary leader speaking to a crowd.

"We don't make pacts with criminals. We want your town to be free of hoodlums. We're part of the Fuerza Rural [police force]. We've got a good relationship with the soldiers and the Federal Police," he yells.

Over the radio, Arturo and his cousins hear some Templario *sicarios* threatening to attack the plaza. They say they're on their way in a Mad Max style caravan of their own. A brief moment of panic ensues as gunmen race to guard the entrances to the square. But, with no trucks seen approaching, it appears to be an empty threat. Beltran calms the crowd. "We have to work together. We invite you to organize yourselves so criminal groups don't stay here," he says.

After the speech, a teacher from Santa Clara nods in approval. "I see them as a group that speaks the truth and wants to help the people," he says.

Below the stage, *autodefensa* gunmen meet with local teens. One guy in his early twenties, who is dressed in a hip-hop style gray outfit and tilted flat-brimmed hat, holds up his skinny arms in a boxer's stance. "We're ready to fight," he tells a vigilante holding a machine gun.

With the sun fading over the avocado fields, the men in Beltran's battalion climb back up into their trucks. "You don't want to be on the roads at night here. There are towns where the Templarios are still strong. They'll stop you and hang you from a tree," one of the gunmen says.

Beltran and his men speed out of Santa Clara in a tight convoy. Unlike previous runs, they didn't face any gunfire, but they feel like they've won the support of many of the locals. They promise to return to set up defensive barricades and work to establish a real sense of security. As the trucks leave and return towards Los Reyes, some SUVs pull off in different directions as they head back to their home communities.

As the remaining trucks approach Los Reyes, however, soldiers stationed at a checkpoint by the town's entrance scramble to their gun stations behind the sandbags in the center of the road. Wide-eyed with fear, the soldiers, aiming their weapons, frantically motion for two civilians in a white Mazda sedan to pass by the checkpoint and flee the area. To the infantrymen, a caravan of luxury SUVs and trucks filled with machine-gun carrying vigilante "police" still looks uncomfortably similar to a cartel death squad.

§ § §

Two years after Beltran passed through for the Santa Clara raid there's a semblance of security in Tancitaro. In the quiet shadows under the thick overhanging branches of the trees of one of the town's family-owned avocado orchards, the sounds of the town and the trucks passing the security brigades on the village's main road are muffled out. Behind the gate, away from the road, among the expanse of trees on his twenty-hectare avocado farm, Javier feels safe. A few days after the Super Bowl in 2016, he's already fought through the biggest rush period of the year. Forty-six years old, Javier graduated from college in 1993 with a degree in Accounting and has helped guide his family's avocado export business through the modern NAFTA era of trade with the U.S. Still, he drives to visit the orchard almost every day to oversee harvests or check on the care his workers are providing for his trees. "February two years ago there was a lot of confusion in society. You couldn't go out and eat with your family. It was still not peaceful. There was a lack of trust," he explains. In 2014 when Beltran drove through town on his way into Santa Clara, Javier wasn't sure if the uprising would succeed. "It was a surprise. When it came it was chaos. I didn't think it would work. We were so oppressed," he says.

Javier had watched the Templarios consolidate their power and turn their attention towards preying on the legal economy operating within their domain. "We paid protection money. All the businesses here paid. If you didn't there were repercussions," Javier says.

The new reality in Tancitaro is, without a doubt, an improvement compared to the terrors of the Templario era. For the most part in 2015, Tancitaro enjoyed a welcome sort of stability. "Now it's more peaceful," he says. Until Michoacan's state government and Mexico's federal government demonstrate they are capable of guaranteeing security Javier would rather live alongside the civilian gunmen than live without them. It's an uncomfortable sort of status quo that was brought to life in late 2013 and early 2014 in part with funding from the avocado growers. "We cooperated to buy guns and build barricades," he explains.[108] Week by week the town's residents armed themselves. "The *fleteros,* people who sell avocados, brought back guns hidden in their trucks. They were old guns, M1s, high caliber AR-15s, *Cuernos de chivo* (AK-47s), M14s. But people had sticks too," Javier says. Absent help from federal authorities residents had to find a way to defend themselves.

"As a community they've achieved a manner of security," he adds.[109]

By 2016, the machine gun carrying citizen police and stone fortresses he passes while driving to his orchard have become just another part of living in Tancitaro. The gunmen, who carry weapons classified for exclusive use by members of the military in Mexico, have persisted nearly two years after Mexico's government tried to regularize the militia members into new state police force called the Fuerza Rural. Javier has some reservations about the civilian gunmen.

"It's a double-edged sword. But what would happen if they weren't here? The government doesn't want community police, but they haven't given us a guarantee of security so the local government hasn't given up control" and disarmed the militia members at the checkpoints, Javier says.

At this point Javier is just trying to accept the new security dynamic as normal and focus on building up his business. Outgoing, but brusque, still radiating the confidence he acquired while playing pro soccer as a teen, Javier has learned to become more comfortable in the anachronistic, almost medieval reality of modern day Tancitaro. Although he insists his kids study it, Javier doesn't speak English. He earns a living exporting to the U.S., but has only visited a few cities north of the border while traveling to play soccer. Mostly he just thinks of the U.S. as the distant market for his produce. He hasn't studied agricultural science, but has picked up the techniques for caring for his trees bit by bit over the years.

"I've had my paws stuck in this since I was a kid," he says, smiling. His guttural, staccato laugh sounds like the warble of an idling Harley Davidson motorcycle.

Guiding his late-model Nissan pickup truck over the rutted trail under a thick canopy of twenty-five-foot-tall trees Javier explains, "In Tancitaro we're the avocado capital. The soil is the best," he says. He and his family have cared for and developed the orchard for over three decades. There are no dry sticks or trash cluttering the ground in line with the strict guidelines of the export program. With farm animals prohibited from roaming the orchards, the avocado farms are a refuge from the booming music and squawking roosters that break the morning calm in the town center. Javier's farm, like the other export orchards in the vineyard, is run with meticulous efficiency like a corporate-owned vineyard. The order of Javier's orchard in Tancitaro stands in stark contrast to the political disarray in the state and the rot that set in to local institutions over the last decade as the federal government turned its attention elsewhere and the criminal groups tightened their grip. Javier looks at what he's been able to build on his property and feels nothing, but disdain for a political system he thinks does nothing to help.

"It wasn't the Ministry of Agriculture, the producers had the initiative. There were people with a lot of vision who created the avocado sector and brought the jobs," he explains.

In general Javier is pessimistic about the Mexican federal government's capacity to operate effectively and help incubate meaningful economic development.

"In Mexico we're short on infrastructure. We need more help from the government in every aspect." Earlier in the year when a hurricane swept through, sending a flood of churning water through the valley and a mudslide of broken tree trunks cascading over the main access highway, the state and federal government didn't come to the rescue. "The government hasn't even fixed the road. The producers had to fix it up to re-open the connection with the nearby city of Uruapan. It's a temporary solution," Javier says. It's part of the culture of individualism and entrepreneurism that defines the state's avocado growers. In Michoacan there are plenty of growers who are proud of the success of the avocado sector, but few who see the government as having played an important role in developing it.

Like the old hacienda owners who once ruled Michoacan before the Mexican Revolution, Javier's family has built up their own small empire behind the fences of their estate. Now eighty two, Javier's father is part of the generation of entrepreneurial landowners who looked beyond corn and beans for alternative crops. Surveying the neat rows of trees, Javier explains, "He was one of the pioneers here in Tancitaro. He brought plants from Israel. Tancitaro was cattle country then. It had agriculture, but planting avocados has made it one of the most productive areas."

He is wearing a black baseball cap, a thick plaid shirt and a puffy red vest. His big metal belt buckle juts up over the hem of his jeans. His beard and mustache are clipped into a neat rectangular goatee. Javier is no longer operating in crisis mode. By 2016, things are just starting to get back to normal. Looking out the window as he eases his truck through the neat rows of tree trunks, Javier explains that after decades of work on implementation, driven by the focus on expanding exports, avocado-related regulations are now strictly enforced in Michoacan.

Javier has seen the evolution of the industry firsthand. He finished college in 1993 just as the avocado export business was starting to take off, and he has overseen the boom years of Tancitaro's avocado sector. "My dad was a producer since the start of the program. It was really good. [The start of the export era] was a catalyst for sales," he says. In the 1995-1996 season following the signing of NAFTA, Mexico exported a record-breaking 45,600 tons of avocado. In 2015, Michoacan exported just under 775,000 tons of avocado, a crop that earned the state more than 1.5 billion dollars. Twenty years earlier as farmers saw the export revenue coming in they were quick to adapt.

"Everybody who had three or five hectares for cattle changed their activity and it was a total shift in the economy. People with cows just got by. But people who changed earned seventy thousand dollars a year with three or four hectares," Javier says. Today a farmer with four hectares of well-maintained trees might earn a few hundred thousand dollars a year in export revenue. In this sector the benefits of following the rules are so great that it pays to abide by the letter of the law. With a clear regulatory framework to follow, and knowledge that the rules are strictly enforced, Javier can focus his time on maximizing his farm's efficiency and profitability.

He drives slowly under the shadow of the heavy canopy of his brother's section of pre-NAFTA era tree and gets out to watch the harvesting operation. Balancing high on the branches, men with bags reach out and grab the avocados they can reach. A worker driving a green John Deere tractor pilots a cherry picker carrying an avocado harvester up nearly thirty feet into the air to pluck the avocados dangling precariously on the outer branches.

With a firm handshake Javier greets a long-time harvester named Juan, who is wearing a cowboy hat and bright red shirt. Juan works at JBR, the avocado packaging facility up the road.

"He brings his people. You make a contract with a packer that's registered for exporting and they bring their workers," Javier explains. Turning to Juan, who has worked for JBR for seven years, Javier points out the work he's been doing trimming. Short trees are easier to manage, safer for harvesting, and more profitable. Javier has learned that it's a mistake to let the trees grow out of control. Careful trimming season by season helps lower the canopy to an easier to reach height.

"It's better to do it bit by bit," Juan says.

"Gradually—yeah 'til they get down to four meters," Javier agrees.

Over time the avocado growers have learned from their mistakes. When the business is well-regulated it is easier to run.

"Before it was like this," he says, clasping his hands, interlocking his fingers and squeezing them tightly together. "It was bad management," he adds. Looking up at the thick canopy of branches overhead, Javier explains, "You make windows so the light comes in." If the trees grow out of control blights become a risk to the whole operation. The reference to letting in sunlight and exposing plagues is an apt metaphor. For decades in Mexico corruption was largely hidden from public view carried out in the shadows. Throughout the Peña Nieto administration more and more scandals have come to light. Visibility is the first step towards eradication, but Mexico still has a long way to go towards improving rule of law.

Javier has implemented a solid management system, but still the pickers have to be careful. One ripe fruit can cause an entire box to spoil before it reaches the U.S. Likewise, one irresponsible farm could destroy the reputation of the state's entire avocado sector. In the early stages of the export era the growers banded together to establish protocols for cultivating, handling, and packaging. They reached out to the government to help them enforce their rules.

"It wasn't a government program. There weren't as many rules. There was a lot of bad management. We had to establish strict rules. The growers planned it out. That's how the export program was born. There was a lack of quality control at the farms," Javier says.

The growers realized that if they could collaborate and collectively enforce a common set of standards they would all be able to sell at higher prices. Now if an avocado falls off a tree and hits the ground Javier's workers will separate it for sale in the local market. They won't try to mix it in with the export fruit. The costs of non-compliance with the export program's strict rules are too great. More than two decades after NAFTA, the process is well established and understood. The harvesting team's leader brings over a document from the packing company. Javier signs his name. "This is to show that it came from this orchard. These are the people who worked," he says, pointing to list of names. "It shows we met the requirements," he adds. Of course there are significant short-term costs to all of the red-tape, but overall the benefits of a properly functioning market are far greater.

Javier holds up a plastic tie and hands it to an employee to pass to an agent from the Junta Local. "He's an inspector. We have a credential that shows we're approved to export. [The plastic tie] shows that all the fruit came from this farm," Javier explains. When the truckload of avocado arrives at the packing facility, the unbroken plastic tie will show that the truck hasn't been opened. It's part of a complicated system of controls to ensure that only the best fruit makes it north to the U.S.

His town is still teeming with gunmen, but life is slowly returning to something resembling normal. "The government doesn't rule here, but it's under control. You can relax," he says.[110]

§ § §

With the afternoon sun already starting to fade over the mountains, a hawk-nosed middle-aged man named Huber picks up his gun and leads his fellow patrolmen from in front of the Jesus statue inside the local headquarters of the Fuerza Rural, a controversial new state-level police force that is composed of former vigilante fighters. In the back parking lot there's an M-16 hanging on the wall next to a row of ripe avocados. The front door of the police headquarters is made from weathered wood. From the doorway a shrine to the Virgin Mary and a row of police trucks are visible. Huber says he joined the *autodefensas* in February 2014, around the time of the Santa Clara raid. When the government regularized the vigilantes into a de jure police force, he signed up alongside Beltran and some of the other original leaders.

He shrugs off the claims that the state government, faced with scandals relating to shootouts and criminal activity by Templarios serving in uniforms, will disband the Fuerza Rural. The group's new police trucks have logos that say "Policía Michoacana," but the personnel are the same. Their uniforms still say Fuerza Rural. Three Fuerza Rural gunmen stand in the back of the truck. One of them has a skull decal pasted onto the clip of his AK-47. The other two commandos wear masks over their faces.

Easing the truck passed the pock-marked adobe brick building in front of the Fuerza Rural headquarters, Huber glimpses briefly in the direction of a blue house built in the style of a U.S. suburban mansion and passes by an A-frame cabin, architectural styles that returning migrants brought back to Mexico. While the patrols that run on the small roads through the farms on the periphery of the city can still be nerve-wracking, rolling through Tancitaro has become more routine. "Before, the municipal police worked with the Templarios," Huber explains. He eases the patrol truck past a building painted with a smiling cartoon avocado with a mustache wearing a straw sombrero and a spray-painted message. "We buy avocado," it says. Tancitaro exports more than a million dollars of avocado every day, but the tax revenues generated by the industry haven't returned in the form of high-quality public institutions for residents. The town lacks quality public schools and hasn't built a world-class public library or cultural center. In general government institutions are only integrated into Tancitaro in the most rudimentary way. Huber thinks the Fuerza Rural is having a positive impact.

The improvement in Tancitaro, he thinks, is obvious. In uniform, driving a late-model police truck, Huber feels like a professional. He now takes advantage of his days off to meet up with friends from the peripheral community where he lives to play basketball. Defending Tancitaro from any Templario invasion has become an almost normal sort of job. "I think we need to keep looking out. You have to stay united," he says. Accelerating up the road that rises from the town center, Huber and the other officers survey the trucks passing them in the street. They roll to a stop at the first security castle on the road out of town.

Jose, a weathered 52-year-old resident with graying black hair and a few silver teeth, volunteers guarding the barricade, sitting lazily in a beat-up armchair underneath the roof of the structure. If a caravan of cartel gunmen is ever brazen enough to try a full-on assault on Tancitaro, Jose's castle will be the last line of defense. But Jose knows that he'll get a warning over the radio. With no chatter on the airwaves, he can relax. By 2016, his shifts at the barricade have become a mundane part of life in Tancitaro.

The men know that if an attack comes they can rush into the fortress and aim through the triangular-shaped turrets, shooting at the attackers without being hit. Manning the barricade isn't too stressful and today Huber's patrol provides an extra level of protection. Huber, who is wearing blue and black commando camouflage pants and a black bulletproof vest marked with the word "POLICIA," cradles his AR-15 rifle and watches the traffic pass. Unlike Huber the gunmen at the barricade don't have uniforms, but, in recognition for their help in pushing out the Templarios, they have been granted a de facto role in the town's security apparatus.

The tense calm of the militarized town is preferable to what residents lived through under the Templarios. "Here it was really buck wild. If you walked around armed you wouldn't wake up the next day," Jose explains. The civilian guards at the checkpoints in Tancitaro don't wear uniforms. Jose, who is wearing a faded maroon jacket, lounges next to a metal bench next to a rifle, a short-barreled machine gun, and a massive, home-modified shotgun that has been fitted with a circular ammo wheel for rapid-fire use during combat.

The burn marks from the grenade blasts have faded from the street, but the men still remember that first day of gun battles, the spark that started the *autodefensa* uprising in town. They call it *la balacera, la chinguiza.* Jose thinks back, "It was a Saturday in November of 2013. A huge movement of armed people came. Mireles and a lot of other people came to defend us," he says. Jose and dozens of other residents accepted invitations from Mireles and Beltran to join the offensive. Working together with locals they drove the Templarios into hiding.

"They ran the bad guys out," Jose adds.

Working together, the gunmen did what the local and state police and federal forces failed to do; they killed and captured the Templario gunmen. At the victory in Tancitaro, some of the men joined up with mobile assault units like the one Beltran led into Santa Clara. On January 12, 2014, the *autodefensa* gunmen engaged in a fierce gun battle, taking over the Templario stronghold of Nueva Italia.[111] On February 8, just under a week after Beltran's raid on Santa Clara, in a negotiated truce orchestrated with help from Mexico's government, they then marched unarmed into the long-time Templario base of Apatzingan.[112] Some cartel members went into hiding. Others were detained and arrested.

Another skinny guard at the fortress named Alejandro, who is wearing a black soccer jersey interjects, "Those that could run, did."

Smiling fiercely with a morbid sort of humor Alejandro explains that there are rumors that some criminals were killed in reprisal attacks. Others are still living in the community. The priests at the church are still looking for ways to repair the social fabric and mend the destruction the Templarios left behind. The town's residents improvised a solution to the Templario's reign and now they are figuring out a way to move forward.

One of the men who helped organize the citizen police in Tancitaro, Jesús Bucio, was killed on August 30, 2015.[113] He was ambushed while returning to town after supervising work at his avocado orchard. Some residents remember him as an honorable man with good intentions and others think he was killed as vengeance for crimes he committed before the uprising began.

"Jesús Bucio—he's the one who organized the *autodefensas*. They killed him. We don't know why. People say different things," Alejandro says. In the long-run for the community to heal the state or federal government will have to build institutions for community outreach to help the town's residents come to terms with what they lived through and find ways to reconcile. For now most locals are just figuring out how to get by on a day-by-day basis. Although both Jose and Alejandro acknowledge that there have been some problems along the way they think that the majority of the town's people support their work.

"Our town has ninety [three] villages. They all help us. The idea was for each pueblo to defend itself, so like that it's peaceful," Jose says, sitting comfortably on a beat-up sofa next to the fortress.

Although the situation in Tancitaro has stabilized, elsewhere in the state the dynamic has only become more convoluted as gunmen who were involved in organized crime joined the Fuerza Rural and began cooking up crystal meth and carrying out murders while dressed in uniform. After dealing with ongoing ambushes from cartel *sicarios*, in April 2015, the Federal Police shot and killed sixteen civilian Fuerza Rural gunmen, alleged members of a Templario splinter group known as Los Viagra.[114] One month later, in May 2015, Federal Police killed forty-two alleged cartel gunmen in an attack in the nearby town of Tanhuato that many witnesses and human rights groups called an extra-judicial massacre.[115]

Tancitaro still hasn't experienced that extreme level of social breakdown.

"Now it's just the town that's taking care of itself," Alejandro says. The men aren't confident that local, state, and federal authorities would be able to protect them if they put down their weapons.

"The problem is if the movement disappears in fifteen days we'd be as bad off as we were or worse. There's no trust in the government," Jose explains.

"People don't want to stop. We aren't going to disarm," Alejandro says.

Mexico's federal government still hasn't found a way to build functioning national police forces or an effective, modern justice system. In 2016 the federal government is focusing on a marketing campaign to promote the image of security in Michoacan and has announced plans to dismantle both the Fuerza Rural and the community police forces. Alejandro says he plans to keep defending the barricade.

He doesn't think the army will try to disarm him and his *compañeros* at the security checkpoints in Tancitaro. "People wouldn't let them. We've won the battle and we're peaceful. In other places there is extortion and kidnapping. Here there's none of that," he says.

Holding up a newspaper and pointing at an article Alejandro says, "After tomorrow they'll detain anyone who's armed." He reads the text out loud, "After this date anyone carrying weapons will be detained."

"So as of tomorrow the *autodefensas* are over?" Jose interjects.

According to the federal government's marketing campaign, the era of vigilante justice in Michoacan is ending. In Tancitaro, however, the daily dynamic isn't changing.

The men are confident that they won't lose their de facto authority. Mexico's federal government seems unlikely to establish real rule of law in rural Michoacan any time soon. Alejandro and Jose are confident they'll get to keep their guns.

Like Javier, they are more comfortable living alongside armed civilians than living without them.

Back in the truck, Huber grips the steering wheel and accelerates up the hill driving past another security barricade.

Cresting over a hill, Huber, who owns an orchard with six hundred trees, can see the expanse of avocado plants, which from a distance look like small yellow-green clumps of broccoli, stretching out into the horizon. He says the patrols have become more routine and less intimidating.

Huber thinks the residents in Tancitaro will continue to support the self-defense movement. "They don't want to disarm because the federal government doesn't provide security and do its job like it should. It was the *comunitarios* who dismantled the cartel," he says.

Pulling to a stop at a small toolshed-sized fortress, Huber looks down over landscape in the distance. "This is the border with Buenavista. It's worse there," he says.

For Huber, the edge of Tancitaro's last ranches marks the end of the "green zone" of safety in avocado territory. Outside it lies the chaos of the Tierra Caliente. "Apatzingan – they've always lived from drug trafficking. That causes problems," he says.

Huber and his men step down from the truck and talk to two pudgy middle-aged men who are guarding the checkpoint. Jesús, a 38-year-old life-long resident of the village of Pareo on the periphery of Tancitaro holds an AK-47 with an extended banana clip.

"I come to take care of the barricades. It's like an obligation. Every neighborhood has a month. You have to come one time per month," he says.

Jesús, whose round belly bulges out from under his

white and blue plaid short sleeved button-up shirt, says he hasn't heard of any plan for the *comunitarios* in his unit to stand down and stop guarding the barricade. The gunmen might be illegal, but for now at least they are accepted.

In Michoacan the overlapping network of official and extra-official security forces is confounding, even for locals. But the dynamic in Tancitaro seems preferable to the problems in other parts of the state. At least there's some semblance of order in Tancitaro.

On the wall of the fortress there's a handwritten set of rules.

"Keep the checkpoint clean," says one.

"Firing weapons unnecessarily is prohibited," says another.

Even in a lawless land it's important to have some rules. "Now it's more peaceful," Jesús says.

By 2016, the community police have become almost institutionalized, although the heavily armed civilians enjoy no official approval from Mexico's legal system. Article Nine of Mexico's Firearms and Explosive Law allows farmers' groups to own .22 rifles and small shotguns, but explicitly bans ownership of military-style weapons.[116] Whereas once they rolled heavy boulders into the street to keep caravans of gunmen from blazing through, now the traffic slows to a stop by the orange cones in front of the checkpoint by the entrance to Pareo. There are speed bumps marked with yellow lines built into the road.

As the sun fades, the sky glows pastel pink and red, and Jesús and Huber watch the approaching trucks slow and roll their windows down, showing they aren't hiding anything as they pass. They look on as an old Volvo transport truck drives by, its cargo hold covered by an orange tarp. The checkpoints look out for gunmen, but they don't frequently carry out inspections to see what the trucks are carrying. Their main concern is preventing violence and repelling cartel gunmen. They still hear reports about groups of criminally-connected former *autodefensa* fighters engaging in wild shoot-outs in Apatzingan.

"I think it's worse to disarm us. People won't let them," he says.

Maybe some time in the future, Mexico's government will finally eradicate the threat from organized crime. Jesús doesn't think it's a short-term goal.

§ § §

Mexico has now been at war with the organized crime groups that operate within its borders for over a decade. Overall, in wide expanses of Mexico's territory, it's still not clear which side has the advantage. Residents in Tancitaro haven't forgotten how former Mexican President Felipe Calderon, an aloof technocrat from the right-of-center National Action Party, started his term in 2006 by donning a baggy, olive-drab military jacket over his dress shirt and pulling a soldier's cap over his erudite, delicate-looking glasses.[117] Calderon made the War on Drugs and the war on Mexico's cartels the center-piece of his administration's policy platform. He wanted to consolidate his reputation as a decisive leader. But as Mexico's Federal Police and army began confronting groups of paramilitary-style cartel gunmen news coverage focused increasingly on the violence, he continued onward even as Mexico earned a reputation for being a failed or failing state, a *narco*-state. Calderon tried using press conferences to convince the world that he was winning his war. He paraded detained cartel capos in front of journalists' cameras. Criminal groups responded by ramping up their attacks on federal police, army units, and local elected officials.

Under Calderon Mexico's military's employment ranks swelled by 70 percent.[118] The death toll was stunning. The total number of annual homicides reported in Mexico surged from 8,867 in 2007 to 27,213 in 2011. Unfortunately for residents in Mexico, as Calderon looked for a military solution he didn't place commensurate attention on the task of building quality local and state police forces to complement the squadrons of Federal Police and soldiers his government sent around the country. Still, by certain metrics, at the end of his term it did seem like Mexico had begun to achieve some important victories against the country's drug cartels. Smashed and decapitated, many of the top organized crime groups splintered up into clans of un-coordinated, geographically limited gangs. By 2012, Calderon's last year in office, the number of homicides recorded in Mexico fell to 25,967, a body-count that is lower than the total recorded in 2011, but still more than three times higher than the murder tally from 2007. Voters were tired of the violence.

Enrique Peña Nieto, Calderon's successor, was elected partially due to the naïve belief among many voters that he and his team of old-school politicians from the PRI could negotiate a peace treaty with the drug cartels and let the technocratic wing of the PRI implement economic reforms and shift the national and global conversation about Mexico away from violence. Once elected, Peña Nieto, a telegenic simpleton who is viewed primarily as the electable figurehead for the PRI political machine, presided over a brief honeymoon period for Mexico. He focused his attention publicly on lauding Mexico's social programs, infrastructure projects, and economic development initiatives. He and his team promised to unleash Mexico's economic potential. Behind the scenes, however, Peña Nieto's team of advisors and political allies did little heavy lifting in the effort to build functioning police forces and establish real rule of law in Mexico. He scored an early victory with the capture of "El Chapo" Guzman on February 22, 2014.[119] He also benefited from the fact that the number of murders recorded in Mexico fell from 23,063 in 2013 to 20,010 in 2014. But, the veneer of positive tidings for Peña Nieto's administration was scraped away relatively quickly, exposing the absence of adequate underlying institutional infrastructure. In September 2014 news broke of a major scandal involving the disappearance of 43 student-teachers from the state of Guerrero, just south of Michoacan. News outlets accused local police and the army of being complicit. More and more media coverage has focused on human rights abuses by Mexican police and soldiers and shocking corruption scandals implicating Peña Nieto and his top advisors. Initial promises to develop a massive new federal police force called the Gendarmería proved to be little more than a short-lived marketing campaign.[120] Throughout 2014 and 2015 news coverage of the *autodefensa* movement in Michoacan undermined Peña Nieto's efforts to present Mexico as a modern economy with a competent government. As splinter groups of cartel gunmen in cities and towns across the country turn their attention to stealing fuel, robbing cargo trucks and trains, and killing, kidnapping, and extorting residents, Peña Nieto's efforts to shift the global dialogue about Mexico away from violent crime are starting to break down. In 2015 the overall number of murders in Mexico started increasing again. By 2016 it already seems like Mexico has regressed backwards towards the dynamic experienced during the bleakest months of the Calderon era. The structure of organized crime has changed, but the impact for residents is largely the same. Mexico now seems more violent than it has ever been. Peña Nieto's government hasn't been able to stop the violence.[121] If the upward trend in overall levels of violence continues into 2017 and 2018 Peña Nieto's term in office may be remembered as the most crime-ridden six years in Mexican history.

Across the country the biggest issue is a fundamental lack of institutional capacity. Mexico's weak tax collection capability undermines the state's ability to finance and train functional police forces. Part of the problem is a shortage of officers. In Mexico the ratio of police officers to residents is 1:373.[122] Over the past century Mexico has built up a problematic and fragmented network of police. As of 2016 Mexico has 134,000 municipal police officers, 113,000 state police officers and 37,000 federal police.[123] These officers are not spread uniformly across the territory or concentrated in high-risk hotspots of cartel activity. Over 88,000 officers work in Mexico City, the central node of Mexico's federal government, the place where state capacity is strongest. It's no accident that many of the places where organized crime enjoy the most power, such as the northern state of Tamaulipas, are also the places where police forces are weakest. Tamaulipas has only 3,000 officers on patrol.

Another issue is funding. On average Mexican officers earn just over a dollar an hour. Many officers in Mexico complain that they have to pay for their boots or repair their patrol trucks with their own money. Departments across the country are under-funded and lack the resources to supply the weapons and equipment officers need to confront cartel gunmen. The temptation for corruption is ever-present and in many cases overwhelming. But, rather than placing police reform at the center of his policy agenda, Peña Nieto has steadfastly shirked away from his promise to build new Fuerza Única state police forces across the country.[124] His Gendarmería force has largely been forgotten.

Mexico's federal government's failure to create, fund, and train effective police forces has created an auspicious environment for organized crime. When impunity reigns and rule of law and institutional capacity are weak, violent criminal groups thrive. In expansive and largely under-developed regions of the country such as Michoacan organized crime groups have encountered little resistance when they move in to fill the vacuum created by the absence of the state in rural stretches of Mexico's sprawling territory. In the hills outside of Apatzingan, Templario leader Nazario Moreno built a clubhouse.[125] It was not an underground casino tucked into a nondescript farm building, but rather a massive steel-and-glass bull ring, a rooster ring, an apartment, and a stable for thoroughbred horses.[126] Locals worked cutting firewood and salesmen hawking flavored ice *raspados* drove by to sell their cold desserts to the cartel gunmen. The people in the ranches nearby saw the army trucks go by, not to investigate and report the facility, but rather to have lunch with Moreno and his men. Moreno sold tickets to his parties there at a travel agency in Apatzingan.

In December 2010, an elite Federal Police squad, a convoy of several dozen officers tried to raid Moreno's facility.[127] They were ambushed by a small battalion of several hundred cartel gunmen and forced to flee.[128] It was a disaster that helped grow the Templario's reputation for military efficiency. While locals forked over extortion payments and saw their neighbors being killed and disappeared, they kept silent. They had all heard the stories about Moreno feeding his enemies to his lion, or even more grotesquely, cooking and serving them as taco meat to his own gunmen. While many municipal police forces in the surrounding area lack funding to supply officers with ammunition and training for target practice, the Caballeros Templarios carry top-of-the-line European and American-made automatic rifles. In rural Michoacan, gunmen from organized crime groups have proven themselves to be efficient tax collectors (of extortion payments) and effective commanders on the battlefield. Residents know not to underestimate the *narco* gunmen that patrol rural parts of the state. Local police forces, on the other hand, are still seen as under-funded and ineffective. In the area around Tancitaro the security crisis is far from resolved.

On February 8, a new group of vigilante police announced their arrival in Michoacan.[129] They released a paradoxical video in which they claim that if the government doesn't enforce its promise to disarm the civilian gunmen the new group's vigilantes will carry out an insurgency of law and order and go out in the streets and fight to do it on their own. It will be a group of heavily armed civilian militants fighting to put an end to the tolerance for heavily armed civilian militants.

Early on, Peña Nieto wanted to be known as the president who catalyzed a new era of economic growth. Now it seems like he'll be a president brought down by his administration's failure to clamp down on illegality. Throughout his term, Peña Nieto has tried to avoid talking publicly about crime and violence. Behind the scenes his team has failed to effectively coordinate security policy or build functioning police forces that extend the state's control into rural pockets of the country. As the general security dynamic in Mexico deteriorates, it seems like the residents manning the castles that ring Tancitaro are the first line of defense against an influx of the turbulence that is still shaking other parts of the country.

§ § §

On Ash Wednesday, the main plaza in front of the mayor's office in Tancitaro has been swept, but is still covered with traces of flour, egg and confetti from a ritualized food fight carried out by the town's children the night before. As the night sky fades to grey the glowing cross on Tancitaro's church burns red. Speaking under a giant golden chandelier in front of a massive, light-skinned Christ figure the priest admonishes the early risers who came out for mass that "He who follows the law of the Lord day and night will receive his reward in due time." The assembled crowd, a handful of women wrapped in blankets and a few fieldworkers in dirty clothes, chants, "Keep us from sin and protect us from wrong."

Across the plaza in the market, the taco stands are closed and the restaurant posts have a variety of meatless options for the parishioners. "It's Ash Wednesday, we just have *nopal* cactus leaves and stuffed chile peppers," a cook explains. In Tancitaro the old dictums of the Church are still faithfully enforced. The area in front of the police office, however, buzzes with activity. Operated by the town's newest police force, the Cuerpos de Seguridad Público de Tancitaro (Tancitaro Public

Security Force) the town's police trucks are decorated with the group's acronym CUSEPT. Formed in 2014 the police force is a supplement to the Fuerza Rural. Although employed by the municipal government they are more like a private police force hired by the avocado growers. They are an atavistic reminder of the armed guards that the area's hacienda owners used to employ before the Mexican Revolution.

The CUSEPT is without a doubt the best armed and best trained small-town police force in Mexico.[130] In other parts of the world, maybe only the guards in the Vatican have more firepower at their disposal. Hugo, a former soldier who joined the force in 2014, climbs inside the side door of a gleaming new GMC Denali, and settles into the plush leather passenger seat. Straining, he pulls the heavy door closed. It locks into place with a jarring clunk. The truck has been fitted with bulletproof metal plates and inch-thick bulletproof glass. It's the type of SUV usually reserved for a foreign dignitary or a cartel boss. It sends the message that the CUSEPT is an elite police force.

Three more commandos climb up into the back of the truck and another officer slips behind the wheel. All of them hold their machine guns close, ready for action. "We do preventative patrols. If there are no alerts we're on standby. If there's an alert we go looking for the criminals. We get reports of trucks filled with armed people so we'll do a patrol and focus on that," Hugo explains.

Tancitaro enjoys a tense sort of peace that might be welcomed by the residents in places such as Apatzingan. Unlike the towns in the Tierra Caliente, Tancitaro wasn't plagued by shootings in 2015. It's been a few weeks since the last report of a shoot-out occurring on the outskirts of town.

"We can just go to the limits of the municipality. We make our presence known and then we return. I think the criminals know that it's difficult for them to enter here," he says looking out the truck's window at a checkpoint where an old man sits, cradling a machine gun.

"The advantage here is that there are *autodefensas, policías comunitarias*. They take care here. We have radios. They can give us reports. There's coordination with the people guarding the security checkpoints," he explains.

The CUSEPT is also unique in Michoacan. Funded by the avocado growers' association, the police force provides its recruits with specialized combat training. After new officers go through the police academy run by state authorities, "we train them in high impact operations, special ops. It's focused on fighting armed groups, rappelling, urban combat, everything that Special Forces do," Hugo says.

The CUSEPT is designed to respond to threats and deter brazen attacks from criminal convoys. Unlike the pitifully trained and poorly paid police in other small towns in Michoacan, the CUSEPT can match the firepower of the cartel hit squads. By contrast, in 2013 the mayor in the distant town of Santa Ana Maya was found dead after he complained that local criminals were charging him monthly *cuota* payments that added up to tens of thousands of dollars every year.[131] In other towns in Michoacan, caravans carrying dozens of cartel commandos arrive to spray bullets in the main plaza and threaten the local politicians and police. Tancitaro stands out for the defenses the town has built up to fight back. Reports of robbers targeting avocado trucks are uncommon. "It happens sometimes, but not really," Hugo says. The resources provided by the avocado growers' association are a big advantage for the municipal government. In Tancitaro the municipal government doesn't have to rely on federally dispersed money to finance local initiatives.

"This truck is bulletproof. When there's a report we go out in bulletproof trucks. We have four," he explains. The CUSEPT is the type of local police force that Mexico needs to build in organized crime hotspots across the country. Until the federal government finds a way to increase tax revenues, however, it isn't clear where the funding for such a massive institution-building effort would come from.

Hugo knows who pays the bills in Tancitaro. Looking out the window, scanning over the avocado fields as the truck rumbles up the road, he says, "All this is avocado—here it's a lot of hectares."

Up in the back of the truck, Daniel Torres, a lean 22-year-old, stands along with two other officers eyeing the houses and checkpoints as the patrol passes.

Speaking loudly over the whipping wind as the patrol winds its way back towards the town center he explains, "It's more peaceful now. There's no more kidnapping. Before it was three or four deaths a day and people getting beheaded."

He knows that in other parts of the state residents are still fleeing the violence; moving to other parts of the country, or migrating to the U.S. Daniel explains that he has spent the last two years working with CUSEPT. Before that, he says he was with the *comunitarios*. Like Huber and some of the Fuerza Rural members, he joined up with the roving *autodefensa* brigades. "We wanted to help. We went to Paracuaro and Uruapan." He had a clear motivation for joining.

"They killed my family members. They killed my uncle, they beheaded another," he says.

The violence in Tancitaro pushed him to join the police. Early on Daniel just wanted to work in the avocado industry. "I worked at a packer called JBR and from there I came here," he says, mentioning the name of the same export packaging facility that harvests and processes Javier's avocados.

But, Daniel isn't sure exactly how long he'll stay with the police. "I'm getting my visa for the U.S. My grandparents are citizens who live in Yakima," he says. He wants to go to the U.S. to try living outside of Michoacan for a while, but only if he gets a visa, "Not as a *mojado*," he says.

Standing in front of the station the officers seem relaxed. But the glass window under the sign that says "Public Security" is still patched over with cardboard, damaged from a shootout from the start of the *autodefensa* uprising. So much about the local power dynamics in Tancitaro seems like a relic of the colonial era, but the town is still strongly connected to the global economy, and in particular, to the U.S. The town that sends more avocado to the U.S. than any other municipality in Mexico has strong connections to *El Norte*.

While Hugo, Daniel and the other officers head into the station, another CUSEPT commando named Emanuel watches traffic in the plaza. A truck drives by blaring a sing-song Eminem hit from Emanuel's high school days. "*I'm Slim Shady, yes I'm the real Shady. All you other Slim Shadies are just imitating,*" the speakers blare.

"I like America, *vato*," he says in Spanglish, using Chicano slang instead of the English word for dude. Switching back to Spanish he explains that during the five years he spent in the U.S., "I learned a lot from your culture."

Emanuel, a hulking six-foot-two tall 34-year-old with giant hands and mini-fridge sized torso, migrated to the U.S.

to look for work and the Michoacan he returned to wasn't the same as the state he left. He had to find a way to interpret the local dynamic and find his own way of understanding it. His re-introduction wasn't an easy one.

"I came back from the U.S. with a truck I bought for six thousand dollars, a Chevy. They kidnapped me. My brother had to sell the truck for the ransom," he says. It was the type of incident that happened so frequently in Tancitaro that Emanuel's demeanor when he talks about is nonchalant, as if it were just another mundane rite of passage rather than a life-altering trauma.

Emmanuel wanted to do something to improve the untenable dynamic in Tancitaro. The CUSEPT force seemed like the best option. Out of the various police forces in the town, the CUSEPT is the most professional and least problematic. The officers have the training and equipment of an elite cartel-fighting Federal Police unit, but they are from Tancitaro so people trust them. Emanuel explains, "I'm from here in the town. Everybody from the force is. It was a requirement to have ten years residency and pass a *control de confianza* background check," he explains. Emanuel feels like he is already making an impact.

"I'm in the transit department, I handle poorly parked cars, fines, license plates," he adds. Slowly, the police force is trying to introduce new standards for parking and encourage residents to respect the handicapped parking spaces in front of the town's market. He also anchors the defense for the CUSEPT's basketball team. The police squad won second place in the last basketball tournament, he says.

When there are no reports about suspicious activity or approaching gun squads, his daily job involves unscrewing violators' license plates and dropping them off at the police station. For first time offenders, "It's just a warning. They pass by the office and we talk. But we make a record. The next time it's a fine. The next time they get towed," he says. He nods toward a man pulling up on a motorcycle wearing a vintage style open-face helmet. "A little while ago we created a rule for helmets," he explains.

Emanuel has been with the CUSEPT since the police force was formed a few days after Beltran's raid on Santa Clara. "Since its beginning. February 17, 2014. Practically two years," he says.

He still remembers the difficult days prior to the November uprising such as the arson attack against two local avocado packing facilities in 2013.[132] "They killed people. They targeted the wealthy people. They burned two packers. That was one of the things that detonated the uprising. It was tense. Now it's safer, but it's delicate," he says. In small ways though, he sees improvement. Kids walk alone to school in the morning and women stroll through the plaza by themselves in the evening.

"Before at seven at night there was nobody in the street. Now there's peace," he says.

Over the past three years, Emanuel watched as the vigilantes logged victories. He saw the momentum turn against the Templarios and watched the *comunitarios* and *autodefensas* settle old scores. "There were times when people would be yelling, 'Shoot him! Shoot him!' And, somebody would walk over and 'BANG!,'" he narrates, making a pistol motion for an execution-style killing.

Still the threat of organized crime hasn't disappeared. "Here the names changed, but it's the same. Familia

Michoacana, Templarios. There was a fight for power. There's a township near here where they used to hang bodies. Like dogs mark their territory they did it with bodies. [There's a rumor] they strung up a pregnant teacher and cut out her baby and left it hanging by its umbilical cord," he says.

In Tancitaro, 2015 was a year of tense stability, aside from the murder of Jesús Bucio.

"Jesús Bucio, they say he killed people. He was with a different group...organized crime. They killed people. His neighbors wanted revenge. They hired gunmen from Apatzingan. They killed him as payback," Emanuel says. Bucio's death, as controversial as it was, did not trigger a spiral of revenge killings. The details of the incident are still unclear because under Peña Nieto's government the justice system is so politicized and profit-oriented that prosecutors in Mexico City will never investigate allegations made against the kingpins behind a billion-dollar-a-year export industry. Residents in Tancitaro have different theories on Bucio's killing.

Emanuel thinks that until Mexico's justice system improves it will be hard to truly establish law and order. "Now there's more stability, but we have to change the culture," he says.

A woman pulls her SUV up in front of the market. "Can I park here?" she asks.

"No, absolutely not. It's marked blue for handicapped drivers," Emanuel explains.

Day by day Emanuel is helping to establish a new kind of respect for the law in Tanitaro's town center. Overall, he thinks there's been a major improvement. Emanuel owns a four-hectare avocado farm with five hundred trees. He explains, "My family has produced avocado for years and we had to pay *cuotas* to bring the avocado to market. Now we're free of all that. Now we own what we produce."

"Before bribes and extortion accounted for 40 to 45 percent of profits. We were practically slaves. Now you can see the change. Now it's more legal and that makes me proud," he adds.

§ § §

Out in the orchards the avocado growers have learned to comply with the strict rules enforced by the Junta Local, the organization that regulates Tancitaro's export farms. It's a meticulously run organization that ensures that each farm in the town complies with all of the norms of the export program. Outside of the office there are two long rows of trucks used by the Vegetable Health Police. The Junta has more than thirty-two specialist technicians and eighty-three assistants who visit the farms and ensure that the rules are followed. Inside his office, Angel Bucio, the Junta's 66-year-old president is like a medieval lord, the chieftain of the avocado realm.[133] The residents call him Don Angel, an antiquated title once reserved for barons, lords, and hacienda owners.

Most days he's at his office by eight in the morning. A slow-moving man with wide shoulders and a heavy, droopy build, Angel is like an ancient sea turtle, Tancitaro's respected elder. His face is round and his cheeks sink below his eyes. He shuffles up the stairs to his office, patiently listening to the local growers' concerns and complaints. Every morning a line of residents waits outside for an audience with him. The town's newly elected mayor was brought into office in 2015 through a negotiation between the three main parties. The local *caciques* selected a trustworthy, but unassuming candidate without the disruption of democratic competition. The deal was designed to prevent outside organized crime groups from backing a candidate and sowing discord. It's clear who holds the power now in Tancitaro.

Don Angel served as the Junta's treasurer for four years and has sat in the main office as the group's president for almost three. Sitting behind his desk he explains, "I'm a producer. I started with the export program to export to the U.S." He owns a farm with about twenty hectares of land.

"As a farmer I have been working for thirty-five years. Before the export program I did national fruit. At that time I was just a producer when the border to the U.S. opened for export," he explains speaking slowly, softly, and deliberately.

He sees the export sector as generating a lot of jobs, not just for the farms, but also for the people who work at the packers. "The harvest is still done with workers. Some businesses cut; the packers hire them. It's private businesses that have the personnel and equipment. The producer doesn't have anything to do with it," he explains.

Don Angel's job is relatively simple. He works to educate farm owners on the requirements set for farms that participate in the export program. "The Junta focuses on avocados. There are rules set by the U.S. to follow," he says.

His fleet of inspectors in the Vegetable Health Police drive out to visit the farms and oversee the harvests. "We've had problems with compliance with the program. All the producers have to comply with the U.S.'s norms. Every month the Junta does a General Assembly of all the producers to give them the information. New producers—we have engineers who teach them how to comply with the norms," he explains.

"When they enter the program they understand their obligation to comply with the phytosanitary norms [relating to pests and pathogens]. There's a work plan of what requirements the producers should complete. There should be no dry branches. At harvest there should be no ripe fruit," he adds.

It's a well-ordered process designed to ensure that growers in the U.S. never find a reason to complain about the production practices and try to block Mexican avocados from reaching the U.S. "The producers they have to comply. When they comply they get certified by the federal government and then they can sell their avocado to the people in the U.S.," he says.

Since the Junta paid to train and hire the CUSEPT police force he's seen an improvement in security too. "Here in the town, yeah. I can't speak about other areas. Here it is better," he says.

Don Angel is happy to talk avocado, but flatly refuses to discuss family business. "I just deal with avocado, nothing more," he says, waving his hand sideways dismissively. He won't address the murder of his nephew Jesús, who ran the town's *autodefensa* movement or the rumors that his brother, Jesús Bucio Bucio, the owner of the JBR packing plant, is deeply involved in organized crime. He just insists that things have improved in Tancitaro.

"I know it's different here. The town is full of orchards," he says.

§ § §

On a sunny Friday morning, there is a row of luxury SUVs and off-road-ready pickup trucks parked outside of JBR's office, a collection that includes a special edition Harley Davidson Ford LOBO and a futuristic looking Jeep Cherokee. Inside the building, Claudia, a 42-year-old executive who handles logistics for the company's export operations, walks from the main entrance towards the packing area. In the front lobby, Angel Bucio's son Pedro, who is wearing an off-brand polo shirt with a giant logo on the chest, chats with a secretary who is wearing a leather jacket and a tiger print skirt.

Pedro has an imposing, almost military presence and the heavily made-up secretary looks like an extra in a *telenovela* soap opera. Some locals whisper that JBR's owner, Jesús Bucio Bucio, a man who goes by the nickname "The Hamburger," is laundering money for drug traffickers. Others say he's behind the torching of a nearby packing facility and was the real boss behind the gunmen who demanded protection money from the town's residents before the uprising. In any case, Jesús maintains a low profile. Most people say they haven't seen him in months. Some people suspect he might be worried that like his son, he'll be killed by a Tancitaro gunman who can't forgive him for some alleged wrong committed during the bad days before the uprising. Regardless of the rumors, JBR hums with activity. While Claudia checks on the packing operation, a refrigerated long-haul trailer truck backs up to the loading dock, ready to bring Tancitaro's avocados up to the border.

From inside the office a silver Ford Raptor monster truck can be seen pulling up. A stocky young man with a short buzz cut and puffy vest, jeans, and brand new sneakers steps down from the truck carrying an AK-47. He enters the office and tucks the gun behind his desk, alongside a statue of Jesús and a photo of a cargo truck near the Golden Gate Bridge. On the wall, there's a framed poster with words spelled out in English that say, "JBR: Mexico's Yummiest Avocados."

Claudia, wearing a black sweater that hugs her slender frame, pulls on a hair net and a white jacket that looks like a dentist's uniform. She walks through a sliding door into the work area. Every year she guides the company's operations through the rush of the Super Bowl to the end of the spring harvest season. She's seen the business grow. "At first we sent six to eight trucks a week. Now the most I've sent in a week is seventy-seven and that was just for the U.S.," she says.

She pulls her jacket close in the chilly air of a refrigerated storage area. "Here's where the fruit comes in from the farms," she says walking by the shipping container-sized blocks of stacked avocado crates.

Claudia knows Javier. She scans over the paperwork on the different loads of avocado and points to his last name. Nodding at the stack of avocado from Javier's farm, she says, "This was cut yesterday so it's here now." After one avocado from each box is sliced open and checked by an engineer looking for plagues, the fruit will be ready for its turn to pass through the packaging line.

She watches the workers sweep the leaves and waste into a pile and a specialist from Mexico's Ministry of Agriculture checks the scraps for any signs of damage from fungus or insects. The fruit from each farm is kept separate. If an issue is ever reported the Ministry of Agriculture specialists and JBR's workers want to be able to know exactly which farm is the source of the contamination. They can't let one producer's problem with parasites spoil the reputation for the entire town's avocado.

"All the avocado passes through here, it's the selection process," she says. Picking up some small golf-ball-sized avocados from a pile of undersized avocados she says, "These are for the national market." Watching the women performing the sorting, she explains, "They select the second class and first class. The more damaged ones won't go to the U.S."

In the next step in the process, the fruit fall into individual caddies and pass under a washing-machine-sized box fitted with bright lights and a camera that is connected to a computer. "This measures the size, the weight," she says.

The fruit passes under a wheel that marks each one with a sticker and then in a cacophonous mix of clicks and clacks launches the fruit into different chutes, sorting them by size. On the ground below the platform, men push the laundry carts full of avocado towards separate workstations where the fruit will be packaged into boxes and loaded onto pallets. Under the oversight of inspectors from both U.S. and Mexican agencies the packer has become a deftly managed operation where rules are strictly enforced. Unlike the local police forces the avocado packers are subject to international oversight and held accountability by multiple government agencies.

In the packing area, Claudia watches the women reach for avocados, toss the fruit from one hand to the other, and delicately place each one in the box. It's a blur of flying fruit and hands in light blue gloves.

She nods towards the traffic jam of full avocado carts piling up in front of the packaging station. "These can't get past to be sorted until the other load is finished. They are really strict. There's a USDA engineer—he's checking to make sure that they don't mix one load with another." The U.S. Department of Agriculture engineers, who are Mexican citizens, travel between export processing plants, visiting each one once a year. It's a system designed to prevent conflicts of interest and relationship building between the engineers and their hosts.

Once the women get the nod of approval from a second engineer from Mexico's Ministry of Agriculture, they begin boxing the next load, pulling down cardboard boxes from an overhead conveyer belt. The women furiously juggle the avocado, loading each box in under a minute while men pile the full boxes onto carts and push them towards the pallet-building station.

"Imagine—it's eight tons of avocado in every truck and every day they're doing thirty-one trucks," Claudia explains.

"The majority goes to the U.S.," she adds.

Working over the steady hum of the conveyer belts, the clickety-clack of the sorting machine and the rhythmic clomping of the box-making machine, the workers fill up more than two thousand cardboard boxes every day.

"We produce for Costco. That's the box for Costco," Claudia explains, pointing to a pallet. The individual boxes will be shipped north and Javier's latest harvest will soon be on shelves. Most consumers in the U.S. will have no idea about the obstacles their avocados had to overcome to make it there from Tancitaro and other parts of Michoacan.

Claudia says her workers also pack avocado for Del Monte and Sam's Club. Once the workers seal the boxes in stacks on the pallets, they cart the load into a refrigerated storage room where it sits before it's loaded onto the trucks.

Watching the workers load up a pallet with avocados in Green Giant brand boxes, she says, "If I get a truck out before 7 p.m. by the next day they'll have the fruit there [in the U.S.]."

Javier's shipment is still waiting to be passed through the sorting machine. "His load came in yesterday. It will take thirty minutes to get processed," she says. After Javier's avocados are loaded onto the truck they'll make one last trip past the gunmen at the castles on the side of the roads leaving Tancitaro.

"In thirty hours a person in the United States can consume it," she says.

§ § §

Inside the packer there's a clear sense of order. Like the rest of the town's avocado sector it's run with clinical precision. Just outside the front door, however, the dynamic is more ambiguous. Giovanni, the stocky man who pulled up earlier in the morning in the Raptor 4x4 stands next to the trucks in front of JBR's facility. He says he's named after a former Pope. "People here are very Catholic," he says.

Asked about the gun behind his desk, he pauses. "It's to go guard at the barricade at night. All men have to go," he says. Giovanni is one of the managers who works for Angel Bucio's sons managing part of the family's avocado growing operation. Pulling out his phone, he shows a picture of himself wearing a camouflage flak jacket and a military-style beret holding up a machine gun and standing in front of a truck. He flicks to another picture of himself in front of a banner. "This one says 'Templarios Get Out,'" he says.

He doesn't think Tancitaro's gunmen will put down their weapons any time soon. "I think it's for life. Or until they find a better solution," he says.

"When the movement started the government wanted to disarm us. I was in jail for two months from August 2014 until October 2014. I was tortured to declare against the *autodefensas*. I never did," he adds.

The *comunitarios* have stuck to their guns.

"It's long term. The government can't provide security like we do," he says.

He says there are now more rules on carrying assault rifles in Tancitaro. "It's regulated." Nodding towards his gun he explains, "Now we can't bring it around. I brought it in here and I dropped it off."

He thinks that the government has finally accepted the *comunitarios*.

"Now they've reached an agreement," he says. "It's like an informal agreement. We don't leave this town. What we asked for was to protect here." In Mexico after all enforcement of the law is selective and the economically powerful enjoy certain privileges.

Climbing up into a late model Toyota 4x4 he explains, "Here there's a military base. There's Federal Police. There's State Police—they were Fuerza Rural, now they're Policía Michoacana. There's CUSEPT; the *aguacateros* formed that. And then there are the *comunitarios* who take care of the barricades," he says.

Giovanni says that it's common knowledge that there are still cells of Templario *sicarios* operating in the area around Tancitaro. But, when there's a problem a fighting force can be assembled with a few minutes notice. "Most people carry radios if they see something suspicious they report it," he says. When an alert goes out SUVs filled with men with their weapons pointing vertically up out of the windows can be seen roaring out of the town as men at the barricades hand over bulletproof vests and rifles to the men in the roving patrols. The CUSEPT and Fuerza Rural also join in.

Giovanni is comfortable with the current dynamic. "People don't trust the justice system," he shrugs.

Approaching a two-story tall, thirty-foot wide castle outfitted with turrets for machine gunners Giovanni explains, "Now Tancitaro is better." Nodding towards the five men standing in front of the barricade holding machine guns he laughs and says, "In the U.S. you can carry guns. Here it's prohibited and people are carrying them." Giovanni knows that Mexico's federal government isn't able or willing to enforce the country's laws. The armed civilian men at the barricade aren't in the mood to chat as he passes. They're talking tensely into their radios listening for warnings.

"They saw something suspicious up the road in Condembaro so they'll send the trucks, *comunitarios* and Fuerza Rural," he says. A CUSEPT patrol truck carrying two commandos in the back roars up the road, passing a metal avocado statue, and heads out towards Condembaro.

Giovanni looks over at the barricade at a wide-shouldered man gripping an assault rifle seeking cover behind the stone wall of the castle, eyeing the traffic coming in. Giovanni's truck pulls to a stop in the town center. A few school children in uniforms giggle and flirt by the gazebo in the center of the plaza. There's a bench with a plaque that says, "DONATED BY THE FAMILY OF ANGEL BUCIO." A pickup truck drives by booming music through a sound system seemingly built to play hip-hop. Its thumping bass bellows and reverberates and the blaring horns of the twangy ranchero song drown out singer's voice.

Only the words "*narco*" and "*seguridad*" are decipherable.

§ § §

After a long day supervising an export harvest at his farm, Javier seeks a quiet moment behind the heavy metal security gate that seals off his office from the street. Javier's office compound is a short drive away from his orchard. It's a property that covers nearly a full block of land and is home to a small garden of avocado trees, a mini avocado packing machine, and a stable and horse training area. "I love horses," he explains with a boyish smile. "Horses are my hobby." As a toddler he followed his father around Tancitaro's center. At that time the streets weren't paved and almost none of the residents drove trucks. "Horses are part of the way of life in Michoacan. Years ago there were no cars. You had to be a horseman," he explains.

Now Javier owns a fleet of trucks, but he's used his avocado earnings to pay homage to his state's rugged equestrian past. On the right side of the complex near the security gate there are three newly-built stalls, each built in an old style with hand-laid stones from the fields forming the front wall. The windows are made from metal and are shaped like old-fashioned wagon wheels. The stable is so new and clean it feels more like a diorama or a model of a rustic barn rather than a real ranch. Javier peeks in through the window at a colt and opens the door. He leads the horse out, cooing, clucking and grunting to control the horse as he pulls the reins.

"He's Spanish. He's a baby," Javier says. Months of patient training have tamed the growing stallion. Javier has been able to teach his horse to kick and clomp in a militaristic sort of dancing motion, part of a tradition local ranchers demonstrate at the village festivals. With a guttural, airy "huh, huh, huh" grunt he pulls the horse's reins, leading it past a row of three bushes his workers have trimmed in the shapes of a cross and two horses, and pats the animal's head with affection.

Javier walks past the immaculately clean training area that has been decorated with heavy wooden chairs carved with horse shapes. On the walls there are cowboy hats, saddles, and other equipment as well as a bar with a massive tequila collection.

Javier nods towards one of his employees, a man who once worked at an auto-body repair shop in Alabama and has an idea for a *maquila* factory that would take advantage of Mexico's low labor costs and repair wrecked cars from the U.S. and then send them back over the border. "He's an ironworker. He knows carpentry, he can build a house. He also moved drugs once. And the job he likes the most is horse training," Javier says.

A grey horse approaches and surreptitiously turns around, backing mischievously towards Javier. "Watch out for his feet," he warns, bracing for a kick. "He's rebellious." Even in his spare time Javier tries to impose order and exert control.

"This is what I do in the afternoon," he says, with an earnest half smile. "I gave up soccer and do this."

As the U.S. market for avocado has boomed, farmers have shifted to sending their fruit north and Javier's packing business has suffered. Nobody wants to sell to the Mexican market anymore. Over the last few years the complex has become an office and a stable rather than a packer. Walking past trees the trees, Javier explains, "It's not for export. When there are loose animals around it can't be exported."

With night falling over the town Javier heads up to his office. He settles into a plush chair and sits imperiously behind his desk, a c-shaped work station with a computer and a printer that looks like a typical accountant's office. He's also put in a small lounge with leather sofas that are dark green like the color of unripe avocado, and added a few photos of horses, a horse statue, and a cross on the wall.

Normally after a long day of work Javier might open a few beers or grab a glass of tequila from the bar downstairs. Today he just wants coffee.

He heats water in a coffee pot and sets up Styrofoam cups filled with instant "cappuccino" mix. Made in Michoacan, the powder contains a combination of cocoa, milk, and instant coffee. If he doesn't have time to make a batch at home in the morning he'll pick up a cup of instant cappuccino at one of the stores in the town's center. None of the stores in town sell high quality coffee from Chiapas. Most residents just want the cheapest source of caffeine they can find.

Javier turns on the TV. It's "El Señor de Los Cielos," a show set mostly in the mountainous state of Sinaloa, the birthplace of Mexico's most famous trafficker Joaquin "El Chapo" Guzman and the center of Mexico's early marijuana and heroin production economies. Throughout Javier's life, he's seen the towns in Tierra Caliente, just outside of Tancitaro's outer limit, come to rival Sinaloa in terms of organized crime activity and violence.

"In Tierra Caliente, it's like Culiacan, Sinaloa—drugs. But Tancitaro has avocado," he says.

Javier insists that although some farmers moonlighted in the drug game over the past few decades, the town's economy "was never based on that." He does acknowledge, however, that in the economic chaos of the 1980s, "There was nowhere to study. In the eighties and nineties there were farms, but a kilo of avocados cost one or two pesos. People left. There was no future here."

In the eighties what had in previous decades been a low, but constant stream of local men leaving to go north to the U.S. turned into a mass exodus. There are now more than three and a half million *Michoacanos* living in the U.S and Javier has a target for his frustration.

He has a distinctly negative view of rural development policy in the post-WWII PRI-led era. "There was never a program for planting avocado. In the countryside there was no structure [of assistance programs.] There was no economy here in the eighties. If there was a program here to help farmers many people would have stayed," Javier says.

At the same time, the growing network of drug smugglers provided an emergency relief fund of sorts for farmers short on cash. "You'd never know who. It wasn't the whole community. But there were people who took advantage of [the opportunities of] the era and made their money. There was a guy—when I left for college he had cows. And when I came back he had thirty hectares and ten trucks," he says.

Out of economic necessity, locals created a sort of moral flexibility when it came to earning money growing poppy or pot or ferrying contraband to the border. "At that time drugs weren't as controlled. It was independent *narcos*, it wasn't cartels."

Historically, Michoacan was one of the most brutally unequal post-colonial societies in Mexico. Landless Tarascan indigenous people worked alongside poor mestizos. Mexico's celebrated twentieth century President Lázaro Cárdenas grew up in Michoacan at a time when the state was home to a deeply divided society. Then as now the rifts were mainly riven along class lines rather than between ethnic groups like in colonial Chiapas. Later Cárdenas used land reform as a tool to split up the big haciendas, but didn't bring many new economic opportunities to Michoacan.

In the nineteenth century, any time a wave of liberalism swept through southern Mexico, local priests and landowners fought back, enforcing the status quo of piety, purity, obedience, and the deification of the light-skinned Virgin Mary. Local landlords funneled money into the church and Catholic education. They appeased the general population by sponsoring village festivals and enforced their property rights by hiring bands of "white guards" to protect their haciendas. Michoacan may have been a lawless state, but local elites always found a way to impose a sort of order. In many towns in the state, churches used their bells to summon workers to the fields and priests used their sermons to urge for humility and respect for the hacienda owners. In one case a priest passed over information gleaned in the confessional to help the local landowners crush a peasant uprising.[134] During parts of the year many of Michoacan's landless farm workers ate mesquite wood when they couldn't afford food for their families. All the while, the priests and bishops, who were paid by the landowners, promised their parishioners that the prize of Catholicism lay in the afterlife. In the late twentieth century, drugs and migration were the first two real sources of social mobility for entrepreneurial individuals looking to break the staid class hierarchy.

"There were no jobs. There was no help from the government. It was a way of life. Some people were good at hiding it in cars. They went to the U.S.," Javier shrugs non-judgmentally. As soon as drug money was funneled into a productive enterprise, a one-time poppy grower or drug mule could take a position of respect within the community. As most wealthy people kept (and continue to keep) their money in banks outside of the town, nobody could ever really be sure of the provenance of the funds local men used for purchasing tractors or snapping up new plots of land.

"Many people had an illegal business and then they went legal. For decades Mexico was a tax haven. A lot of people took advantage," Javier says. The drugs kept the poor from starving.

"Before you could deposit a million pesos and they didn't ask questions. Now if you deposit a hundred-thousand pesos it's a red flag. They ask you what you sold. So now people who launder money make businesses," he says.

The drug money never dominated Tancitaro's economy, but was always there. "Some people made illegal money legal. But the economy was never based on that," Javier says.

The influx of *narco* dollars was tolerated as a necessity after decades of neglect by Mexico's political class. "Here in Mexico the PRI, the PRD, the PAN, they're worthless," Javier says. "Now that the structure of the sector exists they created programs for loans. There's a program for tractors, but it doesn't function," Javier says. Too many of the government programs designed to boost productivity and help farmers are brought down by corrupt officials looking for kickbacks, Javier thinks.

Javier disparages Mexico's conditional cash transfer programs, "There's a program for poverty, Prospera—but a guy can come by with an expensive truck with four doors and they'll give him the aid. It's a mess. That's the state of our country. It's corruption, insecurity, and impunity," Javier says. He thinks it is hard to overestimate how big of a role illegality plays in the way Mexico's economy works. In the absence of real rule of law business owners, ordinary citizens, and even government officials have had to find ways to improvise and survive.

Javier sometimes struggles to reconcile his frustration with corrupt state and federal government politicians with his tacit acceptance of wrongdoing at the local level. He is a deeply religious Catholic who crosses his hands in front of his chest any time he passes Tancitaro's cathedral and criticizes the Church hierarchy for protecting priests who abused children. Still, he harbors a diffident sort of respect for "El Chapo" Guzman, whom he says is loved and protected by the people, and for Michoacan's own version, the Valencia family.

"Valencia, he was like a Robin Hood. He did his business, but he didn't mess with the people," he explains. Back then, Tancitaro was poor, but seen as safe. "There weren't robbers here. It was pleasant. And then it was a shocking change."

At first, for some farmers a brief trip north to work in the U.S. or a season spent cultivating poppy plants or pot could provide the capital to buy more land or invest in avocado tree seedlings or farming equipment. The problem was, like the trees Javier's father planted in the mid-eighties, by the second decade of the 21st century, the criminal activity had grown out of control. Gone were the days of the clandestine growing or smuggling and nonchalant acceptance of newly-generated wealth.

By the time Felipe Calderon entered office in 2006, Michoacan was dealing with fully formed private armies, *caudillos* and *caciques* fighting for control. In Mexico the town square, the plaza, is central to community life in small towns across the country. *Plaza* also has a critical political definition in the world of politics and crime. Dominating local geographic jurisdictions is called "dominating *la plaza*." In rural stretches of states such as Chiapas, Oaxaca, and Michoacan it's clear that the federal government lacks absolute authority. In different areas modern *caudillos*, corrupt politicians or *narco* bosses control *la plaza*. By 2010, the Templarios had established their authority in rural Michoacan. No longer hiding behind the scenes, the organized crime group sent squads of paramilitary-style gunmen on patrols through the outer districts of Tancitaro in trucks marked with the logos of their cartel.

Looking up at the TV, Javier watches two cartel bosses talk.

"You see who's running the country? It's not the government," Javier says.

Fighting for control is expensive and the groups, who had once been content to operate in the shadows, adopted new strategies for generating revenue. Rather than just supplementing and injecting cash into the legal economy, they began to suck the life out of it, charging extortion payments, kidnapping and killing residents who refused to hand over cash. The Templarios made the mistake of crossing the line of the level of criminality that residents could tolerate in their community.

"The critical stage was 2014. The strong control was 2013 and 2014—that's what impacted people. That was out of control. You didn't want to leave your house. It was really difficult. The bad guys, they disappeared people I loved when they didn't pay the protection money," Javier says.

Compared to what preceded it, the new reality of checkpoints and security barricades is an improvement. "Here in front there was a barricade. Everybody went and gave coffee. I paid the electricity for two years. I lent them my restrooms. The people saw a positive change in security and wanted to help. It was a community project that was looking out for our interests," Javier explains. Now when Javier has to drive alone at night he isn't as scared.

Tancitaro might be safer, but it hasn't fully recovered. "Still there are problems. There are people without fathers. People who lost family members. There are kids in school from families that have been torn apart. They can't sleep at night. There were people whose doors were knocked down who were kidnapped in front of their families. Imagine the trauma," he says.

Overall, he thinks the changes are for the better. "We were happy to have the criminal groups out of here. There were a lot of murders. You couldn't go out to enjoy parties," he says. He also acknowledges that the damage wrought during the Templario era hasn't been fully repaired and won't be fixed quickly. "The change wasn't easy. The Church is still working to repair the social fabric. A lot of people who were involved didn't leave. They stayed. They were pardoned," Javier says.

The situation in Tancitaro is extreme, but it highlights a

broader problem in Mexico. In his groundbreaking book *The Politics of Crime in Mexico* John Bailey, a Mexico scholar who teaches at Georgetown University, explains that in Mexico "the wealthy and powerful can manipulate justice for personal, partisan, or group purposes."[135] Both at the national and local level oligarchs can bend the rules and shape laws to meet their needs. Small-scale entrepreneurs are left with few protections. By some estimates security problems currently cost Mexico more than 134 billion dollars a year, or more than 12 percent of total GDP.[136] It's nearly impossible, however, to arrive at an approximation of the true costs of crime and impunity because we can't accurately estimate the amount of investment the country is losing out on due to fears about security problems and rule of law.

Like many rural entrepreneurs Javier just tries to avoid attracting attention to himself. "You can't speak openly here. I don't talk in the street. That's the best way to get in trouble," he explains. Still, a lot of questions remain about who is running Tancitaro. The town has achieved some form of improvised security, but behind the scenes, it's clear there's a near total absence of real law and order.

"There are farm owners who died or abandoned their land, but the farms are still operating. Who owns it? Who knows?" he says.

"Drugs, power, that's the fight there. He who governs the zone has the *plaza*," Javier says. The gunmen at the barricades can focus on threats from outside groups, but residents worry that the citizen defense force could be infiltrated and taken over from within. When it comes to the *comunitarios* and other police forces unlike with avocado, there's no automated process to quickly and easily sort out the good from the bad. The residents simply have to accept that the men at the barricades may or may not have ulterior motives.

"There are honest people and there are people who are involved with *comunitarios* as infiltrators. It's a delicate topic," Javier says.

The current dynamic is untenable, but the effort to build strong, independent institutions and guarantee (near) universal enforcement of Mexico's laws will take decades of earnest and honest effort. Many observers doubt that Mexico's elites will ever put their weight behind such an effort.

Javier doesn't trust the Mexican federal government's plan to create a new professional police force run by the state government. Many academics share his skepticism of the Mando Unico force.[137] "The Mando Unico is coming to the whole country, but some groups want to control *plazas*. If you take away the guns from the population we'll become a target again," he says. It's an institutional crisis. The local people don't trust the state and federal authorities and the state and federal governments don't trust the locals. Both sides make allegations of corruption and complicity in crime. It's a problem that Javier acknowledges, but doesn't know how to resolve.

"You see it here and in the whole state. With more armed people there are risks. But if the police who aren't from here come in they could be corrupt," he says.

Javier sees the current dynamic as an improvised solution. "It was a way to start towards a solution. There are two types of *comunitarios*. One type cares for the community and the other type has it's own interests. There's a saying: 'with friends like these who needs enemies?' But what would happen if these community police weren't here? People are awake, they know there would be chaos. It's really difficult," he says. He thinks the CUSEPT force is a good first step, but he doesn't think it's enough. He hopes that the long-term solution will be more stable.

"How can we pay taxes and not be regulated by the government?" he asks.

§ § §

On Saturday morning, Javier sits settled into a plastic chair at a taco stand near his orchard scooping up chunks of beef from his *birria* soup, savoring the flavor. By 9:30 a.m. he has already escorted another harvesting team to his orchard. He left home at 7:15 and at mid-morning he's ready for a real breakfast.

Above the street, strings of red and white triangular flags flutter in the wind, adding to the medieval vibe. There's a hand-written sign for PROSPERA sitting in between an export orchard and the dismantled carcasses of the cars and trucks lying in front of a chop shop. Just down the hill there's a massive security castle and a covered basketball court. One of the best-known dishes in Michoacan is *carnitas* pork, an unctuous slow-roasted pork dish similar to pulled pork, heaped on soft, freshly-pressed tortillas. Javier prefers beef soup for breakfast. Squeezing a lime into his broth he says, "It's *carne de res*. I don't like to eat grease in the morning."

Reaching for a plate of sliced avocado he says, "Other places don't have flavor like this." He squeezes on lime juice, sprinkles on salt and eats the piece of avocado as if it were an orange slice. The quality, he says, "is the color and the texture.

The color of the skin should be dark and the texture soft, but not mushy. When there's more oil it's firmer."

Watching a frustrated man struggle up the hill pushing a cheap motorcycle that has a Harley Davidson decal slapped onto its gas tank, Javier chuckles. In Tancitaro appearances can be deceiving. It's common to see farm trucks kitted out to look like Cadillacs or decorated with braggadocious decals. It's part of the influx of hip-hop culture and Texan swagger that a previous generation of migrant workers brought back to Tancitaro. Going north to the U.S. as *mojados,* however, is out of the question for Javier's kids.

The new economy has opened up a new realm of jobs. "There's work now. They call avocado green gold for a reason," he says, shrugging.

One of his sons wants to be a veterinarian and the other an engineer. His daughter, who is still in elementary school, might want to study medicine. As Tancitaro's economy booms, the pull of migrating to the U.S. is fading. "It doesn't interest them. The young people have a different way of thinking. They want to study," Javier says.

As an accountant, Javier knows the way businesses' balance sheets implode during an economic collapse. He's lived through the booms and busts that buckled Mexico's economy from the 1970s through the 1990s. He knows how market gluts and price crashes can hurt producers. "There's a lot of interest in exporting to China, but if that doesn't happen with production rising in Jalisco it's going to saturate the market," he says.

Other farmers are happy with the boom and not too worried about the future. Javier knows that in the commodities sector, economic success is ephemeral. He wants to make sure that his kids have careers they can fall back on.

"This will be their patrimony, like a fund, but I don't want them to depend on it," Javier says. He wants his kids to study and doesn't mind if they end up leaving Tancitaro to attend college or look for work. "I want them to be happy and happiness comes from doing what you like," he says. The avocado empire he's built is a means to an end, and not an end in itself. If his kids settle down in a distant city or state, Javier won't worry.

"I'll be happy if they are happy. What you do as a father is for them," he says.

For now, Javier is starting to feel more comfortable letting his sons venture out to the soccer field by the army barracks. The patchwork of police forces in Tancitaro has finally managed to cobble together a sort of security. Javier is enjoying his soup two days after the February 11 deadline for disarmament came and went. The front page of the morning newspaper boldly declares that the end of the *autodefensas* will guarantee peace for Michoacan.[138] The article includes a photo of a shiny new Policía Michoacana state police truck.[139] After years of watching politicians brag about reforms, but never seeing tangible results, residents in Tancitaro are used to seeing this type of simulation. The official story published in the newspapers is just a charade. Local people see a different reality in streets.

By the main entrance to Tancitaro the gunmen are still loafing around a smoldering bonfire with automatic weapons slung over their shoulders. The federal government didn't intervene to disarm the town's gunmen. For now the *comunitarios* continue to guard the checkpoints and carry out their patrols.

"It's delicate. Up until now it's been seen as a triumph by the people. But it's a fragile solution. We're stuck between the government and organized crime. It's not a permanent solution," Javier says.

Conclusion:

How Beer and Tacos Explain Modern Mexico

Jesus helps his workers brew a batch of beer.

A worker holds up a handful of toasted grains at the Minerva brewery

Industrial production equipment inside the massive Grupo Modelo brewery in Guadalajara

Two workers pause from brewing at Minerva

A delivery truck gets a new decal in front of Minerva's office

Jesus helps make an afternoon delivery in downtown Guadalajara

Guillermo sits behind the counter of his neighborhood store on the outskirts of Tijuana

A fish taco at a street stand in Tijuana

Improvised housing on the outskirts of Tijuana

A taco chef cooks steak and tortillas at a road-side taco stand in the Terrazas neighborhood in Tijuana. This neighborhood is home to many residents who moved north from Chiapas and Oaxaca in the 1980s and 1990s

A hillside slum in the Terrazas neighborhood of Tijuana

A mezcal cocktail sits on the table of Mision 19, one of Tijuana's most expensive restaurants

Taco chef Adrian sits down with a plate of food in front of his food truck in Tijuana

An old man and a girl look through the border fence in Tijuana towards the US

Due to a combination of their geographic isolation, weak property rights and general condition of lawlessness, states such as Chiapas, Oaxaca, and Michoacan have mostly missed out on any significant investment in industrial development in Mexico's modern history. These areas of Mexico present extreme examples of communities that are isolated from the global economy and are being left behind as other parts of the country and the world evolve. But, the general story in Mexico is not one of uniform poverty and marginalization, but rather a case study of extreme inequality. Further north up the Pacific Coast from Michoacan in cities such as Guadalajara and Tijuana there has been a boom of construction of new factories and universities and real effort to build new clusters of industrial and technology companies. In both Tijuana and Guadalajara certain neighborhoods have been renovated and rebuilt to resemble Rodeo Drive in L.A. or South Beach in Miami. There are boutique stores, high-end restaurants, and lines of luxury sedans parked on the sides of the road. In these bubbles in Mexico the extreme poverty of Chiapas and Oaxaca and the terrifying violence in Michoacan seem like distant realties.

Still, even in the most successful pockets of Mexico the general truths of Mexico's economy hold. Mexico is often explained as a country of paradoxes where incredible wealth exists side by side with extreme poverty. At the start of 2017 Mexico displaced Brazil to become the top market for luxury goods in Latin America.[140] Mexico is also home to some of the poorest and most marginalized communities in Latin America. It's a country with well-designed laws (on paper at least) that is also frighteningly lawless. The truth is, Mexico is not a developing, middle-income country, but rather a fragmented mix of overlapping first and third world societies where a globalized elite coexists (somewhat uncomfortably) with a mass of poorly paid people who either work in the informal economy or on small family-owned farms or scrape out a living in low-wage, entry-level jobs in the *maquila* industry. There are immense divisions between the more industrialized north and the still struggling south. But, throughout Mexico the basic tenets of inequality, informality, and illegality are the pillars on which society is built.

Across the globe, in countries without real rule of law, monopolies are the only business structure that can protect and guarantee private investment. In Mexico the entire structure of society is based around power, and who has it and who doesn't. It is no surprise that the Modern Mexico of the NAFTA era has been built up around a group of oligarchs and helped exacerbate and entrench the stark divisions between elites and the marginalized masses that have existed since the *hacienda* economy of the colonial era. The struggles that small-time producers of coffee, mezcal, and avocados face when trying to build up their businesses and export their products are not anomalies, but rather exemplary of the obstacles created and built into Modern Mexico's globalized economy.

In Modern Mexico real wealth creation is still the privilege of a small group of politically connected elites. Everybody else just has to try to find a way to fight to survive.

Many of the struggles faced by entrepreneurs in the south also exist in places such as Guadalajara and Tijuana, two of the supposed success stories of the NAFTA era. In particular, Guadalajara's beer industry provides an illuminating case study for the broader dynamics of market concentration in

Mexico's economy. Likewise, the taco vendors that cater to the growing maquila industry in Tijuana also provide an important perspective on the two-tiered nature of Mexico's economy.[141] Beer and tacos illustrate how Mexico's economy works in a way that's easy to digest.

§ § §

Jesús, the ambitious and energetic 38-year-old founder of Minerva beer, a Guadalajara-based brewery that has fought to become Mexico's largest independent beer maker, knows that he is forced to compete on an uneven playing field.[142] With the mid-morning traffic humming by on the wide cement highway outside his brewery, which is tucked inside an industrial warehouse on the outskirts of Guadalajara, Mexico's second largest city, Jesús is focused intensely on his work. The brewing operation is sandwiched between the red-tile roofs of a leafy, upper-income neighborhood and the densely packed cement structures in a humble *barrio* on the other side of the freeway. As his workers remove a heavy pile of spent grains the warehouse fills with the pungent, slightly sour smell of warm grits.

Jesús steps down on the production floor to supervise the beer-making. Soft-spoken and methodical in his work, Jesús has short black hair and a thin, athletic frame. He is recognized for being something of a David figure in Mexico, a businessman who battled Mexico's industrial giants and emerged victorious, at least for now. In an economy that is dominated by billionaires, the clanging, whirring, and hissing of the mechanized operation on Jesús's production line are the sounds of success. Jesús has hired eighty-five employees. He no longer directly supervises the hands-on brewing process every day. Now he usually comes to work dressed in well-worn polo shirts and New Balance running shoes. He looks like he is ready to compete in a track and field event. He is always preparing to fight to protect his business. "I think we're in a difficult time. We have to grow to get to the next level," he says. He needs to concentrate all of his energy on his company's long-term survival.

He climbs up the metal steps onto the elevated platform near the access doors to the *macedor*, a tank about the size of a four-person tent, that serves as a giant stew pot for his brews. The entire warehouse spans the area of a soccer field, but the machinery is clustered into a space that is about the size of a tennis court. The availability of extra floor space is an asset. Jesús needs room to expand.

In Mexico's business world Jesús's company, Minerva, is seen as the rare start-up that has managed to avoid being squashed or squeezed out by the behemoths who control Mexico's industrial sector and the bulk of the country's economy. Jesús is lucky. His father was able to lend him money when he was starting. Other entrepreneurs have to try and fight for loans with crushingly high interest rates from banks such as Inbursa and Banco Azteca, institutions owned by Mexican billionaires Carlos Slim and Ricardo Salinas. The small club of bankers in Mexico reap immense profits, but they also stifle the growth of small and medium enterprises. For small and medium sized businesses bank loans are hard to secure and lending rates average over eleven percent. Overall bank lending as a percent of total economic output in Mexico is only 34 percent, roughly on par with levels of lending recorded in Sub-Saharan Africa.[143] In the U.S. the amount of money lent out by banks is worth around two times as much as annual economic output.[144] Mexico's conservative and insular banking sector is stable and immensely profitable, but has failed to effectively finance and develop Mexico's sprawling collection of small and medium sized businesses.

So far Jesús has carved out a niche for his company, but is still working relentlessly to fight for a permanent slice of the market and achieve some semblance of long-term stability and security.

He's pushing his staff to reach a new production record for the company: twenty-thousand liters of beer by the end of the year. He aims to triple his brewing capacity over the next few years. There's a simple logic to his plans for expansion. "You get economies of scale. You get more efficient production. Everything is risky below sixty thousand," he explains.

Grupo Modelo, Mexico's largest beer company, produces 500 million liters of beer every month in Mexico and is largely responsible for turning Mexico into the world's fourth largest beer maker and number one exporter.[145] Every few minutes Modelo churns out as much beer as Jesús can produce in an entire year. As Modelo continues to expand its reach into the craft beer segment Jesús knows he'll need to bulk up his operation to be able to survive.

Minerva's operation sits just a few neighborhoods away from Grupo Modelo's gargantuan factory in Guadalajara, the city's biggest brewery. Minerva can't compete with Grupo Modelo on price, but like other craft beers they find a way to compete by targeting up-market customers who are willing to pay a premium for a higher quality product.

Minerva's stout is made from a mix of grains from the U.S. and Germany. Over the last two years Jesús has taken a step away from the hands-on operation, but he still appreciates the feel and smell of the slow-roasted, black malted wheat he uses for making his darkest beers. "This is black malt. This gives color to the beer. It smells like coffee," he explains. The kernels of grain have been toasted to the brink of burning and look almost like glossy, dark-roasted espresso beans. They bring a pungent chocolaty taste to the brew. He also adds in a few bags of American golden wheat. As is the case at most of the new generation of factories in Mexico, most of the inputs are imported. The workers merely assemble the product.

"I'm going to throw it in," he says in English, tipping the bag upside down and letting the dry grains cascade in steady, sifting stream into the steaming water inside the tank. He takes a moment to watch the *macedor* churn as the brew begins to roil, exuding a grey, frothy, cap of light brown foam. He has installed sensors and digital displays. His workers can closely monitor and manage the production process on their own. Jesús has built up a team of employees and no longer needs to directly supervise production. He has achieved a level of company growth that few small businesses in Mexico ever reach.

Jesús glances over the railing at the bottles rattling down a conveyor belt on the production floor. The bottles carry out a carefully choreographed mechanized dance as they pass through a series of turn-styles and cogs and machines slap on stickers and clamp on metal caps. Unlike most bottling operations in Oaxaca his production line is automated. His workers help manage the machinery, but they don't perform many rote tasks directly.

Jesús has unlocked the secret to economic productivity. The value of his brand is in his recipes and his distribution network. His workers generate far more revenue per hour than people performing tasks such as sorting coffee beans where output and value added per worker is drastically lower.

Unlike at Mexico's small-town, craft mezcal distilleries everything at Minerva is done with industrial precision. Jesús's employees keep a log of exactly what types of beer they brew and the quantities of ingredients they use. They track cook times on an electronic tablet.

"It's not hard to make good beer. It's harder to sell it and collect payments. Making it profitable is hardest," Jesús explains. He knows that in Mexico the big challenge isn't creating a great product. For entrepreneurs at small and medium sized companies the challenge lies in overcoming Mexico's unique set of obstacles and building up a successful business.

With the stout ready to be pumped up into the fermentation vats, the workers are scrambling to box a freshly-brewed batch of India Tequila Ale, one of the company's signature beers. The bottles jangle together as they pass out of the pasteurizer and rattle down the conveyor belt, receiving a blast of compressed air to shear off any residual water droplets before they reach the end of the production line.

Jesús stands on his loading dock and watches one of his workers gingerly apply a new decal to the side of a delivery truck outside. The panel shows a bottle of Minerva beer with a royal blue label, a tall, elegant flute of amber colored beer and a large slogan that says, "We Carry Mexico's Craft Beer."

§ § §

Jesús slips behind the wheel of his pickup truck and pulls out onto the highway outside the warehouse. Throughout his life he's seen the neighborhood transform from a suburban farming community into one of Mexico's most successful industrial districts. Today there are few signs of the neighborhood's rural roots. The wide, multi-lane highway is lined by factories from IBM, Intel, and Lenovo. On the right-hand side of the road there's a boxy white building from the seventies. "Zapopan was the periphery, but now it has a lot of transnational companies, maquiladoras. There's a lot of retail," Jesús explains.

Over the last two decades he's seen his city, which is located in the state of Jalisco just north of Michoacan, transform. "In general Guadalajara has made the effort to be the Silicon Valley of Mexico. They worked with local universities to get specialized in tech," he says.

"The government gave subsidies to get professors for tech-related degrees. I think it made a great ecosystem," he explains. Unlike in Chiapas and Oaxaca there's a viable domestic market for high-end consumer products. Jesús doesn't have to rely on tourists visiting his neighborhood from wealthier parts of Mexico and elsewhere around the globe. The brew-pub that abuts his factory fills up on weekends and evenings.

"There are good jobs. It's people who work for multi-national companies who have purchasing power," he explains.

Guadalajara has built a tech start-up incubator and an impressive modern office tower for the state's Ministry of Innovation.[146] Maybe more than any other city in Latin America Guadalajara is starting to emerge as a modern 21st century knowledge economy.[147] Companies such as HP and IBM have already moved in and set up sizable operations.[148] Guadalajara is missing out on the newest factories being built by Toyota, Audi and other companies, and is trying to specialize in a niche of jobs that require more education and training. The city is no longer competitive when it comes to wages. Multinational companies focus on cutting costs. Guadalajara's dynamic economic activity drives up wages. It's more profitable to build factories in areas that have only farming and no competition for manufacturing work. Guadalajara is trying to complement and maybe eventually replace the factories that cobble together consumer electronics and other manufactured products with a new generation of higher-value added goods. It's a race to see if the economy can truly evolve before the industries that rely heaviest on low-wages flee for other locales. Optimists see major strides forward in the development of a new cluster of software design, programing, 3D animation, and specialty engineering firms. Pessimists complain that the bulk of the economy is still based on at-risk *maquila*-style assembly operations.

Still, outside of Jesús's brewery there are signs of brisk economic activity. One store front advertises "Glass. Aluminum." Another store has the blue and white logo for Comex, Mexico's largest paint company. When it was founded in 1959, Comex was blocked out of the market by Mexico's established business oligopoly. Barred from stores, Comex's executives built up their own retail network. Today they control over half of Mexico's paint market and are nearly ten times bigger than their next largest competitor.[149]

Unlike Oaxaca and Chiapas, Jalisco, the state where Guadalajara is located, is home to some mega-corporations. Guadalajara's economy also supports a bevy of small and medium sized businesses. The big factory complexes are surrounded by residential streets that are lined with a smorgasbord of small businesses and chain stores. The money generated by local industry and farming exports supports a diverse economy. Jalisco is perennially one of the five fastest growing states in Mexico.[150]

Jesús pulls his truck to a stop at an intersection and looks over at the frame of a new apartment complex rising a block away. Today Guadalajara is also home to an astounding number of new construction sites. "There are a lot [of new buildings]," Jesús explains. The busy highway towards downtown Guadalajara is lined with tower after tower of luxury condos, giant cranes, and skeletons of metal rising from the road. Jalisco has benefited tremendously during the NAFTA era, maybe more than any other state in Mexico. Guadalajara is now Mexico's second largest city. Four and half million people live in the city's metro area. On the outskirts of town, the red tile roofs of the houses in wealthier areas transition to an agglomeration of grey cement buildings in poorer peripheral areas that butt up against a neat grid of well-managed farms.

Overall the state of Jalisco is recognized for being one of the most dynamic regions in Mexico. The state's high-tech sector accounts for 54 percent of Jalisco's economic output. There is clear evidence in Jalisco that investment in technology and mechanization has radically increased output per worker.

The state's tech sector is one example of success in an economy that continues to be defined by low-productivity.

Driving through Guadalajara, it's almost hard to remember how closed off Mexico's economy used to be. Before NAFTA Mexico's government supported a wide range of inefficient firms that made everything from blue jeans to simple electronics and even the paper for the country's print media. Jesús stops to point out the yellow arches of the world's best-known fast food restaurant. "That was the first McDonald's in Guadalajara. They came twenty-five years ago. There were lines and more lines," he explains, smiling wryly at the memory. In the pre-NAFTA era traveling to the U.S. to buy consumer products was a regular aspect of life for Mexico's middle and upper-income families. Middle class families would take an annual road trip to Texas and drive back home with their cars stuffed to capacity with "*fayuca*," a Mexican slang term for contraband.[151] They would bring bags of clothing, sports equipment and household goods. Most of the time these cross-border consumers would offer a small bribe to the customs agents to avoid paying exorbitant import duties.

Jesús thinks back to the pre-NAFTA era. "People from the upper class, we went to the U.S. to shop. I went with my dad. Stores in Guadalajara sold just Mexican clothing and just a few imports, but it was very expensive," he explains.

Going north to the U.S. to shop was just a normal part of Jesús's childhood. "It was very common. We'd even say 'go shopping' in English," he adds. Since the start of the NAFTA-era, however, goods from U.S. companies such as Levis, Converse, and Nike have become available at malls and stores throughout Mexico.

"Now I buy more here. If I need something," he says. In many ways Guadalajara is a petri dish for analysts looking at the effects of free trade on economic outcomes. The aperture of the consumer goods sector led to a rapid influx of foreign brands, but was also the death knell for Mexico's sluggish companies that always relied on government protections and support and never consolidated competitive operations. The new status quo provides residents with easy access to products from brands from the U.S. and other foreign countries, but hasn't helped foster the development of a new generation of Mexican brands. In a free market the strongest companies win. The outcome isn't always beneficial for local producers.

The massive luxury mall by Jesús's house has a cavernous upmarket department store called Palacio de Hierro, a chain that is owned by Mexican billionaire Alberto Bailleres. Palacio de Hierro is one of few Mexican companies that has been able to compete successfully with the influx of American super-stores such as Sears and Wal-Mart. It helps that Palacio de Hierro's owner has a few highly profitable gold mines and a railroad company that in an emergency might help subsidize his retail operations. Even at Palacio de Hierro in Jesús's neighborhood, however, the selection of Mexican-made goods is limited. The mall also has a Nestle store that offers pods of coffee from Chiapas and a U.S.-style seafood restaurant that sells ultra-premium tequila for over two hundred dollars a bottle. They also sell Minerva beer. Overall, however, Jesús struggles to think of the Mexican brands he sees at stores. "Local? It's almost nothing. It's mostly global brands. It's bad. There are only a few local companies," he explains. Some of the only Mexican brands at Palacio de Hierro are in-house brands produced by the company itself. Controlling the distribution network helps the company get its products in front of customers.

In the same way that Palacio de Hierro enjoys the privilege of being part of a billionaire's multi-industry portfolio, a similar company called Oxxo has established itself as Mexico's homegrown competitor to 7-11, the American convenience store chain that has become a powerful force in Mexico's retail sector. Oxxo is owned by FEMSA, the Mexican beverage giant that sold its beer-making division to Heineken in 2009.[152] For decades the network of Oxxo stores has been a huge advantage for FEMSA.[153] They had exclusive access to thousands of stores and in many isolated, rural areas of the country. Through the simple constraints of geography, they effectively dominate the hyper-local beer market in any neighborhood where an Oxxo is the closest convenience store.

Minerva beer is shut out from the shelves at Oxxo. The exclusionary nature of the Oxxo stores is just one remnant of the fiefdoms that Mexico's government traditionally granted to monopolists to help new industries develop. "Oxxo is just for Heineken," Jesús explains.

When he first started Jesús found out that his beer was also blocked from most of the country's supermarkets and bars. Most businesses signed exclusive contracts with one of the beer giants. Shortly after founding his company, Jesús focused on making sure that Minerva found its way onto the menu at brew pubs and gourmet restaurants that cater to upwardly mobile hipsters and wealthy professionals. He targeted the few pubs that carried diverse portfolios of brands and catered to the captive market of tens of thousands of young professionals who are interested in buying and learning about craft beer.

These days as his company's operations have stabilized,

when he drives through the city, Jesús's mind grapples with different business problems. Even though violent crime has spiked in the state of Jalisco throughout the Peña Nieto administration, Jesús doesn't spend a lot of time thinking about organized crime. He's more focused on a different kind of cartel: the monopolies that control Mexico's legal economy.

Accelerating up over a section of smooth, elevated cement highway, Jesús points out at the billowing clouds of steam rising from the smoke stacks at a mammoth manufacturing facility that is the size of a large oil refinery. The hulking facility looks like it is ten stories tall and has the logos of some of the conglomerate's brands painted on the sides of its walls. Its fermentation tanks alone fill up more space than Minerva's entire brewing operation. The Modelo factory churns out thousands of bottles of beer every minute and fills the entire neighborhood with the smell of soggy corn flakes.

"It's the biggest brewer in Mexico. They have 70 percent of the market," Jesús explains.

Together with its largest rival, the Monterrey-based Moctezuma and Cuauhtemoc brewery, Modelo controls 97 percent of the Mexican beer market.[154] There's a similar pattern in almost every major sector of Mexico's economy. Although there has been a lot of talk about opening Mexico's energy industry to new investment, for most of Jesús's life, whenever he wanted to buy gas for his truck he had only one choice. Until 2017 every gas station in Mexico was operated by Mexico's state-owned monopoly, Pemex.[155] If he takes his kids to the movies he has two options. Two companies, Cinemex and Cinepolis control 90 percent of Mexico's movie theatres.[156] Billionaire Carlos Slim dominates Mexico's telecom industry. His company Telmex single-handedly controls 80 percent of

Mexico's fixed line telephones and 70 percent of Mexico's mobile phone market.[157]

The list of major Mexican monopolies is long. A company called Bimbo controls around 90 percent of Mexico's baked goods market.[158] For years Bimbo has paid to sponsor the Club Deportivo de Guadalajara *fútbol* team to have its logo screen-printed in big block letters on the iconic team's red and white striped uniform. The team's owners know that they have a strong fan-base in both the U.S. and Mexico. Rather than relying exclusively on Televisa or TV Azteca, the media giants that together control 98 percent of Mexico's broadcast TV market, the team's owners decided to retain control of their product and sell the broadcasts of their games directly to fans through a Netflix-style streaming service.[159] In almost every sector of Mexico's economy there are just one or two companies that dominate the market. Two giant companies dominate the corn tortilla market. Two companies control 70 percent of the milk market.[160]

Most Mexicans spend over a third of their income on basic consumer goods. If companies achieve a dominant position in the markets for soft drinks, tortilla, baked goods, and beer, it means that shoppers might be forced to pay slightly higher prices every time they go to the super market.

"It's a high cost because competition creates efficiency. Mexicans feel it in their wallets," Jesús says. He thinks that the concentration of power in Mexico's major industries is also a drain on employment.

"Small business generates more jobs. It's well measured. Small businesses rely more on people," he says. But, small businesses in Mexico face long odds if they want to try and expand beyond the neighborhood-level and try and compete with the giants for a larger slice of the national market. Mexico's giant companies are like the colonial era *hacendados* who once controlled the country's largest plantations. Mid-sized family-owned firms are like local *caciques*. They keep tight control over their businesses and prefer to stay small and inefficient (but still profitable) rather than opening their books and welcoming in investors. Informal sector businesses are largely excluded from capital markets and stay small because they have few options for catalyzing growth. It's a dynamic that restricts economic activity and limits the potential for job creation.

Jesús eases his truck onto Avenida Chapultepec, an upper-middle-class area that emerged during the height of Mexico's post-WWII economic boom. The area has become a trendy destination for students and young professionals. It's not an elite demographic, but it's still an important market.

Jesús stops his truck and gets out to help unload a delivery at a newly built pub. The bar manager counts the mini-kegs. Today he's buying ten. "Every month it's sixty," he explains.

Inside the bar Jesús notes signs for Stella Artois and Goose Island, two smaller brands that along with Grupo Modelo are owned by Anheuser-Busch-InBev, the world's largest beer company. His biggest competitor is already evolving to better compete with him and other independent producers. Jesús is still dead set against selling his business to one of the global beer giants such as Heineken or InBev.

For now he's happy to achieve small victories, one at a time. Seeing his beer displayed in glass refrigerators and bar taps along with brands produced by Mexico's two beer giants at the omnipresent American convenience store chain 7-11 is one of his biggest successes.

Jesús was able to get a foothold in Mexico's beer industry in part by following the example set by Oxxo and Comex. He built up Deposito, a chain of craft beer stores. He also joined a lawsuit led by Mexico's Federal Competition Commission to force the beer giants to end the practice of exclusive contracts and open more points of sale for his beer. The court case became a catalyst for the new renaissance of Mexican craft beer and opened the possibility for real long-term success. "We are in 7-11s now. They don't have exclusivity," he explains. He also now has access to a wider market of super-markets and restaurants.

Jesús waits on the sidewalk while one of his employees carries in two more mini-kegs up the street to a café. There's a large sign that says, "Legacy Roasters: Specialty Coffee & Tea: A Cup of Excellence" and a chalkboard that advertises "CERVEZA Minerva *artesanal*" in hand-drawn letters. High quality, small-farm, Mexican coffee is being marketed and sold alongside premium Mexican craft beers.

Jesús's employees say his mind works at a supersonic speed and that he's always thinking several steps ahead. He's focused on fighting to preserve the small slice of the high-end market that he's won and thinking about how to grow his business. He knows that he's now facing new competition from ostensibly "craft brew" brands that are now part of the Grupo Modelo / InBev portfolio. Jesús is worried that InBev has created an e-commerce platform that might come to control an important segment of Mexico's distribution framework. He's planning on revamping the image of his Deposito stores and trying to stay relevant.

Jesús lets his deliveryman finish the day's drop-offs by himself. He's trained his team to handle daily operations on their own. He needs to focus on long-term strategy. After meeting his wife for lunch at a posh Manhattan-style Italian restaurant he'll then need to get back to planning out a potential partnership with a mid-sized (but independent) American brewer. Pushing north into the U.S. might require Minerva to re-brand. The company's name, after all, is a reference to a statue in Guadalajara that faces north in a defensive stance to discourage incursions by raiding armies from the north. Jesús is considering different brand names that might resonate well with buyers in the U.S. while also communicating his beer's roots in Guadalajara. Jesús's work is driven by one over-riding mantra: expand or die. He knows that even though Mexico has transformed over the last thirty years, it's still a country of *patrones* and peons. He has to decide what he wants to become; a plutocrat or a peasant.

"We can't stay small because the market will eat us," he explains.

§ § §

Minerva isn't Guadalajara's only success story. The city has hosted and fostered the rise of a bevy of new small and medium sized companies that do digital animation, website design, and business process outsourcing. As the manufacturing base has grown, a handful of tech startups and outsourcing firms have established themselves. Oracle and IBM both have research and development centers in Guadalajara. HP now employs over four thousand people in the city. In 2016 HP announced plans to invest an additional 15 million dollars in Guadalajara.[161] Total there are over twenty-five thousand relatively well-paid professionals working in tech and IT development in Guadalajara. Over the past few years the regal cobblestone avenues and exquisitely detailed multi-story baroque-style buildings in Guadalajara's historic center have been complemented by some updates. The streets in the main square are swept clean and have been pockmarked with docking stations for the community's shared bicycles, a replica of New York City's Citibike program. The well-balanced combination of old and new creates a sophisticated visual landscape that would fit in in a global financial or academic capital such as London, Frankfurt or Boston.

The centuries-old cathedral and government offices in the historic center are hewn from giant bricks of volcanic stone. Likewise, the modern economy in Guadalajara is built on a solid foundation. Unlike the southern states of Chiapas, Oaxaca, and Michoacan, the state of Jalisco has a long history of industrial investment. By the 1700s several wealthy families had already built colonial tequila factories a hundred times bigger than those used by most mezcal makers. Today Guadalajara is a mass of industrial lots, tightly packed residential neighborhoods, and wide interweaving highways and overpasses that stretches from the airport all the way to the skyscrapers downtown. Unlike cities in the south, the signs of organized economic activity don't end on the urban periphery. The flat expanse that surrounds Guadalajara is crisscrossed with successful farms. The state's agro-industry stretches deep up into the hills. Jalisco is a major producer of meat and is rapidly expanding its exports of new products such as raspberries and blueberries. The state's farmers haven't yet shifted to producing high quality barley for Guadalajara's craft brewers, but the Jalisco Ministry of Innovation is working to help primary goods producers start manufacturing higher-value added products such as avocado oil and natural make-up. In Guadalajara there's a constant churn of new business activity as universities collaborate directly with leaders from the public and private sectors.

During the first three decades after NAFTA was signed, the city has modernized and globalized, but there are still plenty of memorials to Mexico's past. In the main plaza in Guadalajara's historic center there's a statue of the revolutionary priest Miguel Hidalgo holding up a broken chain. In 1810 Hidalgo led a peasant uprising that ransacked cities and butchered Spanish hacienda owners and businessmen. On the monument's base there's a plaque that commemorates "the moment when the brave [Mexican] nation took up arms and removed the heavy yoke that oppressed it for nearly three centuries." In a government office one block away from the plaza there's a massive mural by Jose Clemente Orozco which portrays a brutally explicit picture of the violence wrought during Hidalgo's struggle. While Diego Rivera painted idealized portraits of sanitized class struggle and revolution, Orozco saw the fighting firsthand and portrays the brutal reality of armed conflict. The mural in Guadalajara shows an almost demonic depiction of Hidalgo wielding a torch, imposing over a tangle of grey corpses and assailants stabbing and decapitating their victims. The battle is painted in monochrome ash gray. It's nearly impossible to distinguish the revolutionaries from their victims. The mural is one of many ways Mexico's post-Revolution PRI-led government paid to commemorate and memorialize the bitter class conflict that marked the country's independence and civil war.

Hidalgo's rebellion is a source of pride for many Mexicans, but also a warning about the costs of fighting the status quo.

A few blocks away from the plaza Ignacio, a 56-year-old economist with ruddy cheeks and curly white hair who teaches at ITESO, Guadalajara's prestigious Jesuit university, settles into a chair towards the back of the narrow seating area in La Fuente, one of Guadalajara's oldest and best-known establishments. Equal parts social club and alcohol dispensary, the somewhat dingy and dimly lit space has high ceilings, stone arches, an elevated balcony with a piano in the middle, and a large collection of tequila in front of the old mirror behind the bar. "This is a really famous cantina," he explains.

Ignacio glances over at a group of men coming in from the street and happily scrutinizes the cantina's collection of Mexican kitsch. Behind the bar there's a type-writer style cash register that looks like it could be a hundred years old and a bicycle that's covered with stalactites formed by dust and humidity hung high on the wall in one of the archways. According to local lore, some fifty years ago a hard-drinking patron forgot his bike and never came back for it. The bar is still holding it for him.

Ignacio glances over towards a row of Corona-branded coolers. He orders a Negra Modelo beer and a plate of sautéed beef tongue topped with mashed green tomatillo salsa. It's 2 p.m. on a Monday afternoon, but Ignacio has to shout over the boisterous conversation. The bar's tables are filled with middle-aged men in office attire who have stopped by for a quick lunch and retirement age men who are energetically starting an afternoon of heavy drinking.

"In the 1800s Mexico came to modernity during the Porfiriato. Beer was the symbol of modernity, a product from Europe. Beer became the big new thing. A lot of local brands developed. Big businesses were created," Ignacio explains.

Brews such as Montejo, a Czech style lager originally produced in the Yucatan peninsula on Mexico's Caribbean coast, found favor with locals and visitors. Brewers in other parts of the country built up their own businesses. "Montejo had a good reputation. In Sinaloa it was Pacífico. In Guadalajara we had La Estrella," Ignacio explains.

These regional producers, however, didn't stay independent for long.

"Little by little Modelo went shopping, eating them all up. It became an enormous monopoly. Facing this, Mexico's other big beer companies Moctezuma and Cuauhtemoc merged in the eighties. They had Tecate, DosEquis, Carta Blanca. It created a duopoly," he adds.

"It destroyed a lot of the great tradition of beer-making in Mexico. Until a few years ago the taste for local beer was lost. The tradition of going to a different city and trying new regional flavors died," he explains.

The fight against monopoly control is no longer a Mexican problem. Now it's a global phenomenon.[162] "InBev bought Modelo. Now there's no chance of competition. Moctezuma was sold to Heineken. Now there's no big-brand Mexican beer. Just small businesses," he explains.

Jesús's brewery is an anomaly. "Minerva is Mexican, but it's small. It's for gourmet consumers, people with high income. It's an elite market. It's not the tradition of popular consumption. It's good, but it's expensive. The popular beer is Modelo," he adds.

"It's not just a problem with beer. It's the tendency towards monopoly in all sectors of Mexico. Mexico was a place with variety. There were a lot of candy makers. Now four businesses control the market. It's become a monopolized country. I think it's serious. It means fewer products, fewer jobs, all the problems of monopoly," he explains.

Mexican Monopoly is no longer just a game for local industrialists. After a string of acquisitions, Mars, the U.S.-based sweets confectioner, now controls about 25 percent of Mexico's candy market. The American company PPG acquired Comex in 2014 for 2.4 billion dollars.[163] Now its market power, margins, and profitability help add half a billion dollars of revenue to the American company's balance sheets. Even Mexican banking giant Banamex was absorbed by the U.S. bank Citi. Financial journalists often refer to Comex and Banamex as "the crown jewels" for their American parent companies. Monopolies, after all, are notoriously lucrative for their owners.[164]

Ignacio, however, is also concerned with what Mexico's oligopolies are doing at the local level. He's seen the fabric of society in Guadalajara change as the country's conglomerates have consolidated their market power. "FEMSA destroyed the market for neighborhood convenience stores. The two big chains killed off family stores. Oxxo just sold one brand: FEMSA. 7-11 sold the other, Grupo Modelo," he adds.

Small brewers always faced big barriers to entry and long odds at carving out a niche in the market while Modelo and Cuauhtemoc enjoyed a position of total dominance. "They controlled production and also distribution. There was no competition for beer sales in the huge network of small businesses," Ignacio says.

Ignacio thinks that market concentration presents a big cost for Mexican society.

"What bothers me is the absence of variety and the death of the small producer.

In Mexico it's free market to wherever it takes us, but the small producers are drowning," he adds.

Mexico has a long history of economic domination by a small elite. It's a dynamic that has survived a war for independence, a revolution, and more recently, a transition to free-market capitalism and multi-party democracy.

In the twentieth century Mexico's economy recovered from the destruction of the revolution, endured a binge of oil-financed industrialization after World War II, and more recent shocks as the economy opened to foreign trade in the 1980s and 1990s and the government opened to multi-party competition at the turn of the twenty-first century. Over the last few years a new generation of innovative start-ups has emerged in cities such as Guadalajara, Tijuana, and Monterrey, but it's still not clear whether these ambitious start-up companies represent the trend of the future or are simply an aberration from the country's longstanding traditions.[165]

Ignacio is cautiously optimistic that Minerva will be able to carve out a niche in Mexico's beer market. "I think it will grow. But I hope it won't grow too much. If it does Modelo will buy it! That's the paradox. They have to be successful, but not so much to be absorbed. It's hard to stay on that line," he says.

As the waiter sets down a glass bottle of Pacífico beer Ignacio reflects on whether the brand might offer a warning for Minerva and other new craft brewers. "This was a brand from Sinaloa, but now it's Modelo," he explains.

Ignacio thinks the hegemonic consolidation of production in Mexico's beer sector mirrors the country's more general distribution of income and wealth.

"It's concentration of power. Guadalajara has been developed into a city with poor businesses and rich entrepreneurs. Average salaries are lower than in other cities, lower than the national average. It's a big city where a lot of money flows. But the salaries for the population are low," he adds.

Overall in Jalisco, the state Guadalajara is located, there are just a few thousand people who earn more than twelve thousand dollars per year. There are only 23,862 people in the entire state who earn more than $12,220 a year. By contrast there are 2.7 million residents, nearly 74 percent of the state's economically active population, who earn between $1,222 and $6,110. More broadly, in Mexico as a whole, the wealthiest 1 percent of the population controls over 40 percent of the country's wealth. According to the GINI index, an economic indicator that measures inequality, Mexico is one of the top twenty-five most unequal economies in the world.[166] It's slightly more egalitarian than Brazil, Panama, or Chile, but much more unequal than Russia or China.

Part of the problem is that Mexican politicians have found a way to make the country a desirable location for foreign investment without building the types of strong institutions that might help create a strong middle class. By certain specific metrics Mexico is considered to be one of the most competitive economies in Latin America. The 2017 World Bank Doing Business Index ranks it at number 47 overall, ahead of Chile and Israel.[167] The 2017-2018 World Economic Forum Competitiveness report ranks Mexico at 51st, behind only Panama and Costa Rica within Latin America, but ahead of competitors such as Vietnam, South Africa, and Brazil.[168]

In the NAFTA era, the Ivy-league educated Mexican technocrats who advise their country's federal government have figured out how to tune up the country's regulations to win the respect of Wall Street analysts and economists at multi-lateral agencies such as the World Bank. Ironically, the World Bank considers two of Mexico's greatest strengths to be the ease of access to credit and the ability to enforce contracts. On paper Mexico has great regulations. In the real world, however, the underlying quality of Mexico's institutions leaves much to be desired. For instance, in terms of Math and Science education Mexico is ranked among the world's worst countries.

While Mexico is respected for its market size and lauded for its stable macroeconomic policy the World Economic Forum ranks the country 123rd out of 137 countries in terms of the strength of its public institutions.[169] In terms of institutional quality Mexico is considered to be ahead of Venezuela and Nigeria, but behind almost every other country in the world, including Sierra Leone, Russia, and the Philippines. Mexico scores particularly poorly in the categories of public trust in politicians and business costs of organized crime. Judicial independence and favoritism in decisions by government officials are also weak points. Modern Mexico is a place where the regulations make it relatively easy to start a business, but don't do much to reign in monopolies. In terms of extent of market dominance the World Economic Forum ranks Mexico as 103rd, as one of the planet's countries that is most controlled by oligarchs.[170] Finally, if there's one other area in which Mexico stands out, it's corruption. Transparency International ranks Mexico at 135th in its corruption index, as one of the most corrupt countries in the world, roughly on par with Russia and Honduras, but worse than Liberia, the Philippines, and Pakistan.[171]

Ignacio sees Mexico as a free-market economy that allows well-trained Olympic sprinters to compete head to head with old, frail men in sandals. The field of competition favors the chosen few. Small-time coffee, mezcal, and avocado producers in southern Mexico know just how many barriers there are to real free-market competition in Mexico.

In one of his papers Ignacio calls Guadalajara a "Banana Chip Economy." He sees the city as a recalibrated version of the historic Latin America banana republic that now relies on low wages to produce electronic products instead of fruit. Ignacio thinks that understanding Mexico's economy requires a mix of quantitative and qualitative analysis. His recent fieldwork has taken him deep out into the urban periphery.

"I've rediscovered the city. What surprises me is the size. It's mostly lower middle class. People on the poverty line. They have electricity, they have small houses. It's thousands and thousands of houses. There are no medical clinics, few schools, no parks. It's deplorable conditions. It's not poor people, but it's people with a lot of economic problems. At the same time there are huge houses, luxury cars, expensive restaurants," he says.

In the still rustic district of Tlaquepaque, a twenty-minute drive to the city center, locals still gather on weekends at La Parian, Mexico's biggest cantina, to eat platefuls of local delicacies such as succulent beef *carne en su jugo* and hot-sauce slathered pork sandwiches called *tortas ahogadas*. The main avenues in the neighborhood now have 7-11s and Oxxos, but the residential streets are packed with narrow single-family houses. Many of the old, family-owned convenience stores have closed. The last few small shops in the neighborhood sell only Modelo beer. The customers in the neighborhood are mostly construction workers. They never ask for craft beers. The big brands produce the beer for the masses. By contrast the posh bars in downtown areas have become a meeting places for engineers, bankers, and tech entrepreneurs who work in nearby office towers. On most weekday afternoons bars in the wealthier pockets of the city packed with small groups of professionals and the street out front is lined with late model sedans and sports cars. Some tech entrepreneurs joke that craft beer is the best friend of the tech industry. Some managers host "Craft Beer Fridays" at their offices. Others bring out their colleagues for *cervezas* after work. Mingling and sharing ideas over bottles of expensive beer and platefuls of tacos is one of the ways knowledge is transferred throughout the tech eco-system. Overall, however, craft beer is still the exclusive niche market that caters to the upper echelon of Guadalajara's two-tiered economy.

"Every day it becomes a more polarized city," Ignacio says.

Ignacio isn't convinced by the strides Guadalajara has made in developing a cluster for high tech services, software design and research and development. He sees it as a highly localized niche trend rather than a fundamental shift in the city and surrounding state's economy.

"Mexico is a maquila economy. That's the advantage of Mexico: cheap labor," he adds.

Well-paid knowledge economy jobs are just a small fraction of the labor market in the same way that craft beer accounts for just 1 percent of the Mexican beer market.

"It has to do with education. In Mexico we don't need researchers. In Mexico we need disciplined, cheap labor. The electronics industry has exams. What they care about is finding the people with creativity, intuition, and intelligence and *NOT* hiring them. It's terrible. The electronics industry brings people from rural areas two hours outside of Guadalajara. Those are the people who put up with it. It's hard conditions," he explains.

"The top ten percent here earns thirty thousand dollars a year. Unskilled workers earn a hundred and twenty dollars a month," he says.

Ignacio sees one culprit as being largely responsible for the country's current limitations: monopolies.

"They're protected by the state. The biggest monopolies are businesses that used to be government owned," he explains.

Whether it's the telecom empire of Carlos Slim, the mining conglomerate run by the Bailleres family, airlines, railroads, or soda companies, Ignacio thinks Mexico's biggest businesses benefit from a dangerously close relationship with the government. When a small group of businessmen wield so much concentrated power public policies and regulations inevitably favor their interests.

"They get huge tax breaks. What they pay in taxes is minimal," he says.

In theory the government has the power to break up and regulate monopolies. But in Mexico trust-busting isn't likely to occur until the overall quality of rule of law improves and people start to believe that they have a guarantee of protection in the courts. Many scholars see monopolies as the inevitable outcome in an environment of weak rule of law.[172] When courts can be trusted and the law is applied uniformly investors are more willing to take risks and compete against other companies. Absent strong guarantees for their rights industrial magnates need special incentives to invest in new sectors. They might be willing to take the risk if the government guarantees them monopoly power and profits. Mexico won't develop into a fully-functional market-oriented economy until the federal government finds a way to guarantee rule of law and protect entrepreneurs as they work to expand their businesses.

Right now, successful, medium-sized, family-owned companies in Mexico mostly prefer to self-finance. They tolerate immense inefficiencies and miss great opportunities to grow to keep their wealth in-house and avoid paying taxes. There are tens of thousands of strong family-owned companies that could transform into modern corporations, but don't do so because providing more transparency about their finances and letting outsiders into their board rooms would give tax authorities greater leverage to collect larger payments.

It's a difficult dynamic that spurs some industrial development, but also restricts the formation of a more robust, multi-tiered economy. Over time industrial conglomerates can expand across multiple sectors, self-finance their growth and always enjoy fat profits. Small entrepreneurs face stiff competition from the outset and steep costs from Mexico's concentrated and conservative banking sector.

"It's not just beer. The process of domination by a few firms is pervasive. Mexico is a country of 55 million poor and more than fourteen fortunes bigger than a billion dollars. Since liberalization [which started in the 1980s] a lot of small businesses failed. At the same time enormous fortunes have grown. It's the polarization of Mexico," he says.

In Mexico and elsewhere around the globe the presence of strong monopolies corresponds with the existence of immense income inequality and deep divisions in society. A society that creates brawny interest groups will inevitably create rules and laws that protect the powerful. In Mexico this overall dynamic has existed since the colonial era conflicts between massive hacienda owners and the landless farm-laborers they employed. Mexico's overall economy still looks a lot like the beer industry. There are a few interesting start-ups that are beginning to attract attention, but overall the market is still dominated by monopolies. Optimists might look at it as a glass half full situation, but even so, in Mexico the glass is still filled with big brand beer. Independent producers are just a small dollop of foam on top.

§ § §

The basic dynamics of the stratified economy in Guadalajara are also seen on the border in Tijuana, a city just south of San Diego that has grown rapidly and fitfully during the NAFTA era. In the 1920s Tijuana, which is located in the state of Baja California on a peninsula that connects with the U.S. state of California, was a dusty border town. The main street, Calle Revolución, was little more than a small village for tourists coming across from the U.S. After WWII the city began to grow and in the 1970s as manufacturing companies in the U.S. began to globalize their operations the small outpost south of San Diego started to boom. Some companies moved south from the U.S., but many companies came in from

Japan. Tijuana first specialized in building big, bulky TVs for Japanese manufacturers. Over the years Tijuana's economy has been hit hard by competition from China. The collapse after the 2001 recession in the U.S. corresponded with a major exodus of factories that moved out to Asia. Tijuana managed to move on, letting certain industries such as toy and clothing production leave while trying to foster the development of new sectors. Now Tijuana produces medical devices, automotive components, and solar panels. Like Guadalajara Tijuana is missing out as a site for the construction of new automotive factories. But, city officials hope that as cars become more complex, battery-powered, and reliant on technology, that Tijuana's base of engineers, universities, technical schools, and established electronics sector might leave it poised to succeed in the 21st century.

For now, however, the reality of industrial Tijuana seems to be lagging behind the vision described by the city's politicians, city planners, and business leaders. Across Tijuana inside the football-field-sized factories lines of workers furiously crimp and cut copper wiring and solder simple circuits. Whether it's people sorting coffee beans in Chiapas, hacking at agave leaves in Oaxaca, sorting avocados in Michoacan or working at a factory in Tijuana many aspects of the job seem similar. Over the last thirty years the factories have switched from making TVs to producing increasingly complex and specialized electronic equipment, but for the people on the production line the basic tasks are largely the same. Each person performs a single, robotic, repetitive motion, and together the line works at a furious pace. They are racing to compete against inexpensive producers in Asia. They are racing against the inevitable forces of automation. Eventually fully mechanized production lines might become more cost-effective. Eventually these entry-level jobs for automatons might disappear.

§ § §

In the steep, silty hills on the outskirts of Tijuana the precariousness of the city's modern manufacturing economy is hard to miss. In a neighborhood called Terrazas that sits in between Toyota's Tacoma-producing factory and the downtown area, in one of the city's last fringes of residential housing, Guillermo, a stocky 55-year-old resident with a close cropped grey stubble mustache and goatee, stands behind the metal bars of the small shop he built in the front of his house. He has lived at this location for almost thirty years.

"In the time I've been here I have gotten to know the people. One woman, I met her when she was young. Now she has kids. I know everybody," he says.

The entire neighborhood is watched over by a Virgin Mary hand painted onto a four-by-eight-foot sheet of plywood on a partially built church that sits on a hill overlooking the district. Parishioners have been building the chapel bit by bit, year by year. The bell tower is still unfinished. Some sections of the hillside are girded with stacks of old, tread-worn, sand-filled rubber tires. The simplest structures are built using small, irregular squares of old discarded boards. Most people in Guillermo's neighborhood have real wooden doors. One of the humblest houses in the neighborhood just has a sheet of plastic hanging over the main entrance.

It's not uncommon to see residents using old political billboards as walls of their homes.[173] It is still slightly jarring, however, to see people living in a structure made from a highway sign that announces, "Tijuana Deserves Better!" Most of the streets in Guillermo's neighborhood are lined with fences made from old wooden pallets, detritus from the factories and warehouses in the surrounding area. Most of the structures are no bigger than small cabins. As is the case in the isolated mountain towns in southern Mexico, some of the houses have small storefronts facing the street. Just like in rural villages in Chiapas and Oaxaca, there are a few walls that have hand-painted signs advertising Coca-Cola and blocky letters declaring, "We sell tortillas." There are only a few structures that are made from cement or sheets of corrugated steel. Guillermo thinks most of his neighbors avoid bank loans. They prefer to build piece by piece as the years pass.

In many ways, Tijuana's working-class neighborhoods are like a hastily built copy of the poor mountain communities that many residents left behind in Chiapas and Oaxaca. But the community isn't temporary. Many residents have lived there for the duration of the NAFTA era. Guillermo thinks that most people move in and stay. Entrance into Mexico's mythologized middle class seems like a distant dream. Few people move on to better jobs and nicer homes. Over the last few years Guillermo has watched as the houses in the lower part of the barrio have been connected to the electrical grid. Other homes are still basically just shacks for squatters. "In services we're screwed," he says. He nods towards the rows of houses that jut out from the sides of the dirt road on the steep slope that leads up to the church. "Up there the services are terrible. There's no water, no sewage, no pavement," he adds.

Every day Guillermo feels the effects of one of the immense questions for Modern Mexico. Trying to consummate the myth of a plural and diverse mestizo society that combines industrialization with indigenous traditions, Mexico's government still tries to turn the ideals of Diego Rivera's murals and Octavio Paz's prose into reality. Mexico's federal government still devotes massive resources to the impossibly isolated communities in the south. Neighborhoods like Terrazas in major industrial centers don't receive enough funding. Increasing tax revenues might help assuage this conflict, but a bigger government budget wouldn't resolve the question about where resources should be allocated.

Guillermo's community has a graffiti-covered cement basketball court which is lined with rough cinder-block walls. The local kids mostly play soccer on a patch of gravelly dirt down the street from Guillermo's store. Sometimes the players stop by for snacks after their games. Guillermo is wearing an old, navy blue t-shirt with a large logo from Tijuana's soccer club on the front. He's been in the neighborhood for thirty years. In the barrio he feels like he's a bona fide local. Like him, many of the neighborhood's other residents, are originally from Mexico's south. Guillermo grew up in Oaxaca's capital. One of his neighbors who lives just up the hill is from Chiapas. Her son now works at the Toyota factory down the road.

For Guillermo there's a quiet rhythm to his days inside the shop. He chats with neighbors and watches Bimbo vans deliver baked goods and bright red Coca-Cola's trucks drop off cases of soda. He prefers it to the time he spent on the factory floor. "I worked at a maquila as a welder," he explains.

"It was Hyundai, trailers for cargo trucks," he adds. He doesn't miss the stress and long hours he had to put up with. He prefers the instability of the informal economy. At least he's able to enjoy some solitude now. At Hyundai he struggled to see the benefit, beyond the guarantee of a steady pay check.

In 2015 Mexico exported more manufactured goods than the rest of Latin America combined.[174] Unfortunately for the workers, the boom in new investment in factories hasn't translated into upward pressure on salaries. Tijuana is lined with big box factories decorated with banners that say "Now Hiring!" but factory managers are always looking for ways to bus in workers from rural Mexico, always trying to keep labor costs down. For line workers the career prospects are often dim.

"There were no raises. The salary stayed the same, but they had a lot of requirements for production. There were a lot of demands and low pay. I wanted to try being my own boss," Guillermo says.

Back in Oaxaca Guillermo had studied Business Administration. He took six semesters of classes, but never finished his degree. Instead, in 1988 he set off, planning to migrate north and look for work in the U.S.

"I wanted to cross to the other side," he says.

After being deported to Tijuana after just six months in the U.S. Guillermo decided to stay at the border rather than go back home to Oaxaca. "I saw there was a lot of work here," he says.

"There was work for people with no experience, no education. That was me," he adds.

He quickly found a good job as a supervisor at Sanyo during Tijuana's early boom as an electronics assembly hub.

"From there I did one year sewing at a clothing factory. Then one year at Panasonic. I was doing carpentry for two years at a factory. Then I was at Hyundai thirteen years," he explains.

He started in the Hyundai factory in 2000 and worked

there for over a dozen years. Finally he had had enough. Unlike the previous boom in the nineties, Tijuana now had to compete with producers in China. Factory jobs now only offered twelve-hour shifts, a few dollars a day, and few chances for career advancement. Guillermo says he isn't the only one who left.

"A lot of people quit. I had ex-coworkers who have done the same to earn more and get better working conditions," he adds. Many of his neighbors now prefer to improvise jobs in Mexico's sprawling informal sector. "A lot of people sell clothes or perfume at home. That's informal," he says.

The work might be unsteady or unpredictable. But at least they don't have to venture out on two to three hour journeys to get to work every day on the old rickety school buses that serve as Tijuana's public transportation system. The neighborhood has its own local, cash-based economy. "Tire shops, *taquerias*, people who sell candy in the street, all those people are informal. They don't pay taxes," Guillermo says. Total, around 40 percent of the people in the surrounding state of Baja California work at micro businesses.[175] In 2017 informal employment dipped to historic lows in the state, but the sector still employs nearly four out of every ten people. (In Chiapas and Oaxaca the rate of informal employment is nearly twice as high.)

Guillermo estimates that around a third of the people he knows in his neighborhood work at the Toyota plant down the road. He thinks that the maquila industry is his barrio's biggest source of employment and knows that the residents who work in factories help bring in money to the community and sustain the informal retail economy. Still, over the years he's seen his neighbors move in and out of the informal sector, periodically making the trade-off of longer hours and low pay for a steady paycheck and a guaranteed income. Guillermo doesn't think it's worth it. "It's hard to support a family earning just five or six dollars a day," he says.

Running his store selling snacks and drinks to his neighbors, Guillermo might make three for four times more in a single day than he made on the production line. The data on income backs up Guillermo's bleak assessment. In 1994 when NAFTA came into effect the minimum wage in Mexico was worth about five dollars a day. By 2017 Mexico's minimum wage fell to 4.46 dollars a day, a 14.5 percent drop for the previous twenty-three years.[176]

"When I got here it was excellent. That was '88. Now I see it as worse. They ask a lot from workers," he says.

"It's a lot of work, but the salaries are low. I think there's a lot of competition. There's a lot of people who need work. So they have a limit they won't pay more," he adds.

Before China emerged as a global manufacturing powerhouse factory jobs in Tijuana were seen as great opportunities, especially for people coming up from small towns in Chiapas and Oaxaca.

"It was good work and you got paid in dollars. In that era I got thirty dollars a day. It was really good," he says. Over the years, however, Guillermo saw the costs of living rise and wages stagnate. Right now a Mexican earning minimum wage earns about 8 percent of the salary of a minimum wage worker in the U.S. Guillermo doesn't see how it makes sense to try and get by on factory wages.

Still, even though his own experience inside Tijuana's factories didn't work out the way he would have hoped,

Guillermo isn't totally pessimistic. He hopes his kids will study and build careers.

"Maybe there are good jobs for people who study," he says.

He wouldn't want his son to look for an entry-level post on an assembly line. Jobs for the generalized pool of unskilled laborers seem like a dead-end. "There are well-paying jobs, but you have to study. I think in the economy in Tijuana there are places that pay well, but you have to be well trained," he says. Over time Mexico has been trying to move up into more complicated, higher value-added, better paid industries. As a whole though it's going to be hard for Mexico to move beyond low-wage labor. In Mexico right now only a fifth of all prime working age, 25 to 34-year-old men and women have a college degree.[177] In South Korea over 70 percent of this vitally important age group have a university education. The U.S., by contrast, ranks behind Japan, Australia, Canada, and Norway, but above the OECD average. Mexico, unfortunately, sits dead last in the OECD in this category.

Guillermo's perch among the improvised houses and simple shacks that line the steep dirt roads on the slopes in Terrazas provides him with an excellent viewpoint for judging Modern Mexico's industrial society.

"The economy isn't equal. There are jobs that pay well and jobs that pay less," he says.

§ § §

Just before the start of the NAFTA era Mexican academic Guillermo Bonfil Batalla published a celebrated book on the rift between Mexico's wealthy, well-educated, urban elites and low-income, rural, indigenous population. "The recent history of Mexico, that of the last five hundred years, is the story of permanent confrontation between those attempting to direct the country toward the path of Western civilization and those, rooted in Mesoamerican ways of life, who resist," he wrote.[178] Bonfil Batalla saw the schism between Mexico's two cultures as a divide between what he called the "imaginary" Mexico that was built following the example of European and U.S. institutions and ideals and what he called "Mexico Profundo," the deep Mexico, the rural, indigenous Mexico, the real Mexico.

Ever since independence from Spain the Mexican state has performed a delicate balancing act of trying to create liberal, democratic institutions, but no national government has ever found an effective strategy for bridging the gap between the two halves of Mexican society. On paper, Mexico's constitution aspires to codify and materialize high-minded and socially progressive ideas of the country's founding fathers. In practice, in the rural hamlets of Chiapas, Oaxaca, and Michoacan and the peripheral neighborhoods of Guadalajara and Tijuana, the reality still falls short of these ideals. In his book *Democracy in Mexico*, which was first published in 1965, Mexican anthropologist Pablo Gonzalez Casanova explains that in Mexico the aspirational, liberal constitution of 1917 as well as decades of subsequent laws and reforms, play a largely ritual role in attempting to encompass and govern Mexico's economic and political reality.[179] Mexico's founding fathers imported political theories and institutional designs from the U.S. and Europe into a country with an economy that Gonzalez Casanova calls "semi-feudal" and a political system based around the de facto power of local and regional *caudillos* and *caciques*. "In our country we are accustomed to comparing the legislative ideas and models with reality. Every citizen acquires the habit of comparing the 'orthodox' model with the 'pagan' reality in which he lives," Gonzalez Casanova explained.[180] He saw Mexico as a country defined by conflict in which de facto power doesn't always correspond with de jure authority.

Today the myth of Modern Mexico persists on paper. It is used in marketing materials that present the codified, intellectualized Mexico that exists tenuously in a new generation of reforms, legislation, and World Bank reports. Although this mirage does seem to actually exist in a nascent form in certain pockets of Guadalajara, Monterrey, Tijuana, and Mexico City, it belies the darker dynamics that better explain Mexico's current reality.

In mid-2018 during the final months of the Peña Nieto presidency Inter-American Development Bank economist Santiago Levy published a book called *Under-Rewarded Efforts: The Elusive Quest for Prosperity in Mexico*. Levy wades though reams of data from recent economic surveys and labor market reports and concludes that Modern Mexico's economy is weighted down by an over-abundance of small, unproductive firms. The disparate and disorganized way in which coffee and mezcal are produced in Chiapas and Oaxaca are representative of Mexico's economy as a whole. Levy calls Mexico's ecosystem of companies "scattered."[181] After all, more than nine out of every ten businesses in Mexico operate in the informal sector.

The economic dynamics on the outskirts of Guadalajara and Tijuana show that informality isn't just a problem in Mexico's under-developed south, but rather a defining characteristic of Mexico's economy as a whole. Mexico's labor laws and tax structures have the perverse effect of punishing entrepreneurs for expanding and creating jobs. "To elude or evade various regulations, they modify their size, failing to achieve economies of scale or scope," he explains.[182] Business owners who do want to grow face challenges posed by a small, monopoly controlled financial system. But until Mexican legislators find a way to clamp down on corruption and illegality, for most business owners it's still better to stay small and protect long-term viability rather than take the risks and opportunities that come from seeking out capital and growing. In all of Mexico there are just over ten thousand formal sector companies that have more than fifty employees. By contrast, Mexico's federal government counts nearly three million tiny, informal sector companies that operate from a permanent location. There are also an uncounted number of micro businesses that operate from street stands or other impermanent locations. Mexico's federal government doesn't even try to tally the number of businesses in the country's smallest and most isolated towns. The data that is available, however, suggests that Mexico's current political, economic, and regulatory dynamic has led to a far from ideal allocation of resources and contributed to decades of disappointing growth. A number of factors drive the current economic outcome. There is no clear guideline for the best path Mexico should take to address its structural economic problems, but it's clear that the current dynamic isn't sustainable. Investing in education or infrastructure won't be enough. Mexico needs to re-work and improve the entire framework of regulations that manage its economy. Levy argues, "what Mexican workers need most are productive firms that can offer them stable jobs where they can take advantage of the education that they have invested in."[183]

Creating an environment in which more businesses can develop and grow will require a bevy of reforms to address the root causes of inequality, informality, and illegality. Up until now Mexico has patched together an improvised solution, and found a way to connect with the global economy without fully addressing its longstanding political problems. In the first eighteen years of the twenty-first century the federal government has tried to diffuse rising social tension by shifting tax revenues generated by manufacturing operations in states such as Jalisco and Baja California to under-developed states in the south such as Chiapas and Oaxaca. But residents in both the north and the south have become frustrated with the status quo.

§ § §

Modern Mexico is inscrutable, but if there is any single item that can help summarize the country's identity, it's the taco. Given the prevalence of informal economic activity in Mexico, the most representative Mexican worker isn't an industrial technician like Rosie the Riveter. The most representative example of a Mexican worker would have to be an informal sector laborer, perhaps a street stand taco chef. It's fitting to argue that tacos help explain Modern Mexico.

Throughout Peña Nieto's presidency from 2012 through 2018 food trucks have boomed in Tijuana. The trucks are a glorified version of Mexico's informal taco stands. Perhaps there's no better way to understand Mexico than through the tacos that form the basis of most people's diets. In Mexico everybody eats tortillas. They are either the fourth utensil in the table setting at formal restaurants or the only utensil at roadside stewed *barbacoa* or *pastor*-style spit-roasted pork carts.

Adrian, a 25-year-old food truck chef, finished culinary school in Tijuana three years ago. After working at Applebee's and saving his paychecks he first bought a small cart. A year ago he graduated to a boxy van in a food truck park down the road from a Chili's and an IHOP. He's now trying to promote a slightly more gourmet version of Mexico's celebrated street food.

Throughout Mexico informal taco stands help feed the local community. In many cases they might steal electricity by splicing power cords into the electrical cables overhead. They accept cash only and in most cases won't pay taxes or provide benefits for their employees. In mountain towns in Chiapas and Oaxaca and on the street in front of the maquilas in Tijuana vendors sell their tacos at rock bottom prices. They keep costs low and try to pass the savings on to their customers. In most cases at the street carts you can usually buy a plate of five meat-packed tacos for a dollar or two.

Adrian jokes, though, that there's always a risk. Patrons have to laugh off the idea that the dirt that blows in from the street is extra seasoning. There's also macabre humor that the meat might be from street dogs, *tacos de perro*. "You have to just risk it. But we always say a little dirt doesn't kill you. We joke around," he says.

On the other hand during the early 21st century restaurants such as Tierra y Cielo in Chiapas, Casa Oaxaca in Oaxaca, and Misión 19 in Tijuana have helped bring Mexican food onto the global stage. These eateries have been recognized for being some of the world's best restaurants. At Tierra y Cielo a plate of three small *chorizo* and *longaniza* sausage tacos costs more than five dollars. At Misión 19 in downtown Tijuana the "Glutton" taco dish, a decadent mix of udder, tripe, and steak tartare, costs just under eight dollars. Factoring in the cost of several entrees, tacos, and a few glasses of mezcal and beer, the bill for a dinner for two at one of these restaurants could easily top the monthly wages of a factory worker in Guadalajara or Tijuana.

Thus, the lens of "taconomics" is useful for understanding the deep divide that defines Modern Mexico's economy.

At his food truck Adrian sees a mix of people from different backgrounds. The factories in Tijuana tend to have small parking lots. Managers, accountants, engineers, and consultants can drive to the plant. Assembly workers take the bus and don't have the mobility or income to leave the job for lunch.[184]

Overall, in Baja California, the state where Tijuana is located, the overwhelming majority of residents earn just a few thousand dollars a year. Most people in the state make somewhere between the minimum wage of $4.70 per day and a salary worth five times the minimum wage. In other words, 67 percent of the state's 1.6 million economically active residents earn annual salaries that are roughly worth between $1,222 and $6,110. Only 14,081 residents (or 0.9 percent of Baja California's economically active population) earn salaries worth more than $12,220 a year. Adrian knows he has to focus on a small segment of locals who have some type of meaningful disposable income.

"We sell to a lot of factory employees. Not the line workers, but engineers, managers, architects. It's middle, middle high, to high income levels." he says.

He tries his best to keep prices low and create lunch packets that are accessible. Still, his most expensive taco costs around two dollars. Three of his gourmet-style tacos would eat up a day's wages for one of the city's typical line workers.

For young entrepreneurs like Adrian there are challenges when it comes to building a formal sector business. For now Adrian is still figuring out how to acquire all the permits he needs. He pays bribes to a few inspectors, but hasn't yet submitted the paperwork to register with Mexico's Treasury or pay taxes. Right now he just has to pay operational costs, rent, and utilities. Operating informally is a risk, but it's helped him get his start.

"I'm currently registering my business. When I get done with that I'll start with taxes and all that," Adrian says. He thinks that regularizing his business will open access to bank loans. Eventually he might like to open a formal, sit-down restaurant. But he also worries that becoming more established will expose him to the risk that public officials will come by for more than a bite to eat. Mexico after all ranks as the worst country in Latin America in terms of the incidence of bribery. Total more than half of all residents reported paying a bribe in 2016.[185]

"Here in Mexico it's all bribes. Everything is bribes. The guys that give you permits, they sell some. Even if you try to do things right they still try to get money out of you. There's no way around it. That's one of the bad things about starting a business here. You have to know the people. Give them money. They'll let you work. We have that issue here. We have to give money to a permit guy. He said, 'if you don't cooperate we'll shut the place down.' So we are paying," he explains.

The downside to the bribes is that, like the extortion payments business owners in Michoacan sometimes have to pay, the money goes into the pockets of law-breakers rather than towards public services that benefit the community as a whole.

Overall Mexico struggles to collect taxes. Even counting royalties from oil production, Mexico's government manages to capture less than a fifth of the value of total economic output. In terms of tax collection Mexico sits in last place in the OECD.[186] While billionaires and special interest groups in the U.S. lobby to abolish the estate tax, in Mexico the moneyed elite has already achieved that concession. Overall Mexico only captures just over 6 percent of its annual output in income taxes, around half as much as the OECD average.[187] Society lets the wealthy club of oligarchs avoid paying taxes and in return elites don't push to widen the tax base or crack down on more mundane and low-level forms of tax avoidance. The government is left with limited resources and, especially after politicians pocket their take, there are limited funds available for providing basic public services or helping to foster meaningful, long-term economic development. Across Mexico people complain about the government's failures, but still do everything they can to avoid paying taxes.

"Here in TJ we don't have trashcans on every corner. We are missing a lot of things. TJ is one of the most important cities in Mexico and we don't have a decent transportation system," Adrian says.

Mexico has radically transformed in Adrian's life. But he still sees poverty and corruption as two of the most important obstacles the country faces. He's encouraged that more people seem to be earning more money, but still sees immense problems.

"As long as we have bad leaders we'll be working hard

to earn little, just surviving. We're not getting help from our government to progress," he says. Unfortunately, even people who do pay taxes can never be sure their contributions will benefit the public good. The shocking series of corruption scandals that were exposed during the Peña Nieto administration have eaten away at the public's already fragile confidence in elected officials. In Tijuana small business owners see a very clear dynamic unfolding in the local economy.

Mexico's economy keeps evolving, but like meat in an over-loaded tortilla too many people fall out to the side. The formal economy isn't nearly big enough to absorb the entire labor force and over half of Mexico's population is largely excluded from the benefits of the modern economy. Optimists say that over time the formal economy will expand, pull in more workers, and help the struggling rural economy. Pessimists complain that the current model is based on low wages and can't create a real middle class without collapsing.

To Adrian the economic development model seems to benefit the professional class and the owners, but not the workers.

It's hard to see how Mexico can really become a middle-income economy when the entire model seems to be based on low wages for workers.

From behind the counter at his food truck, Adrian sees some signs for optimism. He thinks that if Tijuana continues to attract investment the additional jobs will lead to better pay for workers. Still, he has his doubts about Mexico's future.

"Mexico could be one of the strongest economies in the world. But we're selfish. One guy gets fat while a thousand starve. That's how it works. That's how it is," he says.

Acknowledgments

This book is based on field work and articles I've written over the last few years. A lengthy list of wonderful editors at publications including *The Guardian, Foreign Affairs, Fortune, Forbes, The Atlantic, Americas Quarterly, Monocle, Univision, Outside, The Global Post,* and *Pacific Standard* helped me improve my writing and sharpen my reporting and story-telling skills. A long list of writers publishing work in *Harper's, The New Yorker, Pacific Standard,* and *The New York Times Magazine* motivated me to pursue this project and with their brilliant narrative non-fiction writing.

I first started kicking around the idea for this book in January 2013. I had already read and been inspired by Ed Villiuamy's *Amexica,* Charles Bowden's *Murder City* as well as more academic texts like Shannon O'Neil's *Two Nations Indivisible* and Jorge Castañeda's *Mañana Forever*. I wanted to do a project that mirrored the style of Villiuamy's cross-border journey, but brought in the diversity and complexity that one sees when comparing Mexico's south and north. Reading Brian Kevin's *The Footloose American* inspired me to put together an outline of my idea and start thinking more seriously about the project. My friend Eli Altman helped me consolidate the concept and put together a plan for fieldwork. He encouraged me to build on the profile-based style of Judith Adler's *Mexican Lives* and Patrick Oster's *The Mexicans*. Katie Zanecchia helped me further develop the concept. Daniel Duane and Cynthia

Anderson gave me great advice along the way. Stephanye Hunter played a huge role in helping to consolidate and improve the text. Many other friends and fellow Mexico scholars reviewed particular chapters including Luis Vivanco, Shannon O'Neil, Casey Lurtz, Weston Phippen, Sarah Osten, Jessica Zarkin and Michael Lettieri, my sister Louise, and my *amigos* Seth Bowden, and Adrian Thompson. Thank you as well to Lloyd Belton, Miriam Wasser, Danielle Renwick, Patrick Corcoran, Mat Youkee and Ariel Stulberg. Finally, a big thank you goes to Roberto Cabello-Argandoña and the rest of the team at Floricanto Press for believing in, helping to edit and improve, and publishing this book.

Books like Julia Preston's *Opening Mexico*, John Womack's *Zapata and the Mexican Revolution*, Alexander Dawson's *First World Dreams*, Alan Riding's *Distant Neighbors* and George Grayson's *Mexican Messiah* helped spark my interest in Mexico. I have an entire bookshelf of other texts about Mexico, Latin America, globalization, and inequality that also shaped my ideas. Over the years I've relied on the work of Mexico-focused journalists and writers Adam Williams, Isabella Cota, Jesse Cottrell, Jude Webber, Martha Pskowski, Alex Alper, Nathaniel Janowitz, Anthony Esposito, Nacha Cattan, Robbie Whelan, David Agren, Jon Lee Anderson, Cecilia Balli, David Luhnow, Ioan Grillo, Patrick Radden Keefe, Parker James Asmann and the entire Mexico teams at The Associated Press, Bloomberg, *The New York Times, The Guardian, The Los Angeles Times, The Washington Post* and Reuters. Over the last decade I've had so many conversations with Mexico scholars and experts including Tony Payan, Shannon O'Neil, Jesse Wheeler, Grant Sunderland, Carlos Petersen, Eric Olson, Andrew Selee, Eric Farnsworth, Viridiana Ríos, Patrick Iber and Duncan Wood.

Mexico has phenomenal statistics published by the Instituto Nacional de Estadística y Geografía (INEGI) and hundreds of brave, talented, and dedicated journalists who work for local media outlets across the country. While working on this book I met with journalists, writers, and editors from media outlets including *Animal Político, Horizontal, Nexos, Letras Libres, Gatopardo, Lado B, Chiapas Paralelo, Zeta, La Jornada, Proceso, El Universal, Chilango, El Financiero* and countless other organizations. I've seen firsthand how investigative reporters and critical journalists helped open a new chapter of active public debate and criticism in Mexico. Brave local reporters often help draw international attention to major scandals and human rights abuses and more mundane, but still terrifying instances of violence. During the years I worked on this project between 2013 and the end of 2018 the Committee to Protect Journalists recorded eighteen reporters killed in Mexico. The sacrifice these journalists made needs to be acknowledged.

I'd also like to thank my professors at Columbia University's School for International and Public Affairs (SIPA) and in particular Pablo Piccato and Tom Trebat at the Institute of Latin American Studies. Anya Schiffrin and the entire International Media (IMAC) program, as well as John Coatsworth, Maria Murillo, Jorge Castañeda, and José Antonio Ocampo. I also have to thank all of my Mexican classmates at SIPA, (Edgar, Vladimir, Brenda, Mónica, MaFer, Laura, Pedro, Ramón, Ernesto and so many others) who over innumerable dinners, tequilas, and late-night discussions explained countless aspects of Mexican politics and society. And, from my undergraduate studies I have to thank the late Ross Thompson, Luis Vivanco, Elaine McCrate, and Moustapha Diouf who led the intense, challenging and rewarding residential Integrated Social Sciences Program (ISSP). Stephanie Seguino from the Department of Economics also played a big role in encouraging me to study economic issues from a variety of angles and ideological viewpoints. My two study abroad programs, Boston University's International Honors Program and the School for International Training's program at the Universidad de Chile, helped me start to investigate the effects of globalization across multiple continents and gave me my first introduction to field work and foreign adventures.

This book is the result of a long process. My basketball team and bicycling buddies helped me keep my sanity while working on this project. Viviana Ibieta's love and humor kept me grounded and inspired. And, finally the people in Mexico have proven to be peerless hosts and ambassadors, opening their homes to me, sharing their time and their stories, helping me to understand a country that is often as beguiling as it is beautiful.

I wrote this book during the administration of Enrique Peña Nieto (2012-2018). The first edition is being published early in the administration of Andres Manuel López Obrador (2018-2024). López Obrador's election marks a major milestone for Mexico, but the country will no doubt continue to confront the problems of inequality, illegality, and informality that I address in this book.

Working on this book has been an immensely rewarding experience. Juan Carlos, Antonio, Pedro, Javier, Jesús, and so many other people invited me in to hear their stories and document their lives. I'm excited to see the moves these entrepreneurs make in the future. I can't thank all of the people who participated and helped me out along the way enough. *Gracias a todos.*

Endnotes

1 Nathaniel Parish Flannery. "Central American Migrants Face Deportation Long Before They Reach U.S. Border." *Fox News*. July 1, 2014. http://www.foxnews.com/world/2014/07/01/central-american-migrants-face-deportation-long-before-reach-us-border.html

2 Nathaniel Parish Flannery. "The New Frontier." *Monocle*, March, 2014. 70.

3 Laura Quintero. "Empleo informal reina en la region sur del pais." *El Economista*. June 6, 2016. https://www.eleconomista.com.mx/estados/Empleo-informal-reina-en-la-region-sur-del-pais-20160606-0086.html

4 Dan Levy, Ricardo Hausmann, Miguel Angel Santos, Luis Espinoza, and Miguel Flores. "Why Is Chiapas Poor?" CID Working Paper No. 300. Center for International Development at Harvard University. March 2016. https://growthlab.cid.harvard.edu/files/growthlab/files/cid_wp_300_english.pdf

5 "Mexican government says poverty rose to 46.2 percent in 2014," *Reuters*. July 23, 2015. https://www.reuters.com/article/us-mexico-poverty-idUSKCN0PX2B320150723

6 Ana Langner. "El 43.6 percent de los Mexicanos viven en situacion de pobreza: Coneval," *El Economista*. August 30, 2017. https://www.eleconomista.com.mx/economia/El-43.6-de-los-mexicanos-vive-en-situacion-de-pobreza-Coneval-20170830-0151.html

7 Nathaniel Parish Flannery. "What's The Real Story With Modern Mexico's Middle Class?" *Forbes*. July 23, 2013. https://www.forbes.com/sites/nathanielparishflannery/2013/07/23/whats-the-real-story-with-modern-mexicos-middle-class/#2fac7f741d42

8 Dainzú Patiño. "Mexico, el pais con mas emigrantes de America Latina: Cepal," *El Financiero*. November 11, 2014. http://www.elfinanciero.com.mx/sociedad/mexico-el-pais-con-mas-emigrantes-de-america-latina-cepal.html

9 Rodrigo Aguilera. "On the Margins: Why Mexico's Southern States Have Fallen Behind." *The Huffington Post*. August 10, 2015. https://www.huffingtonpost.com/rodrigo-aguilera/on-the-margins-why-mexico_b_7967874.html

10 Eduardo Bolio, Jaana Remes, Tomas Lajous, James Mayika, Eugenia Ramirez, and Morten Rosse. "A tale of two Mexicos: Growth and prosperity in a two-speed economy." McKinsey Global Institute. March, 2014. https://www.mckinsey.com/global-themes/americas/a-tale-of-two-mexicos

11 Nathaniel Parish Flannery. "Dodging Bullets to Make the World's Best Coffee in Mexico." *Pacific Standard.* November, 2018. 64.

12 Marc Lacy. "Ten Years Later Chiapas Massacre Still Haunts Mexico." *The New York Times.* December 23, 2007. http://www.nytimes.com/2007/12/23/world/americas/23acteal.html

13 Rafael Victorio. "Chiapas primer lugar en produccion de café organico." *Cuarto Poder.* August 3, 2017. http://www.cuartopoder.mx/chiapasprimerlugarenproducciondecafeorganico-211890.html

14 Kenneth Weathers and Nadine Weathers. *Diccionario Español - Tzotzil.* (Mexico City: Instituto Linguistico de Verano: 1949). 3.

15 Alma Guillermoprieto. "Losing The Future." *The New Yorker.* April 4, 1994. 55.

16 Fredy Perez. "EZLN también se moviliza en Chiapas por caso Ayotzinapa." *El Universal.* October 8, 2014. http://archivo.eluniversal.com.mx/estados/2014/ezln-ayotzinapa-marcha-1044567.html

17 Nathaniel Parish Flannery. "Looking Back At Mexico's Masked Guerilla Uprising." *Forbes.* July 22, 2013. https://www.forbes.com/sites/nathanielparishflannery/2013/07/22/looking-back-at-mexicos-masked-guerilla-uprising/#4c487ab230a3

18 John Womack Jr. *Zapata and the Mexican Revolution.* (New York: Vintage Books, 1968), 372.

19 Harvey. 177.

20 Ibid.

21 Mexico. Ministry of Agriculture. "Estratificacion de productores por superficie: Chiapas." Mexico City. May 2018. https://twitter.com/NathanielParish/status/1010147389913665537

22 Jose Woldenberg. "La desigualdad en Mexico." *Revista de la Universidad de Mexico.* Nueva epoca. May, 2011. No. 87. http://www.revistadelauniversidad.unam.mx/8711/woldenberg/87woldenberg.html

23 Alan Riding. *Distant Neighbors: A Portrait of the Mexicans.* (New York: Knopf, 1984), 22.

24 John Womack Jr. *Rebellion in Chiapas: an historical reader.* (New York: The New Press, 1999), 74.
25 Ibid. 77.
26 Alan Knight. *The Mexican Revolution: Volume 1.* (Nebraska: University of Nebraska Press, 1986), 78.
27 Julia Preston. *Opening Mexico.* (New York: Farrar, Straus and Giroux, 2004), 4.
28 Octavio Paz. *Labarinto de Soledad.* (Madrid: Catedra, 2011), 206.
29 Paz. 209.
30 Paz. 210.
31 Paz. 176.
32 Enrique Krauze. *Mexico: A Biography of Power.* (New York: Harper Perennial, 2013) e-book edition. Loc 9050.
33 Patrick Oster. *The Mexicans: A Personal Portrait of a People.* (New York. William Morrow / HarperCollins, 2009.) e-book edition. Loc 2762.
34 Neil Harvey. *The Chiapas Rebellion: The Struggle For Land And Democracy.* (Durham: Duke University Press, 1998), 177.
35 Jacqueline Mazza. *Don't Disturb the Neighbors: The U.S. and Democracy in Mexico, 1980-1995.*(New York. Routledge, 2001), 22.
36 Oster. Loc 4672.
37 Oster. Loc 4688.
38 Alexander Dawson. *First World Dreams: Mexico Since 1989.* (Nova Scotia: Fernwood Publishing, 2006), 30.
39 Mary Beth Sheridan. "Zedillo Leaves Behind Great Achievements—and Significant Failures." *Los Angeles Times.* December 1, 2000. http://articles.latimes.com/2000/dec/01/news/mn-59741
40 Anahi Rama and Gabriel Stargardter. "Chronology: Checkered history of the PRI's rule in Mexico." *Reuters.* June 28, 2012. https://www.reuters.com/article/us-mexico-election-pri/chronology-checkered-history-of-the-pris-rule-in-mexico-idUSBRE85R12C20120628
41 Javier Brandoli. "En Chiapas, la Coca-Cola es Dios." *El Mundo.* May 12, 2012. http://www.elmundo.es/espana/2015/05/12/5550dc1bca4741ba5b8b457a.html

42 Oscar Lopez and Andrew Jacobs. "In Town With Little Water Coca-Cola Is Everywhere. So Is Diabetes." *New York Times*. July 14, 2018. https://www.nytimes.com/2018/07/14/world/americas/mexico-coca-cola-diabetes.html
43 Patrick McDonnell. "1968 Massacre in Mexico Still Echoes Across Nation." *Los Angeles Times*. October 2, 1993. http://articles.latimes.com/1993-10-02/news/mn-41447_1_tlatelolco-massacre
44 Isain Mandujano. "Echan de una cafeteria a indigena estudiante de doctorado tras confundirla con vendadora ambulante." *Proceso*. November 13, 2013. http://www.proceso.com.mx/357788/echan-de-una-cafeteria-a-indigena-estudiante-de-doctorado-tras-confundirla-con-una-vendedora-ambulante
45 Gerardo Esquivel. "Extreme Inequality In Mexico." Oxfam Mexico. June, 2015. 5. http://www.socialprotectionet.org/sites/default/files/inequality_oxfam.pdf
46 Kerry Dolan. "The World According To Slim." *Forbes*. March 7, 2012. https://www.forbes.com/forbes/2012/0326/billionaires-12-feature-telecommunications-mexico-world-according-carlos-slim.html#7b6655483b8d
47 Edgar Hernandez. "Falla en Chiapas combate a pobreza." *Reforma*. April 1, 2016. http://www.reforma.com/aplicacioneslibre/articulo/default.aspx?id=807160&md5=815676549e970542b0500314f22e00b0&ta=0dfdbac11765226904c16cb9ad1b2efe&lcmd5=abea5250ef9e49ec49c690fc731f5ea8
48 Jathan Sadowski. "Why Silicon Valley is embracing universal basic income." *The Guardian*. June 22, 2016. https://www.theguardian.com/technology/2016/jun/22/silicon-valley-universal-basic-income-y-combinator
49 Larry Rohter. "Man In The News; A Mexican on the Fast Track: Carlos Salinas de Gortari." *The New York Times*. October 5, 1987. http://www.nytimes.com/1987/10/05/world/man-in-the-news-a-mexican-on-the-fast-track-carlos-salinas-de-gortari.html
50 "Bloqueo en Chiapas impide paso de ambulancia; mueren 2 niños." *El Imparcial*. April 30, 2016. http://www.eluniversal.com.mx/articulo/estados/2016/04/30/bloqueo-impide-paso-de-una-ambulancia-mueren-2-ninos

51 Issa Maldonado. "Maestros se enfrentan a policias en Chiapas; hay 18 detenidos." *Milenio*. April, 15, 2016. http://www.milenio.com/estados/maestros_detenidos_Chiapas-protesta_maestros_Chiapas-bloqueos_Chiapas_0_719928200.html

52 David Agren. "Mexico's top politician has the right fluff." *Macleans*. February 20, 2014. http://www.macleans.ca/news/mexicos-top-politician-has-the-right-fluff/

53 Paul Friedrich. *The Princes of Naranja*. (Austin: University of Texas Press, 1986), 134.

54 Viridiana Rios. "Chiapas, peor que ayer." *Nexos*. January 1, 2014. https://www.nexos.com.mx/?p=15676

55 Ibid.

56 Ibid.

57 Christian Jimenez. "Oaxaca, en los primeros lugares de inseguridad alimentaria." *El Universal*. October 17, 2017. http://oaxaca.eluniversal.com.mx/estatal/17-10-2017/oaxaca-en-los-primeros-lugares-de-inseguridad-alimentaria

58 Ana Laura Martinez. "Desigualdad y corrupcion: el caso Chiapas." *Expansion*. July 14, 2015. http://expansion.mx/opinion/2015/07/13/desigualdad-y-corrupcion-el-caso-chiapas

59 Rios.

60 Selene Alvarez. "Chiapas ocupa el primer lugar en analfabetismo." *Suceso Chiapas*. August 7, 2017. http://www.sucesochiapas.com.mx/cultura/chiapas-ocupa-el-primer-lugar-en-analfabetismo/

61 Rios.

62 Oscar Gutierrez. "Muere policía en desalojo de carretera en Chiapas." *El Universal*. September 26, 2015. http://www.eluniversal.com.mx/articulo/estados/2015/09/26/muere-policia-en-desalojo-de-carretera-en-chiapas

63 Angeles Mariscal. "Maestros chocan con policía federal en Chiapas, al menos 22 son detenidos." *La Cañada*. April 15, 2016. http://www.cdanoticias.com/notas/1166/maestros-chocan-con-policia-federal-en-chiapas-al-menos-22-son-detenidos

64 "Arriban a Chiapas mas de 9 mil policias federales." *La Razon Online*. May 17, 2016. https://www.razon.com.mx/arriban-a-chiapas-mas-de-9-mil-policias-federales/

65 Angeles Mariscal. "Indigenas de Chenalho secuestran a diputados de Chiapas." *El Financiero.* May 25, 2016. http://www.elfinanciero.com.mx/nacional/indigenas-de-chenalho-secuestran-a-diputados-de-chiapas.html

66 Oscar Gutierrez. "Asesinan a alcalde de San Juan Chamula." *El Universal*. July 27, 2016. http://www.eluniversal.com.mx/articulo/estados/2016/07/24/asesinan-alcalde-de-san-juan-chamula

67 Isain Mandujano. "Renuncia la alcadesa de Oxchuc tras seis meses de protestas." *Proceso*. February 5, 2016. http://www.proceso.com.mx/429057/renuncia-a-su-cargo-la-alcaldesa-de-oxchuc

68 Nathaniel Parish Flannery. "Dodging Bullets to Make the World's Best Coffee in Mexico."

69 Patrick J. McNamara. Juarez, Diaz, and the People of Ixlan, Oaxaca, 1855-1920. (Durham: University of North Carolina Press, 2012), 102.

70 Humberto A. Torres. "Persiste informalidad laboral en el estado de Oaxaca." *El Imparcial*. November 15, 2017. http://imparcialoaxaca.mx/oaxaca/85483/persiste-informalidad-laboral-en-el-estado-de-oaxaca/

71 Denisse Garcia. "Peña Nieto and the Unions." *Harvard Political Review.* May 28, 2013. http://harvardpolitics.com/world/pena-nieto-and-the-unions/

72 David Agren. "Mexico's Dissident Teachers Union CNTE Proves Tough to Tame." *Vice.* June 16, 2015. https://news.vice.com/article/mexicos-dissident-teachers-union-cnte-proves-tough-to-tame

73 Lizette Mendoza. "En Oaxaca la mayoria de escuelas no tiene acceso a internet." MVI Noticias. December 20, 2016. http://www.nvinoticias.com/nota/45114/en-oaxaca-la-mayoria-de-escuelas-no-tiene-acceso-internet

74 Laura Poy Solano. "INEE: solo 4 de cada 10 escuelas primarias tienen computadora." *La Jornada.* December 23, 2016. http://www.jornada.unam.mx/2016/12/23/sociedad/029n1soc

75 Nathaniel Parish Flannery. "How Boutique Mezcal Makers Are Taking on Tequila". *Fortune.* December 28, 2015. http://fortune.com/2015/12/28/mezcal-export-boom-mexico-us/

76 Ibid.

77 Ibid.

78 Blanca Heredia. "Lo que sabemos y no de la educacion en Oaxaca." *El Financiero.* July 29, 2015. http://www.elfinanciero.com.mx/opinion/lo-que-sabemos-y-no-de-la-educacion-en-oaxaca.html

79 Laura Poy Solano. "Mexico, sin avances en matematicas, lectura y ciencia en una decada." *La Jornada.* December 6, 2016. http://www.jornada.unam.mx/2016/12/06/sociedad/040n1soc

80 Heredia.

81 Ibid.

82 McNamara. 7.

83 Carlos Ramirez. "Encuesta Oaxaca: sociedad usará violencia contra CNTE." *Debate.* August 4, 2016. https://www.debate.com.mx/opinion/Encuesta-Oaxaca-sociedad-usara-violencia-contra-CNTE-20160803-0156.html

84 Nathaniel Parish Flannery. "Mexico's Unfinished Education Reform Key to Pena Nieto's Economic Agenda." *World Politics Review.* October 28, 2014. https://www.worldpoliticsreview.com/articles/14287/mexico-s-unfinished-education-reform-key-to-pena-nieto-s-economic-agenda

85 Virgilio Sanchez. "Toma PF installaciones de IEEPO." *Reforma.* July 21, 2015. http://www.reforma.com/aplicacioneslibre/articulo/default.aspx?id=596378&md5=986cf1ac30c3a45c9065fc436d43e84d&ta=0dfdbac11765226904c16cb9ad1b2efe&lcmd5=3572c3f3730086a026de9410b57b3646

86 Jo Tuckman. "Elba Esther Gordillo – Mexico's famed union boss – accused of embezzlement." *The Guardian.* February 27, 2013. https://www.theguardian.com/world/2013/feb/27/elba-esther-gordillo-mexico-union-embezzlement

87 Oscar Rodriguez and Victor Hugo Michel. "Recupera CNTE escuela 'Hermanos Flores Magon." *Milenio.* November 28, 2013. http://www.milenio.com/estados/CNTE-SNTE-seccion_22-maestros-seccion_59_0_198580499.html

88 Seis de cada diez rechazan marchas de la CNTE," *Carta Paramétrica.* http://www.parametria.com.mx/carta_parametrica.php?cp=4896.

89 Mexico. Ministry of Public Education. "Sistema interactiva de consulta de estadistica educativa." Mexico City. June, 2018. http://www.planeacion.sep.gob.mx/principalescifras/

90 United States. Department of Education. National Center for Education Statistics, Common Core of Data (CCD), "Public Elementary/Secondary School Universe Survey," 2004–05, Version 1a. https://nces.ed.gov/pubs2007/overview04/tables/table_2.asp

91 Fredy Martin Perez and Marcos Muedano. "Muere maestro durante protesta contra evalucaion." *El Universal.* December 9, 2015. http://www.eluniversal.com.mx/articulo/nacion/seguridad/2015/12/9/muere-maestro-durante-protesta-contra-evaluacion

92 Ibid.

93 Minh Tran and Peter Burman. "Rating the English Proficiency of Countries and Industries Around the World." *Harvard Business Review.* November 21, 2016. https://hbr.org/2016/11/research-companies-and-industries-lack-english-skills

94 "Sweden at Top, Middle East at Bottom of EF's Global Ranking of English Skills." PRNewswire. November 3, 2015. https://www.prnewswire.com/news-releases/sweden-at-top-middle-east-at-bottom-of-efs-global-ranking-of-english-skills-539730692.html

95 Rafel Montes and Eugenia Jimenez. "SEP detecta 44 mil maestros 'aviadores'" *Milenio*. July 17, 2017. http://www.milenio.com/politica/sep-aviadores-magisterio-conago-aurelio_nuno-miguel_angel_mancera-milenio-noticias_0_994700719.html

96 Ibid.

97 "Mexican education: Flunking the test." *The Economist.* March 5, 2015. https://www.economist.com/news/americas/21645748-failing-schools-pose-big-challenge-president-enrique-pe-nietos-vision-modernising

98 "FOTOGALERIA: Maestros recuperan a la fuerza escuela de Oaxaca." *Excelsior*. November 14, 2013. http://www.excelsior.com.mx/nacional/2013/11/14/928787

99 Leticia Robles de la Rosa. "Mexicanos tienen nivel de secundaria; se va 9.2 años a las aulas." *El Excelsior.* April 20, 2016. http://www.excelsior.com.mx/nacional/2016/04/20/1087672

100 Carlos Ramirez. "CNTE pelea poder, no la educacion." *El Financerio.* September 24, 2013. http://www.elfinanciero.com.mx/opinion/cnte-pelea-poder-no-la.html

101 Nurit Martinez Carballo. "De 478 dias, salario de maestros en Oaxaca." *El Universal.* August 30, 2013. http://archivo.eluniversal.com.mx/nacion-mexico/2013/impreso/de-478-dias-salario-de-maestros-en-oaxaca-208716.html

102 Louise Story and Alejandra Xanic von Bertrab. "Mexican Political Family Has Close Ties to Ruling Party, and Homes in the U.S." *The New York Times.* February 10, 2015. https://www.nytimes.com/2015/02/11/nyregion/jose-murat-casab-mexico-pri-luxury-condos-us.html

103 "Mireles y Autodefensas son atacados con granadas en Pareo, Michoacan." YouTube video, 3:09, posted by "Grillonautas2," November 16, 2016. https://www.youtube.com/watch?v=4RB5DPDSOH0

104 Nathaniel Parish Flannery. "Riding Along With Vigilante Leader 'Papa Smurf.'" Fusion. March 24, 2014. https://splinternews.com/riding-along-with-vigilante-leader-papa-smurf-1793841084

105 Ibid. Note: All material from the 2014 patrol with Pitufo is based on "Riding Along With Vigilante Leader 'Papa Smurf.'"

106 Daniel Hernandez. "Calderon's war on drug cartels: A legacy of blood and tragedy." *Los Angeles Times.* December 1, 2012. http://articles.latimes.com/2012/dec/01/world/la-fg-wn-mexico-calderon-cartels-20121130

107 Ioan Grillo. *Gangster Warlords: Drug Dollars, Killing Fields, and the New Politics of Latin America.* (Bloomsbury Press, 2016), 249.

108 Nathaniel Parish Flannery. "Mexico's avocado army: how one city stood up to the drug cartels." *The Guardian.* May 18, 2017. https://www.theguardian.com/cities/2017/may/18/avocado-police-tancitaro-mexico-law-drug-cartels

109 Ibid.

110 Ibid.

111 Ernesto Martinez Elorriaga. "Tras balacera, autodefensas toman Nueva Italia, bastion de templarios." *La Jornada.* January 13, 2014. http://www.jornada.unam.mx/2014/01/13/politica/004n1pol

112 Jose Gil Olmos. "Advierten autodefensas que se quedaran a limpiar a Apatzingan de criminals." *Proceso.* February 9, 2014. http://www.proceso.com.mx/364477/autodefensas-esperan-tomar-el-control-de-apatzingan

113 Carlos Arrieta. "Asesinan a fundador de autodefensas de Tancitaro." *El Universal*. August 30, 2015. http://www.eluniversal.com.mx/articulo/estados/2015/08/30/asesinan-fundador-de-auto-defensas-de-tancitaro

114 Laura Castellanos. "'Fueron los federales', matanza de 16 personas a manos de la Policia Federal en Michoacan." *Vice*. April 29, 2015. https://www.vice.com/es_mx/article/nnp3ed/fueron-los-federales-matanza-de-16-individuos-desarmados-a-manos-de-la-policia-federal-en-michoacan

115 Christopher Woody. "One of Mexico's biggest gunfights in a decade may have been a cold-blooded massacre." *Business Insider*. May 29, 2015. http://www.businessinsider.com/mexicos-biggest-gunfight-drug-cartel-massacre-2015-5

116 Nathaniel Parish Flannery. "Dispatches: Xaltianguis, Mexico.) *Americas Quarterly*. Winter, 2014. https://www.americasquarterly.org/content/dispatches-xaltianguis-mexico

117 Nathaniel Parish Flannery. "Calderon's War." *The Journal of International Affairs* 66, no 2. (2013). 181. https://jia.sipa.columbia.edu/calderons-war

118 Hector Molina and Ruben Torres. "Insisten en falta de capacitacion de las policias." *El Economista*. February 27, 2018. https://www.eleconomista.com.mx/politica/Insisten-en-falta-de-capacitacion-de-las-policias-20180226-1135.html

119 Randal C. Archibold and Ginger Thompson. "El Chapo, Most-Wanted Drug Lord, Is Captured in Mexico." *The New York Times*. February 22, 2014. https://www.nytimes.com/2014/02/23/world/americas/joaquin-guzman-loera-sinaloa-drug-cartel-leader-is-captured-in-mexico.html

120 Nathaniel Parish Flannery. "Mexico's Scaled-Back Gendarmerie Force No Security Panacea." *World Politics Review*. August 1, 2014. https://www.worldpoliticsreview.com/articles/13970/mexico-s-scaled-backed-gendarmerie-force-no-security-panacea

121 "Why Mexico's murder rate is soaring." *The Economist*. May 9, 2018. https://www.economist.com/the-economist-explains/2018/05/09/why-mexicos-murder-rate-is-soaring

122 David Saul Vela. "En Mexico, cada policia debe cuidar a 373 personas." *El Financiero*. July 12, 2017. http://www.elfinanciero.com.

mx/nacional/en-mexico-cada-policia-debe-cuidar-a-373-personas
123 Alejandro Hope. "Los policias que no estan." *El Universal.* July 9, 2018. http://www.eluniversal.com.mx/columna/alejandro-hope/nacion/los-policias-que-no-estan
124 John Holman. "Mexico police officers 'underpaid, under-equipped.' *Al Jazeera.* August 2, 2018. https://www.aljazeera.com/news/2018/07/mexico-police-officers-underpaid-equipped-180729120903772.html
125 Marco Antonio Coronel. "'La Fortaleza' de 'El Chayo.'" *Milenio.* March 17, 2014. http://www.milenio.com/policia/El_Chayo-Nazario_Moreno-El_mas_loco-Caballeros_Templarios_0_263974127.html
126 Nathaniel Parish Flannery, "Are Vigilante Groups The Answer To Combat Drug Cartels In Mexico?" *Fusion* video, 5:48, 2014. https://fusion.net/video/2192/are-vigilante-groups-the-answer-to-combat-drug-cartels-in-mexico/
127 Eduardo Ferrer and Ernesto Martinez. "Narcoviolencia: No paren hasta acabar con ellos." *La Jornada.* December 11, 2010. http://www.jornada.unam.mx/2010/12/11/politica/002n1pol
128 Arturo Cano. "La PF actua sin avisar...y la rescatan Ejercito y Marina." *La Jornada.* December 14, 2010. http://www.jornada.unam.mx/2010/12/14/politica/002n1pol
129 "Encapuchados presentan a IRIS, nuevo grupo armado en Michoacan." Proceso. February 8,
2016. http://www.proceso.com.mx/429265/surge-nuevo-grupo-armado-en-michoacan-
amenaza-con-acabar-con-grupos-criminales
130 Katy Watson. "The avocado police protecting Mexico's green gold." *BBC News.* November 28, 2017. http://www.bbc.com/news/world-latin-america-41635008
131 Ernesto Martinez Elorriaga. "Muerte del edil de Santa Ana Maya, impune." *La Jornada.* November 7, 2014. http://www.jornada.unam.mx/2014/11/07/estados/040n3est
132 "Grupos armados incendian empacadoras de aguacate en Tancitaro, Michoacan; no se reportan heridos." SinEmbargo. April 25, 2013. http://www.sinembargo.mx/25-04-2013/601633
133 "Angel Bucio Bucio nuevo president de la JLSV de Tancitaro." *La Opinion.* Posted on the website of Mexico's

Secretaria de Agricultura. http://www.sicde.gob.mx/portal/bin/nota.php?from=90&accion=buscar&subrutina=pagina_1&-column=2&busqueda=&orderBy=Notas.FechaNota&order=AS-C&fecha=&notaId=1672804255519ce500814d0

134 Marjorie Becker. *Setting the Virgin on Fire: Lazaro Cardenas, Michoacan Peasants, and the Redemption of the Mexican Revolution.* (Berkeley: University of California Press, 1996), Loc 317.

135 John Bailey. *The Politics of Crime in Mexico: Democratic Governance in a Security Trap.* (Colorado: FirstForumPress, 2014.) 11.

136 Camilla Schippa. "This is how much violence costs Mexico's economy." World Economic Forum. May 2, 2016. https://www.weforum.org/agenda/2016/05/this-is-how-much-violence-costs-mexicos-economy/

137 Jessica Zarkin. "Centralizing the Police Force: What It Means For Mexico's Narco Violence." *Cornell Policy Review.* October 5, 2016. http://www.cornellpolicyreview.com/centralizing-the-police-force-what-it-means-for-mexicos-narco-violence/

138 Angelina Arredondo Elizalde. "Fin de autodefensas; garantizan paz estatal." *Provincia: El Diario Grande de Michoacan.* February 12, 2016. 1.

139 Ibid.

140 Miguel Angel Pallares Gomez. "Mercado de lujo titubea, pero logra crecimiento." *El Universal.* April 24, 2017. http://www.eluniversal.com.mx/articulo/cartera/economia/2017/04/24/merca-do-de-lujo-titubea-pero-logra-crecimiento

141 Nathaniel Parish Flannery. "How Tacos Explain Mexico's Labor Market." *The Atlantic.* October 4, 2013. https://www.theatlantic.com/international/archive/2013/10/how-tacos-explain-mexico-s-la-bor-market/280288/

142 Joshua Partlow. "Mexican microbrewers step out of the shadow of the country's beer giants." *The Washington Post.* July 13, 2015. https://www.washingtonpost.com/world/the_americas/mexi-can-micro-brewers-step-out-of-the-shadow-of-the-countrys-beer-gi-ants/2015/07/12/58c3cf22-23ec-11e5-b621-b55e495e9b78_story.html

143 Leticia Hernandez. "Credito en Mexico alcanzaria 40 percent del PIB en 2019." *El Financiero.* March 22, 2017. http://www.elfinanciero.com.mx/economia/credito-en-mexico-alcanzaria-40-del-

pib-en-2019.html

144 "Domestic credit to private sector (percent of GDP)." The World Bank. https://data.worldbank.org/indicator/FS.AST.PRVT.GD.ZS

145 Roberto Morales. "Mexico se consolida como el mayor exportador de cerveza." *El Economista.* May 17, 2017. https://www.eleconomista.com.mx/empresas/Mexico-se-consolida-como-el-mayor-exportador-de-cerveza-20170518-0098.html

146 Nathaniel Parish Flannery. "Mexico's Silicon Valley." *Americas Quarterly.* March 7, 2012. http://www.americasquarterly.org/mexicos-silicon-valley

147 Gabriela Chavez. "El Silicon Valley Mexicano Innova Para Multinacionales." *Expansion.* April 30, 2015. http://expansion.mx/negocios/2015/04/27/zapopan-el-silicon-valley-mexicano-que-innova-para-otros

148 Nathaniel Parish Flannery. "The Tequila Trail: What Can Jalisco Mexico Teach Us About Migration?" *Forbes.* October 27, 2014. https://www.forbes.com/sites/nathanielparishflannery/2014/10/27/the-tequila-trail-what-can-jalisco-mexico-teach-us-about-migration/#2a5d64371f22

149 Axel Sanchez and Adrian Arias. "La CFC 'pinta su raya' a Comex." *El Financiero.* July 19, 2013. http://www.elfinanciero.com.mx/archivo/la-cfc-pinta-su-raya-a-comex.html

150 Gerardo Villafranco. "Los estados con mayor crecimiento economico en Mexico." *Forbes Mexico.* February 11, 2015. https://www.forbes.com.mx/los-estados-con-mayor-crecimiento-economico-en-mexico/

151 Jorge G. Castañeda. *Mañana Forever: Mexico and the Mexicans.* (New York: Alfred A. Knopf, 2011), 154.

152 Ben Berkowitz and Philip Blenkinsop. "Heineken buys FEMSA beers, cements Latam alliance." Reuters. January 11, 2010.

153 Ibid.

154 Anabel Manzano. *Animal Politico.* June 15, 2015."Cerveza artisanal, el 'boom' invisible en Mexico." http://www.animalpolitico.com/2015/06/cerveza-artesanal-el-boom-invisible-en-mexico/

155 Jude Webber. "Exxon to make $300m push into Mexican gas station business." *Financial Times.* May 17, 2017. https://www.ft.com/content/becee692-92a3-3c9d-925a-a7146deeaf61

156 Vicente Gutierrez. "Cinepolis y Cinemex: dueños de la exhibicion del cine en Mexico." *El Economista.* February 9, 2016. https://www.eleconomista.com.mx/arteseideas/Cinepolis-y-Cinemex-duenos-de-la-exhibicion-del-cine-en-Mexico-20160209-0103.html

157 Christine Murray. "Carlos Slim bows to Mexico telecoms reform." Reuters. July 8, 2014. https://www.reuters.com/article/us-slim-america-movil/carlos-slim-bows-to-mexico-telecoms-reform-idUSKBN0FD2KR20140709

158 Dan Mitchell. "Bimbo Takes Big Part of U.S. Bread Market." CBS News. December 11, 2008. https://www.cbsnews.com/news/bimbo-takes-big-part-of-us-bread-market/

159 Ximena Cassab. "Chivas Signs on with Univision for U.S. TV Rights for One More Year." Portada-Online. February 23, 2017. https://www.portada-online.com/2017/02/23/chivas-signs-on-with-univision-for-u-s-tv-rights-for-one-more-year/

160 Ivette Saldaña and Miguel Pallares. "Ley contra monopolies, poco eficaz hasta ahora." *El Universal.* September 18, 2015. http://www.eluniversal.com.mx/articulo/cartera/economia/2015/09/18/ley-contra-monopolios-poco-eficaz-hasta-ahora

161 "Empresa HP invertirá 15 MDD en Jalisco." *El Informador.* August 5, 2016. https://www.informador.mx/Economia/Empresa-HP-invertira-15-MDD-en-Jalisco-20160805-0089.html

162 Dwyer Gunn. "Is Antitrust Policy The Next Frontier?" *Pacific Standard.* October 27, 2016. https://psmag.com/news/is-antitrust-policy-the-next-frontier#.xzg6h5nny

163 Axel Sanchez. "Mercado de pinturas tendrá un valor de 44 mil md pen un lustro: Comex PPG." *El Financiero.* December 8, 2015. http://www.elfinanciero.com.mx/empresas/mercado-de-pinturas-tendra-un-valor-de-44-mmdp-en-los-proximos-cinco-anos-comex-ppg.html

164 Dan Freed and David Henry. "Citi struggles to bring back shine to its Mexican crown jewel." Reuters. May 24, 2017. https://www.reuters.com/article/us-citigroup-mexico-turnaround/citi-struggles-to-bring-back-shine-to-its-mexican-crown-jewel-idUSKBN18K0EX

165 Shannon K. O'Neil. *Two Nations Indivisible: Mexico, The United States, And The Road Ahead.* (New York: Oxford University Press, 2013), 4.

166 Mark Deen. "Chile, Mexico, U.S. Have Highest Inequality Rates, OECD Says." *Bloomberg.* November 24, 2016. https://www.bloomberg.com/news/articles/2016-11-24/chile-mexico-u-s-have-highest-inequality-rates-oecd-says
167 "Doing Business 2017: Equal Opportunity for All." World Bank. October 25, 2016. http://www.doingbusiness.org/~/media/WBG/DoingBusiness/Documents/Annual-Reports/English/DB17-Report.pdf
168 Klaus Schwab and Xavier Sala-i-Martin. "The Global Competitiveness Report 2017-2018." The World Economic Forum. September 26, 2017. http://www3.weforum.org/docs/GCR2017-2018/05FullReport/TheGlobalCompetitivenessReport2017 percentE2 percent80 percent932018.pdf
169 Ibid.
170 Ibid.
171 "Transparency Index 2017." Transparency International. February 21, 2018. https://www.transparency.org/news/feature/corruption_perceptions_index_2017?gclid=EAIaIQobChMI9Lvgu-vWD3QIVjrbACh0zYwq9EAAYASAAEgJ1BvD_BwE
172 Stephen Haber, Herbert S. Klein, Noel Maurer, and Kevin J. Middlebrook. *Mexico since 1980 (The World Since 1980.)* (New York: Cambridge University Press, 2008), Loc 198.
173 Nathaniel Parish Flannery. "How Trump's Bullying of Mexico Could Backfire." *The New Republic.* February 23, 2017. https://newrepublic.com/article/140831/trumps-bullying-mexico-backfire
174 Santiago Levy. *Under-Rewarded Efforts: The Elusive Quest for Prosperity in Mexico.* (Washington DC: Inter-American Development Bank: 2018). 4. https://publications.iadb.org/handle/11319/8971
175 Esther Hernandez. "Trabajo informal avanza en BC al 41 percent." *La Cronica.* March 29, 2016. http://www.lacronica.com/EdicionEnLinea/Notas/Noticias/29032016/1065209-Trabajo-informal-avanza-en-BC-al-41.html
176 Eric Martin and Nacha Cattan. "The U.S.-Mexico Wage Gap Is Actually Widening Under Nafta." *Bloomberg.* November 28, 2017. https://www.bloomberg.com/news/articles/2017-11-28/nafta-s-ugly-reality-u-s-mexico-wage-gap-is-actually-widening
177 "Education at a Glance 2017: OECD Indicators." OECD.

51. http://www.oecd-ilibrary.org/education/education-at-a-glance_19991487

178 Guillermo Bonfil Batalla. *Mexico Profundo: Reclaiming A Civilization.* (Austin: University of Texas Press: 1996) xv.

179 Pablo Gonzalez Casanova. *La democracia en Mexico.* (Mexico City: Ediciones Era: 1965) http://ru.iis.sociales.unam.mx/jspui/bitstream/IIS/5208/1/La_democracia_en_M percentC3 percentA9xico.pdf

180 Gonzalez Casanova. 17.

181 Levy. 21.

182 Levy. 7.

183 Levy. 284.

184 William Booth. "Mexico is now a top producer of engineers, but where are jobs?" *The Washington Post*. October 28, 2012. https://www.washingtonpost.com/world/the_americas/mexico-is-now-a-top-producer-of-engineers-but-where-are-jobs/2012/10/28/902db93a-1e47-11e2-8817-41b9a7aaabc7_story.html

185 "Mexico, el de mas 'mordidas' en AL." *El Universal.* October 10, 2017. http://www.eluniversal.com.mx/mundo/mexico-el-de-mas-mordidas-en-al

186 David Bradbury. "Revenue Statistics 2017-Mexico." OECD Centre for Tax Policy and Administration. https://www.oecd.org/tax/revenue-statistics-mexico.pdf

187 Leticia Hernandez. "Mexico, de los paises de la OCDE con menores ingresos fiscales." *El Financiero.* June 28, 2018. http://www.elfinanciero.com.mx/economia/mexico-de-los-paises-de-la-ocde-con-menores-ingresos-fiscales

Made in the USA
Coppell, TX
27 April 2020

21904639R00169